All Honor to You

The Journey of Faith Toward

Love and Life

By
Peter Quang Nguyen

All Honor to You

The Journey of Faith Toward Love and Life

Published by Peter Quang Nguyen

Printed in the United States of America

Library of Congress Card Number: 2002094325

ISBN 1-931947-04-X

Foreward

All Honor to You—The Journey of Faith Toward Love and Life—
is an ordinary personal story. It is written to honor Almighty God,
who gives me a new life with His blessing. It is God who loved me
before I was born. It is God who strengthens me and is always with
me on my journey. My journey of faith is one of many other journeys
that my brothers and sisters have in their lives. Each of us begins our
own journey to the Holy One who is the Love and Life of the world—
of yours and mine.

All Honor To You—is a personal short story. It is short because I
don't think that I will have enough paper and ink to print it out. But,
it will be long story as yours and mine. If you wish to have a wonderful intellectual insight, you won't find it in this book. If you wish to
read the story of a hero, you won't find it in this story. But, if you
want to have a friend, an ordinary friend, who loves to walk with you
in your pilgrimage toward love and life, you will find one.

All Honor To You—is a story of the poor who long to see the face
of God and live. It is a story of the one, you and me, who seeks freedom to love and to serve God and His People. It is a story of an ordinary person who hopes to be faithful to God's promise. It serves as a
reminder of God's love for you and for me. Also, it gives you a gift of
perseverance to honor God and yourself in the difficulties of daily life
as I came to believe. It serves as a reminder of your own struggles and
it encourages you to live your life with your faith so that in your own
journey of faith you will come to know that God loves you very much
and you love God. He is always present and walks with you, side by
side, to lead you to the fullness of love and life. So please, don't give
up living your life, even in the moment of suffering and hopelessness, and don't let go of God's love for you.

All Honor To You—is an expression of thanksgiving to the Lord
our God and to you, my brothers and sisters, that God sent me to

love and to serve. It is an expression of thanksgiving for God's blessing to me. I want to share God's blessing with you in my journey of faith toward love and life as I received it from my teachers. They were sisters, priests, bishops, and friends, who taught me to be faithful to God's promise as they were the true testimony of what they taught me. I want to honor them with my gratitude.

All Honor To You—I want to honor YOU, the readers, the benefactors, children of God, students, faculty and staff, grandparents, parents, brothers and sisters at St. Mary's Catholic Church and School, and to the extended family of each of us. You're God's blessing to me. I honor you, all my friends, for your love, prayers, and support. Without your love, prayers, and support I cannot become who I am in the family of the People of God, in the community of the Mystical Body of Christ as you are. Thank you for believing in me.

All Honor To You—is serving as a soft voice of hope to remind us of God's love and mercy. I wish you love and peace. Live your life and you will find out that the Lord our God is with you always. Love God and allow God to be with you in your journey and you will find out that it is good to go on with your journey of faith toward love and life. Don't be surprised that the Lord is walking side by side with you because God loves you very much.

Fr. Peter Quang Nguyen
St. Mary's Catholic Church and School
Greeley, Colorado – August 15, 2002
Feast of Assumption of Mary

Acknowledgements

My deep gratitude to:

Dr. Betsy Hall—For your precious time and effort to motivate and help me to begin to write this book. Most of all, thank you for sharing your journey of faith with me in friendship, love, prayers, and support.

Cherie VanPortfliet—For your many hours in a labor of love and your enthusiasm to type this book with your compassion and love. Your support to me is always as God's blessing for me. I wish you peace, health, and love.

Rev. Mr. Joseph Meilinger—For your time and computer skills to generat the draft of the book. Thank you for your assistance.

Dr. Richard Kemme, M.D., and Mrs. Mary Kemme— Mr. and Mrs. John and Carol Saeman and Family— Patsy Lyness—For your encouragement, love, prayer, friendship, and financial support to help me to print this book.

My faculty and staff of St. Mary's Catholic Church and School—For your encouragement and patience to work with me in the ministry for the People of God at St. Mary's. Most of all, thank you for your support and assistance.

My Friends, Sisters, Priests, Bishops, Teachers, Professors, especially, Rev. Msgr. James W. Rasby and Rev. Roger Mollison—For your enthusiastic teaching, compassion, understanding, love, guidance, and prayers. You are the courses for me to learn to love God and to serve others.

Fr. Peter Quang Nguyen
His very first Mass, celebrated at St. Vincent de Paul Church,
Denver, Colorado on July 1, 1990

Dedication

I dedicate this book to:

The Almighty God who loves me and has chosen me to serve His people in the Priesthood.

My grandparents, parents, and family.

The People of God at St. Mary's Catholic Church and School — Greeley, Colorado

The People of God at Notre Dame Church and School — Denver, Colorado

The People of God at Immaculate Heart of Mary — Northglenn, Colorado

The People of God at St. Vincent DePaul Church and School — Denver, Colorado

My benefactors, teachers, professors from my childhood to this present time.

Contents

Introduction

Geography

Vietnam is a small country in Southeast Asia. Shaped like an elongated S, it stretches the length of the Indochina peninsula, bordering the South China Sea. It shares its frontier with China in the north, and Laos and Cambodia to the west. Mountains and forests make up more than three-quarters of Vietnam's total land area of about 127,000 square miles. Vietnam's territory encompasses a vast sea area, including many islands from the Tonkin Gulf to the Gulf of Thailand.

As the bird flies, from Nam Quan to Ca Mau, Vietnam stretches about 1,000 miles from north to south. The widest point in the north is about 370 miles from east to west. The narrowest part is about 30 miles across. The 1,500 miles of coastline have many beautiful beaches. Indeed, Vietnam is a land of great geological beauty and diversity. North Vietnam has chains of mountains and carved valleys that separate it from China. The Red River delta provides a source of rice. Central Vietnam forms a long, convex curve. There are many small plains wedged between the South China Sea and the high plateaus of the Truong Son Mountains. Dunes and lagoons in the east, toward the coast, characterize the terrain. The Central Highlands, rich in volcanic basalt soil, constitute the most important forests and growing regions for tea and coffee. South Vietnam is blessed with the Mekong River. Over many centuries, the Mekong's deposits collected on a shallow, undersea shelf, forming an immense, low-lying alluvial plain; the Mekong Delta. This large, rich delta produces rice, grains, and orchard crops for the country.

Located between the Tropic of Cancer and the Equator, Vietnam is characterized by a strong monsoon influence. Generally, there are a considerable number of sunny days, a high rate of rainfall, and high humidity. Some areas located near the tropics or in mountainous regions are endowed with a less temperate climate. The winter season in North Vietnam usually has drizzle during the months of January and February. The summer is quite hot, with abundant rain and occasional typhoons. The provinces of Central Vietnam vary in climate, depending on their altitude and proximity to the sea. From November to March, it has a cool, humid season during which it can rain, uninterrupted, for a whole week. The climate in South Vietnam is distinguished by constant hot temperature. However, this suddenly changes at the beginning of the monsoons. The humid season begins in May and ends in October; the dry season lasts from February to April.

Brief History

The history of Vietnam reads like a series of variations on the same theme: invasion followed by occupation, rebellion followed by independence, internal squabbling followed by another invasion. Vietnam's ancient history also reads like a book of legend and fairy tales. Although the historical record is not complete, it offers a good presentation of the origin of Vietnam.

The source of these legends began over four thousand years ago with the Han (China) and the Viet (Vietnam) cosmogony. This perspective viewed the world through the concept of Five Elements: metal, wood, water, fire, and earth. Ngu Hanh represents Five Regions: center, south, north, east, and west. The earth, with yellow color, represents the center; fire, with red, represents the south; water, with black, represents the north; wood, with green, represents the east; and metal, with white, represents the west.

From ancient times, a kingdom controlled the heart of the Asian continent. The rulers based their power on these concepts of Five Elements and Five Regions. The kingdom's power center was located in the Five Mounts (Ngu Linh) Territory, and its people comprised many races; the two major ones being the Han and the Viet. The Viet

2

settled south of Yellow River and developed agriculturally. The Han located in the northwest and became expert in hunting and battle skills.

The people of Vietnam regard themselves as descendants of Than Nong, who taught his people to grow rice. According to Vietnamese historical folklore, De Minh, a third generation descendent of Than Nong, fled to the southern territory of the Five Mounts. He married the goddess Vu Tien. Their son, Loc Tuc, became king of the South, Kinh Duong Vuong. He married the daughter of Dong Dinh Quan, a king of Dong Dinh territory. Sung Lam, their son, became King Lac Long Quan, the Dragon Lord of the Mighty Seas. He married the goddess Au Co, who was the daughter of King De Lai. Their union gave birth to one hundred children.

Because of the precariousness of their earthly lives, Lac Long Quan and Au Co decided to separate from each other. They divided their children into two equal groups. Lac Long Quan took fifty children and went down to the eastern sea, to the fluvial plains and riverside lands. Au Co went up to the mountains and jungles with the other fifty children.

Later, the dynasty of Hong Bang (2879 B.C. – A.D. 258) was established. King Hung Vuong named it Van Lang. Then, Emperor Gia Long (nineteenth century) renamed it Viet Nam. The symbolism of Lac Long Quan's lineage from the Dragon Lord and Au Co from the Immortals holds significance for the Vietnamese. The Dragon symbolizes yang and Immortals symbolize the yin. Until now, even after many dynasties, the Vietnamese believe they are the descendants of Rong-Tien, the Immortal and the Dragon. These symbols constitute the earliest totems for the Vietnamese people.

The People

According to a commonly accepted hypothesis, the Vietnamese people are comprised of a number of tribes who first established themselves in the valley of the Yang Tse Kiang, the longest river in China. In the third century they moved southward and settled in the

Red River Delta. They radiated into the lowlands of current northern and central Vietnam. Continuing their expansion for almost 2,000 years, they reached the Gulf of Thailand around in 1700.

The following list summarizes the most important dynasty successions in chronological order:

Hong Bang Dynasty	2879 B.C.
First millennium B.C.	Period of Hung Kings and the bronze civilization.
Second century B.C.	Annexation by the Han Empire.
Revolution led by the two Trung sisters.	
Ly's insurrection.	
Bach-Dang victory.	
Ly Dynasty.	
Tran Dynasty.	
Invasion and occupation by the Minh.	
Le Dynasty.	
1600s and 1700s	Trinh-Nguyen's secession war.
Tay Son Movement.	
Accession to power of the Nguyen Dynasty by Emperor Gia Lang.	
French attack on Da Nang.	
South Vietnam annexed by France.	
Popular armed struggle against the French.	
Patriotic and renovation movements.	
Insurrection led by King Duy-Tan.	
Founding of the Communist Party.	
General revolutions throughout the country.	
July 20, 1954	The Geneva Agreement on Vietnam.
New Year, 1968	Tet of Monkey offensive.
January 27, 1973	The Paris Agreement.
April 30, 1975	Fall of Saigon.

Under the Nguyen dynasty, in the nineteenth century, the Vietnamese reached the borders of Cambodia, Laos, and Thailand. As time went on, Vietnam became a unified country in terms of language, customs, and traditions. In spite of a tripartite geography, the

Vietnamese are an ethnically and culturally homogeneous people. The people of these three regions speak the same language, but with different tones and dialects.

There are three regions of Vietnam: north, central, and south. The northern people have been reputed as aggressive and overly ambitious. Historically, royal families dominated the central portion of the country. The royal dynasty was strongly established in the central area, mainly in the city of Hue. The old imperial capital was built in the central region. The people of Central Vietnam always found it more difficult to make a living than people in the other two regions. Nevertheless, they are proud to remain. Perhaps the austerity of life and land motivates them to be more attached to their cultural heritage. In South Vietnam, the people live in a rich land and this also influences their attitudes about life. Life in the south has always been slow and relaxed. They are less traditional than those born in the north and central regions. The southerners are also more responsive to western culture and adapt it in their lives.

Philosophy and Way of Life

Vietnam is a predominantly agricultural country and is polite and peaceful by nature. From the beginning, the people who maintained the culture were the peasants. They hold a preeminent role, but have always led a very simple life. Furthermore, the strong sense of morality of the Vietnamese people has been their most powerful weapon for self-defense and survival: constant, faithful, fair, sincere, and truthful. They live in the midst of virtuous folk songs, proverbs, legends, old fairy tales and stories. They use these teachings as guidance and principles in their daily lives. They prefer moral beauty to the material world. They prefer to perceive the depth of soul rather than the surface appearance. They are a most hospitable and generous people. There is a tradition to reserve their best facilities and best food for their guests. Their saying, "The guest comes first, the host comes second," demonstrates their wise and noble concept of relationship among human beings. They work seven days a week. All the work of plowing, harrowing, sowing the seeds, and transplanting the rice seedlings is carried out by hand with utmost care and patience. They live a life of thrift and austerity. At the same time, they are among the most valiant people in the world, for their collective spirit has helped them survive from the time of old. The Vietnamese learn from childhood to be acquainted with and to endure suffering. They are taught to endure in the hope of better days ahead; to endure for the good of their children, extended family, and country; and to endure for one's own survival.

A Personal Experience

Due to over 30 years of continuous war, from 1945 to 1975, some areas of Vietnam became very poor and the people could no longer survive by farming. The only way to survive was to study hard, so their future depended on education. In this way, it was hoped, the young people would be able to take care of themselves and their families when they grew up.

Many of the present generation's parents and grandparents did not have an opportunity to go to high school or college. Some did not even have a chance to go to school and never learned to read and write. These folks endured the hard work of farming, especially in Central Vietnam; although the people were willing to farm to nourish their family, the yield of the soil was poor. Even if they worked all year long, there still might not be enough to eat. From this kind of background many parents would get very tough and force their children to go to school no matter what. The parents would work very hard to give a bright future to the children because, in their lifetime, they had experienced the hardships and suffering of not knowing how to read and write. Definitely, they did not want their children's lives to end up like theirs. The next generation had to be successful in education, economy, and prosperity.

In many parts of Vietnam there are historical monuments that honor famous heroes and heroines. They were accomplished people. They are honored for their examples of piety and lives of virtue. Although each region raised its heroes and heroines, it seems that

North and Central Vietnam had more famous figures than the south. This may be true because it is not as necessary for southern people to work long, hard hours to sustain a pleasant and prosperous life. The soil is so rich in the south that people work very little and abundantly harvest anything they choose to plant. The farming is good, and farmers get over one-hundred-fold return on what is planted. The people from the south primarily study literature. They focus on liberal arts or business, and become poets or musicians rather than mathematicians. However, many of them invest in science and technology.

Traditionally, children inherit land from their family and the pattern of life goes on. They live in their family's house and treasure it as their own home. In their lifetime, they may not want to move from one city to another, due to their devotion to their ancestors' land. On the other hand, during time of war, people may live one day at a time, for they know not what will happen tomorrow. Whenever it is possible, however, they take time to enjoy life. They relax along the banks of the many nearby rivers and talk to their friends. These farmers might work for an hour and then sit down and talk to their friends for two hours. They do not mind long breaks. The personality of the southern people is sincere and "easy." They take it easy with many things and say, "Easy come, and easy go."

In other words, they just enjoy the day in its fullness. If they like, they talk to their friends for a couple of hours, they take a nap for an hour, they work for another hour and just enjoy the routine of the day. They go fishing while they are working. When they feel like working, then they work. They are generally content and pretty much laid back. Again, they live in the fullness of their spirit. They don't worry about getting rich, because they are automatically becoming rich from their fertile land. They have learned to live their lives with a calm and relaxed spirit. Even though they struggle occasionally, they don't have to worry about their education.

For the people of Central Vietnam, the soil is so bad that no matter how hard one tries, no matter how much one fertilizes the soil, the yield of the harvest is very little and of very poor quality. As a result, the young people in Central Vietnam study very hard. These children are taught it is through education that they can take care of their future. I didn't realize this until I went from South Vietnam to Central Vietnam to study in the seminary. All my classmates from the central area studied very hard. I wondered why on earth they kept studying day after day, hour after hour. I was much more relaxed. I am fairly intelligent and can read something once or twice and remember it right away.

Once I asked a few of them, "Why do you study so hard? What makes you study so much?"

They answered, "If I don't pass this class my parents will give me a lot of trouble. I will be in trouble with the faculty of the seminary. I will be in trouble with all the people who support me for my vocation."

I didn't understand at that time that the deeper reason was they wanted to get out of the impoverished situation in which they grew up, and education seemed the only way out.

When we live in a country broken down by war, where so many things are uncertain, education seems like the only guarantee of our future. Sometimes it is the only thing we can do for ourselves and the only thing we can take with us.

I never lived in the north even though my grandparents and family were from there. It seems to me that the people in the north study very hard, even though their land is very rich. They have many natural disasters, and often suffer from floods and famine. For example, when I studied the history of Vietnam, I learned that in 1945 approximately one million people died in the north due to famine.

In many different ways these facts helped me make comparisons and appreciate my diverse blessings, especially the gift of education. This also helped me to balance and enjoy life, too. I can see why my friends studied so hard. Even when some of them came to the soccer field they would have a little book or a little quotation or notes to memorize. For example, when we studied Latin, it was not easy to understand and therefore some of us had to write it down on a piece of paper and just memorize it. Even when we were playing soccer they were memorizing Latin. I never had to do so, and would just laugh at them and say, "Don't do that."

I really did admire them, though, for their willingness to study hard. Our teachers encouraged their students to study hard, and they didn't have any problems with us. We had no choice but to make the decision to study hard if we appreciated our family's efforts, if we recognized the goodness of the people who loved and supported us so we could receive an excellent education. Some might have better living conditions than others, but to have a natural desire and be given an opportunity to go to school was never an easy blessing. However, I learned to appreciate others and myself better through the gift of education, and tried not to take those blessings for granted. It made learning always easy and exciting for me.

Religions

The development and stories of Vietnam have been recorded for 4,000 years in literature, religion, and history. To succeed, the Vietnamese have had for centuries to be conscious of the forces around them – the seen and the unseen, the favorable and the hostile – and to understand their nature and intentions, to resist them if necessary and co-exist with them if possible, but to never provoke their anger. To comprehend this immense web of influences and matrix of powers, the Vietnamese have looked to what is in heaven, on earth, and amongst the people themselves. To penetrate the mysteries of heaven, to understand the workings and movements of the earth, and to establish relationships with people, the Vietnamese have traditionally sought the highest form of knowledge: the way in which things emerge, exist, progress, disappear, and re-emerge. They seek religion.

Generally, the people are very proud of their ancestors and remember how they gave up their lives in order to protect their lands and nurture succeeding generations. This line of thinking is commonly called, "Ancestor Worship." They honor the spirits of their ancestors with deep respect and sincerity. Within many Vietnamese homes, and inside all pagodas, one can find an altar dedicated to their ancestors. On anniversaries of deaths, and on traditional festival days, the relatives of the deceased gather together to offer food and incense. Then the entire family visits the grave of the deceased.

As an ideology, Confucianism is based on the teachings of Confucius. He was born around 550 B.C. and lived in a time of great political turmoil. As a teacher and unsolicited adviser to kings, he compiled sets of ideas about relationships between rulers and subjects, parents and children, husband and wife, student and teacher. Confucius was more of a moral and ethical guide than a spiritual leader. He was primarily interested in a social order based upon compassion, etiquette, loyalty, knowledge, and trust. Although many years have passed, Confucianism has remained a pillar of Vietnamese moral and spiritual thought. It is taught with five obligations or five ordinary duties: Nhan – love and humanity; Nghia – right actions in expressing love and humanity; Le – observation of the rites or rules of ceremony and courtesy; Tri – duty to be educated; Tin – self-confidence and fidelity toward others.

Another religion that contributed to the molding of Vietnamese culture over many centuries is Buddhism. It came from India and China around the second century A.D. Between 1010 and 1214, the Ly Dynasty made Buddhism a national religion. There were many pagodas built under the Ly Dynasty. Buddhism extended the question of knowledge from the social order to the general human condition, in an attempt to reach a rational analysis of the problems of life and a way to their solution. It holds to the Four Noble Truths: existence is unhappiness; unhappiness is caused by selfish desires; unhappiness ends when selfish desires end; selfish desires can be destroyed. Attaining the last of the truths can be done by following the steps of the eight-fold path: right understanding, right purpose or aspiration, right speech, right conduct, right vocation, right effort, right alertness, right concentration. "Right" means conforming to the

Four Noble Truths.

Into this rainbow of institutionalized religions, philosophies, and animist beliefs came Catholicism. In 1533, the first missionaries set foot in Tonkin, North Vietnam. By 1596 they were in Central Vietnam. In 1615 Portuguese Jesuits founded the first permanent Christian missions in Hoi-An, Da-Nang, and Ha-Noi. Under several dynasties of Vietnam, Catholicism was considered a foreigner's religion. The introduction of Christianity and its perception as a foreigner's religion generated many misunderstandings and conflicts in the country. However, Catholicism contributed two major transformations to Vietnamese culture: the adaptation of the Roman alphabet to the written language and the introduction of modern scientific method and Western logic.

Many Vietnamese, from all classes of society, converted to Catholicism. This development worried the mandarins and ruling classes, who saw the new religion as a threat to the traditional order of society and its rites. Between 1712 and 1720 a decree forbidding Christianity was enforced in the north of Vietnam. Under Emperors Minh Mang (1820-1840), Tu Duc (1848-1883), the Catholic Church was assaulted by a wave of persecution. Many of Christ's followers paid with their lives for their faith. More than a hundred thousand faithful were persecuted, including missionary Catholic clergy and laity. The persecution ended in 1885, with the French conquest of the entire country. Many Catholic religious orders established themselves throughout the country with convents, schools, colleges, hospitals, and seminaries. Despite persecution, the church in Vietnam has continued to grow. Today, there are over five million practicing Catholics.

American Protestant missionaries began working in Vietnam in the Mekong Delta area during the early 1900s. Protestant churches continue to grow, although with smaller communities of ethnic minority groups who live in the high plateaus of Central Vietnam.

Several more religions exist in Vietnamese communities: Islam, Hinduism, Cao-Daism, Hoa Hao.

Vietnam's small Muslim community consists mainly of ethnic Khmers and Chams. Their religious practices are not fully Islamic. They do not make the pilgrimage to Mecca. They do not eat pork, but they do drink alcohol. They pray only on Fridays and observe Ramadan for only three days. Their rituals co-exist with animistic and Hindu worship.

Like the Muslim community, Vietnam's Hindus make up a tiny percentage of the population. The Hinduism practiced today is an adaptation of the original form that reached Vietnam from India at a very early date.

In 1926 Cao-Daism, meaning literally, High Terrace or Supreme Being, was officially recognized by the French colonial administration. It was created in South Vietnam and attempted to bring all existing faiths in Vietnam under one single supreme creator. Cao-Dai still has many followers in South Vietnam.

Created in South Vietnam, Hoa Hao, unlike Cao Dai, means literally, Peace and Kindness. It avoids glamorous and complicated ceremonies in favor of a return through prayer, meditation, and fasting to early Buddhism's essential purity and simplicity. Even though it is a variant of Buddhism, its followers did not build any temple or set up a religious hierarchy. Hoa Hao has about a million followers.

When I did this research it was a great lesson for me. It helped me to appreciate the different points of view expressed in religion, sociology, history, and political psychology. All of these perspectives give me a deeper understanding and appreciation of life and faith. They are very rich in the collective spirit and meaning of Vietnamese culture—a culture, fortunately, that I was born and raised in—a land I call my dear homeland.

CHAPTER ONE

The Headline Means "Spoiled"

If there had been even a small newspaper headline on January 11, 1956, the day I was born, it might have read, "Finally a Son." You see, I was the fifth child and the first son of my parents. Little did anyone suspect that I would have five more sisters in the years to come!

My father was in the military, so we moved around the country with his various military assignments for many years. We all moved along with him to wherever he was assigned. And so it happened that when he was stationed in Da Nang my parents gave birth to me.

My father married my mother in North Vietnam. In 1954, the Geneva Peace Agreement divided our country into two parts. The north belonged to the Communist Party and south belonged to the Republic of Vietnam. The religious background of my family was Catholic. Before I was born my ancestors were converted to Catholicism and I received the faith with baptism at the time I was born.

Due to the experiences of my grandparents during the time of Christian persecution by the Vietnamese communists, the fear that communism would continue to suppress the religious practices of the Catholic faith caused my parents to uproot themselves and my three oldest sisters and flee to South Vietnam. At that time, my mother was pregnant with my fourth older sister. My father re-established in the south with other families in the military. At this time my father was in the army and worked for the southern government. It was not only for reasons of religious persecution, but also for political freedom, that my parents uprooted us and moved south. They did not want to live under communism.

Transportation of any sort was very difficult, risky, and expensive in 1954. In the midst of this evacuation, all of my other relatives, including my father's parents, his six brothers, and a sister, were left behind in North Vietnam. In 1963, I learned that my grandfather was imprisoned and killed by the North's People Court because he had worked for the French colonial administration before 1954. My grandmother and my uncles and aunt were forced to give up their home and other properties. They had a new beginning from emptiness and poverty.

I often consider the evacuation of my family from the north and the suffering they endured in their lives as the new journey of faith. In the early months of 1954, they left everything behind, including their loved ones; my parents began their journey of faith and left a trail for me to follow. I want to understand what they went through in their lives so that I can live my life in a deeper appreciation of my faith and freedom. In my family, we used to tell each other that in 1954 my parents uprooted themselves because of the fear of oppression and persecution of the Communism. In 1975, when the Communists took over the south of Vietnam and closed the seminary, I too, was uprooted and searching for freedom. Each of us was challenged to choose and to seek the so-called "freedom land," to live with human dignity and to have an opportunity to exercise our religious freedom. Historical events repeated themselves for political and religious reasons in my family as well as in Vietnam itself.

In 1956, the city of Da Nang received a vast influx of people. They were families of military personnel. They shared similar backgrounds and gathered together to live in small villages. The people of the north gathered together with their priests and began to establish their community of faith. Fortunately, they spoke the same dialect, shared the same cultural customs, religious festival celebrations, and their own unique traditions. Most of the families who lived in the parish were Catholic and had just arrived from North Vietnam.

14

In the beginning, we lived on the military base with other military families. Then, my parents moved us into a small village, Thanh Bo. The military base did not have a school, and it was not a good place for my family to live. My parents wanted to live near the church and school where there was a better environment to rear us. Frankly, they did not want us to see the behavior of the soldiers when they were drunk. My parents also wanted us to live in a safe place, since the military base was becoming a target for enemy attacks and rockets. My family built a house in a quiet area where they had a small farm to raise chickens and plant vegetables for our daily food. In this house, a peaceful and a loving home, I was born and lived until I was seven years old. My parents and older sisters always provided a world of love for me. No wonder I was so "spoiled."

Of course, my father was a very important person in my life. I loved him very much, but I didn't really appreciate his way of disciplining me as he tried to get me in order and to be organized. Because of his military background he would give orders that were short, concrete, and direct. I didn't want to be directed in that manner; I wanted a softer, gentler approach. For example, he would say, "Go and do your homework now." I did not like that. Instead, I wanted to hear, "It is about time to go and do your homework." For me, that was a gentler and a softer way.

This desire to relate to people still influences me today as I work and live with others. I am willing to take correction and accept criticism from people if they do so with gentleness. When I first learned English I would always tell others that if I don't pronounce some words correctly, or, if I say something incorrectly, please let me know so I might say and do it right. I really do appreciate when people correct me with gentleness rather than in frustration. I can excuse rudeness one time, but after that I avoid listening to such people. I liked my mother and older sisters' attitude better. They were nice and gentle. For me, I think it isn't really important what people share with me but how they share it. This is a result of my childhood experiences: I like a soft way of relating to others and don't like to be approached in a hard way.

Church as Center

The church in the village where I grew up was called Thanh-Duc Church, a combination of the names of two villages, Thanh Bo & Duc Loi. Commonly, we do not call the church by the name of a saint or a religious name. When we call the name of the church it means the name of the village also. The church and the community are one. The name of our church was dedicated to the Sacred Heart of Jesus. Our village was considered a Catholic village because most of the people who lived there were Catholic, but, they also had a Buddhist Pagoda named after the village. The Buddhists liked to stay in a Buddhist residence area so they could support one another and feel more at home with their religious practices and celebrations. It was easier for each group to gather together for religious activities when they lived close to one another. In addition, because it was a time of war, it was difficult to walk very far from home to church, or from home to pagoda. So this living arrangement worked out well for all residents.

When I was young my mother always took me to church. I had been baptized about a week after I was born, and, I went to church daily, not weekly, but each day. There was a strong devotion to the Blessed Sacrament and to the daily Mass among the Catholics and particularly among the Catholic military families. The priests also had been uprooted from the north and moved south with their people. These shepherds brought their own sheep with them and gathered them together into a community of faith. They were discouraged by the new regime's policies established in the north, and came to live in the south with their own people, hoping to continue their vocation in peace.

Attending church was a way of receiving information of all kinds about conditions and news outside our immediate village. The church community offered her members an opportunity to remain bonded to one another and to receive support and instruction on how to survive in what seemed a foreign land. It may seem strange, because Vietnam is such a small country, but the people in the cen-

16

tral areas are quite different from those in the north. They have different local customs and speaking tones that caused confusion. The priest, became not only the religious, spiritual leader and shepherd, but also the leader of our social life. He became the teacher, protector, and translator for families who were assigned to his care. He was our link to what was going on in the local community, around the country, and in the war.

The church bell rang early in the morning, around four o'clock. It rang three times before the Eucharist was celebrated. The first bell rang to wake up people. I mean it woke up everyone, and every other living being. The roosters crowed, dogs barked, children cried. Newspaper carriers ran to deliver the papers. The venders began to walk to alleys and routes to advertise their products were ready for their customers. All was alive! Fifteen minutes later, the bell rang again, and people began to walk to church. The third bell rang at 4:30 a.m. Then, the rosary was said and other prayers offered, followed with the Mass. The church remained open all day long for the adoration of the Eucharist until the Evening Mass for children at six.

Daily devotions of the Eucharist and the rosary were stabilizing forces in our lives. Mass was celebrated in the very early morning for adults so people could go back home and have breakfast before they went to work. After having breakfast with parents, children walked to school. All students were in their school uniforms. Of course, I had to walk to school with my sisters and their friends. Most of the time, I became an object for others to laugh at. Why? Culturally speaking, girls walk with girls, boys walk with boys; I was not supposed to walk with girls alone. However, it did not bother me at all. Besides, I needed to protect my sisters from other "Romeo" boys.

At the time of war, in Da Nang, there were only two public high schools; one for boys and one for girls. The rest of us studied at parochial or private schools. We went to school from Monday to Friday and a half-day on Saturday. After school, we walked to church for daily devotion and the Eucharist. It began at 5:30 with the rosary and other devotions to the Blessed Virgin Mary, the saints, and the

Sacred Heart of Jesus, and followed with the Eucharist at six o'clock.

The daily devotion of the rosary and attending the Eucharist was a requirement for children, not only from the perspective of the church but from the parents as well. All parents expected their children to be at church at 5:30 in the evening. After Mass, children went home and had to remember what the priest had shared in the homily or sermon. Parents would ask which priest said Mass. Who were the altar servers? What were the readings? What was it the priest said? They were just checking to make sure you attended Mass. Sometimes, I would skip Mass because I was having a good time swimming in the river. I would then have to rush home by a different route in order to meet some of the boys and girls who had attended Mass so I could know who were the priest and altar boys, and what the homily was about. I fooled my mother for a while, but in the end some of the other kids said, "Quang wasn't at Mass today."

After church, we went home and had dinner together. Then, we did our homework. The older siblings were expected to be tutors for the younger ones. We did not have television or any other types of entertainment at all. We told stories and fairy tales and even listened to my older sisters practicing songs for their choir. Then we gathered before the altar, thanked God for the day and prayed for peace and the safety of my father and others. Finally, we rested together in the same bed at ten o'clock. Half asleep, I could hear my mother's prayers amid the background of airplanes and bombing.

Play

We came to know most of the people who lived in our village. The setting was quite peaceful. Surrounding the house was an abundance of planted sugar canes. Around the well were different fruit trees. In the back yard of our home were plenty of lively chickens, several kinds of ducks, and fish in the pond. Our lives were quite good in the late fifties and early sixties. Water from the rivers was easily accessible for working in the fields. The irrigation equipment was built by hand. We raised corn and other vegetables. I especially remember and miss, the potato field, fishpond, and the river near the house. The potatoes were grown in lines, or rows, and they made a wonderful playing field for us children. My friends and I played a lot under the burning sun in the potato field. We would often dig out potatoes, catch a fish from the pond and wrap it with wet clay, then build a fire and cook ourselves a snack, even a good meal on a Saturday afternoon.

We usually swam in the river and skipped lunch. My mother did not like me to do that at all. She was afraid that I would get sick or drown. I was grounded many times. However, after lunch, the excitement of being a kid made me sneak out of bed and my mother's arms to meet my friends at the riverside.

None of us had any formal swimming lessons. We would just jump into the river and keep moving our bodies and all our muscles, trying to get to the surface. We would move our feet, our legs, and our hands like a flying bird, or perhaps doggy style. In my case, my oldest sister brought me to the river and taught me to flap my hands and legs. I don't remember how much water I swallowed learning to swim. There were many afternoons when we played and practiced and I don't know when I finally learned to swim; it just happened. We were not totally unsupervised. Normally my two older sisters were always near. In Vietnamese families the older brothers and sisters take care of the younger siblings most of the time.

There are two seasons in Central Vietnam: hot and rain. In the rainy season we looked forward to a bath under the rain. Children ran out of their houses and tried to catch the fresh water from on high. Under the rain, we sang folk songs and played a game of cat and mouse. It was fun!

During the dry season we gathered along the riverbanks, peeled sugar canes and ate them. Sometimes, we would challenge each other to dive into the water from the tops of the trees along the riverbanks. Eventually, I became a good diver because I had no fear at all. It didn't seem like a fearful situation. Each time, I would climb up higher and higher to show off. I just wanted to know what it looked like from up high and how it felt to fly down. When I think back I realize how foolish I was, but that daring character came to me naturally and it must be the hand of God that protected me. I wonder if anyone ever checked to see if the water was deep enough for diving. We were so lucky that none of us ever broke his neck.

During my childhood, I created my own toys. It is not surprising that there were a lot of wooden guns. When our fathers had permission to return home they would carry all their weapons with them. We boys, especially, wanted to be like our fathers and so we created our guns by hand because we had no access to modern factory-made toys. Sometimes we would make spinning wheels cut from food cans. We made a connection between them with a rubber band and would twist the rubber band to spin the wheel. Sometimes we tried to make cars out of a piece of wood or cardboard. These were our toys. There were times when we would cut the Y branches of a tree and make slingshots so we could hunt ducks; we even shot at each other. We didn't know how dangerous that was.

We didn't have anything to play with except what we created. I don't remember having many toys. Most of the kids didn't have fancy toys because no one had any money to buy them. Another reason was that most families moved quickly and often, so they tried to pack lightly. It happened again and again, depending on the assignments of their fathers, so most of the parents didn't worry much about having toys for their children.

When I was young, I would play "saying Mass" in the field with the other kids. A thin piece of potato substituted as the bread, and a little cup of red berry juice substituted as wine. With as few wild flowers, a broken table, a can of beeswax, a cross made from dried grass, and my sister's handkerchief, we began play of saying Mass. The chasuble was made up with my two bath towels that clipped together at both ends so that I could put my head through. I was always chosen to be the priest because I remembered and I could intone some of the Mass parts in Latin. It impressed my oldest sister a lot—she later became a nun.

I became an altar server in third grade. I had to learn the responses for the Latin Mass and the order of the Mass by heart. In our playing, I did exactly what the priest did in church, step by step, even though I didn't understand much of it. I remembered it all by heart. I didn't have any idea that I wanted to be a priest at that time. I did realize, though, that by being a priest you drew a lot of attention and the priest—baby one as I was—could have fun with his friends. Priests, somehow, were important and respected people in the community as my mother always showed to her pastor. I liked that part.

Sometimes in our play we would perform a wedding. We would pick out some girl and boy, force them to kneel down and then ask them the questions just like the priest asks the bride and groom when he marries them. I sometimes protested to my friends, "How come I can never play the role of a groom?" They answered, "Because you play priest better."

We played like this because we didn't have any movies, television or toys. We had to be creative. Obviously, we associated with the church a lot because it was so central to the activities of our lives, and so in our play we often dramatized situations that occurred in church and in school.

School

From the beginning, my first day in the school was not at all exciting. Waking up early in the morning, leaving home, and going to school regularly was a bit of a shock and a difficulty for me. Even though I really liked Sister Margarita, who taught me in kindergarten, and Sister Rosa, who taught me in the first grade, my mom had to stand at the door of the classroom because without her presence I would just run home. I would not stay in school. Mom would ask me to try to behave myself and would reassure me that everything would be fine, but I just would not stay. I was a pain in the neck for my mother. My father experienced none of that with me. He was off to battle all the time. It was my older sister, now a nun, who helped my mother to assure me. I needed to be assured. I needed that sense of security.

Sister Margarita was my very first teacher. She was young and beautiful in every way. She tried to calm me down and assured me that I would do all right in the classroom with my friends. But I would not listen to her words. First, she used a strong approach by raising her voice a little bit, but I didn't care. That approach did not in any way influence me to stay. Later on, she put her hand into the pocket of her habit and pulled out a lollipop to sweeten the situation and that worked a lot better. First she had used a hard way and got no results, then she used a soft way and it worked. It took about two weeks for me to adjust and after that I was fine. I began to open up and to have positive experiences in learning and making friends. Whatever the nun asked us to do I would always do the best I could.

Education in Vietnam is patterned after the European style where everything is memorized. Information is learned by heart rather than by thinking and processing as in the more modern Western system.

After I was ordained, I assisted a teacher at St. Vincent de Paul School in Denver. The teacher was very eager for the students to learn but she wanted the students to learn a subject matter for themselves. Teachers gave instructions and encouragement but the students had to learn to do things by themselves; they even had to learn how to spell and to write. In my childhood school, I remember Sister Margarita held my hand and helped me to write the alphabet. She would help me to spell and to write carefully. It did turn out that we had very clear handwriting. Teachers wanted to make sure that what we wrote was good and clear handwriting. Even in the crafting hours the teacher would demonstrate for the students and we would have to learn that way. We observed well and did it carefully, for we had to use well our limited resource of paper and other supplies.

I always liked being the center of attention and thought that I was rather clever. I often made our class a little exciting by pulling little tricks. I was often told that the school was a little more fun for everyone if Quang was there. My friends would let me know that if I was sick and didn't go to class for a day I was missed. I don't know why. Maybe it was because I laughed a lot or because I would help them with their homework. When coloring, I learned how to do it perfectly, the way the Sister had asked me to do. Colored pictures had to look real to me. I went very slowly and attended to every detail. I enjoyed doing this artistic stuff.

In the classroom, I was allowed to help the other kids even though I was spoiled and a kind of stinky guy at that time. I would often do whatever I wanted. Very often I wouldn't listen to the orders of the teachers. I was very lucky to have those nuns as my teachers. I had nuns from kindergarten all the way up to fifth grade. It was from them that I became familiar with the image of religious life, but I never thought of becoming religious myself. Like most people, I used to wonder, "What do they look like behind the habit?"

Later on, I was impressed when my older sister got her habit. After that, even when she would come home from her convent, I never saw her in regular clothing. Becoming a religious person was truly a transforming and mysterious experience for me.

For many years, I was president of my class. My duties included organizing visits to the teacher and classmates when they were sick. Sometimes, if a student didn't have money to pay tuition and had to drop out of school, I would organize my classmates to raise a little money to help that friend and family. Another way we helped our friends was to volunteer after school, helping our friends by working in the fields with them. There could be as many as thirty to sixty of us volunteering at one time. We were young and little, but with many hands to help, it made a significant difference when weeding was the job. Volunteer classmates, the more accomplished ones, would tutor students in their classwork after school. In this way the student wouldn't get too far behind and would be able to continue to study with us after the fieldwork was done. I used to do these things. We all helped out however we could. We never asked about what we were doing, or asked, "Why do I have to do this?" It was just the way we were brought up.

The first language I learned was my native tongue, Vietnamese. My early education was in French. In the Vietnamese language, we have only twenty-two characters. Spelling alone made learning a bit different and difficult for many of us. We don't have the characters z, w, f, and j. When I was in high school seminary we were exposed to many different ancient languages. We learned Latin because many church documents were often written in Latin. I learned English in 1982 when I came to this country.

The relationship of individuals, family, church, and school community was very close. If I got in trouble with school, my parents would experience trouble as well. If the priest called my parents into his office and gave them a moral lecture on my misbehavior, then I, in turn, would be in trouble with my parents. I remember my mother being called into the principal's and the pastor's offices many times. My parents didn't enjoy this at all. They really tried hard with every single effort to make sure I didn't get into trouble again, but only God knows why. I could never understand how I got in trouble with the rules all the time.

War

The worst thing I remember about my childhood is the death in 1965. It was a bad battle. The Catholics and Buddhists were in a conflict that had been provoked by local politicians. Mr. Ngo Dinh Diem was the first Catholic president in the southern government, and as a result there was a lot of unhappiness among the Buddhists.

I don't know how it all happened. One-night Buddhist men and women surrounded our village, Thanh Bo. Molotov cocktails were thrown into the houses of the village. The fire started. Children were crying. Adults were screaming at each other, and they used a lot of bad words. Women and children were evacuated and led to the church. The townspeople, Catholics, fought back with very primitive weapons created from containers and bamboo sticks. There were a few knives, swords, and guns. People were fighting and killing each other all night long.

On this night my mother woke me up because of the fighting. We had to evacuate. Whenever we had to evacuate, we went to the church because we felt it was the safest place. When we got there the church was packed with people. The priests, sisters, seminarians, and a few adults were working to see that it was the "right" people who were getting into the church. The local Catholics were let in and helped to settle down. Young men were standing guard around the church, making sure no one got in the church to harm us.

I observed and recognized those "Shepherds of the People" in these many helpful individuals, but I didn't understand what that title meant until the time I made the decision to pursue the priesthood. Those memories and images have often flashed back to my mind—how good our old priest was and how he wanted to make sure that all the people were safe. He walked among people and was asking questions like, "Where is your daughter?" or "Where is your grandson?" He remembered the names of all his people. I was so impressed. He used to call me, "The son of Mr. Thoa." Thoa is my father's first name. He didn't remember our first names but he knew who we were and what family we belonged to. The old priest really tried to make sure his people were safe and the nuns tried to give comforts to children to stop them from crying. The atmosphere was filled with fear and anxiety. We were afraid to turn on any lights in the church. We were afraid to even light candles for fear they would draw attention to the church. Just a few candles lit the sanctuary at the tabernacle and a few flashlights were used so people could move around and not step on each other.

This was the first time I saw dead people. In the morning, we went to check on our home. I saw bodies hanging on the fence and laying on the ground. This scene became a nightmare for me. I was only eight or nine years old. After that night, I was afraid to be in the dark. The images would appear in my mind. When I would wake up in the night to drink water, one of my sisters would have to walk with me to the kitchen or to the well to draw water for me. I wouldn't walk alone. If it wasn't my sister then it was my mom. I kept those dark memories for several years.

Later on, I often saw people dying from war and conflict as I had in 1965. It made me wonder why—why people have to die and what is the meaning of life and death. It all looked so scary and so ugly. These and many other childhood experiences formed in my mind a real hatred for violence, war, and death. I didn't know how to express it. I only knew that it was sad to see someone dead and it was painful to lose loved ones.

Death

My very first personal experience with death was the loss of two good friends in fifth grade, Vinh and Ly. It happened one afternoon when one of the sisters got sick and we were allowed to go home early from school. A group of ten of us young boys made a decision to go to my house. The sugarcane was available around the property and fruits were on the trees. The typically hot weather also made it enjoyable to jump into the river and cool off.

We swam for a while and then decided it was time for a snack. We chopped sugarcane and peeled it. Some of us picked fruit from the trees and laid it on the riverside. We ate and swam again. It was a great day.

Most of the time we swam pretty well. I used to be the last one to come out of the water, for I loved to swim far from the riverbank. But, that day I didn't feel good enough to stay in the water. I went into my home to dry myself. When I came out I saw that two of my friends had gone out to the deep water. They screamed out loud for help. I thought their screaming was a game. As young and innocent boys we were often fooling around like that just to have a good time. It was a stupid game that we played. We pretended that we needed help but we didn't. We were just teasing and just being kids. I didn't know that this time it was real.

Their reactions were not the same as usual. Indeed, they were in serious trouble. I sat there on the riverbank and yelled at them to cut it out and stop fooling around. Then, I realized they had bobbed up and down several times and were not coming up to the surface any longer.

I jumped into the river and swam as fast as I could to where I had last seen them. There were several inflatable tire tubes that we used to rest on after we were swimming awhile. The wind blew one of the tubes farther away. I didn't know what to do. I thought, "Should I go after the tube or should I go down to the water to find them first?"

The rest of my friends were on the riverbank. They cried for help, too. I decided to go after the tire tube first. I pulled it back with me to the place where my friends had disappeared. I was already exhausted. Taking a deep breath, I dove under the water. I tried to open my eyes to look around, but the water was mixed with mud, and I couldn't see them. I tried again and again. Finally, I grabbed one of my friends and brought Ly to the surface. I made sure that he held on to the tire tube. Turning around, I quickly dove under the water to find Vinh. The river was very active that day and there was so much silt I could not find him. I enlarged the searching area but with no luck. Vinh had vanished.

The adults of the neighborhood finally saw us and came to help. One of them brought Ly to the riverbank. There they tried to restore his breath. While others tried to help Ly, several adults and I continued to search for Vinh. About a half-hour later we finally retrieved him. We rushed Vinh to the riverside. They held him upside down by his legs, then tossed him on their shoulders and ran up and down along the riverbank. They tried to get the water out of his lungs and stomach. There was no sign that Vinh was going to make it. When we got to the hospital, Ly was pretty stable but Vinh had already passed.

I remember that the parents of Ly and Vinh rushed into the hospital and pushed the doctors and nurses away to embrace their sons. They cried. Suddenly and immediately, blood rushed out from Ly's nose. In the end he also died. I didn't know why. It was a great shock for my friends and me. It was a terrible and devastating experience for all of us who played and swam at the river that day. My friends and I witnessed the death of two of our dear friends on the same day.

It was difficult for me to understand and accept their deaths. How could we, the eight of us who survived, be all right and go on normally with our lives? My mother went to work in the field that day. My father was at war. After the accident, day after day, I spent a lot of time sitting on the riverbank with a little blanket wrapped around myself. I was shaking even though I wasn't cold. I was so scared. I couldn't believe what had happened. I couldn't understand why it happened or how. I didn't have an answer. One moment, ten of us were swimming and yelling and racing with each other. We were happily at play, eating sugarcane and fruits. Just one minute later everything changed and there were eight of us left.

Ly and Vihn had been a part of my life. In the classroom, one used to sit at my right hand and the other in front of me. They were important to others as well. We gathered money as a class and gave all the money we collected to their families to help with their burial services. The teacher of our class asked me to write a little discourse to express to the family how sorry we were about what happened. We thought it was a good idea for us and for them to express how much we missed our friends. I also wanted to sincerely ask the parents of my friends to please consider that we were still their children, too. We wanted to remain close to one another and to them.

After the funeral services, I found myself trembling with sadness and fear. I could not get hold of my emotions. I barely finished the discourse and a farewell on behalf of my class. We were raised with the mentality that boys don't cry no matter what. I couldn't help it and I broke down and cried. The whole class and the people cried, too.

At the time of my friends' deaths our small community didn't have a mortuary or a funeral home. Bodies were kept for several nights at home. The warm climate made it difficult to keep the body exposed longer than that. Each night my friends and I would gather together and go to one house for the rosary and prayers and then to the other house for the same type of prayer. There were many grieving family members and friends. This was the darkest moment of my life. I blamed myself for their death. I was very sad and felt guilty for taking my friends home for swimming. What if I didn't take them home that day? What if I kept my eyes on them at all times? What if I didn't allow them to go to the deep water? I trembled in fear and frustration, and I kept wondering, "Why?"

At the graveside, we again read the discourse I had written. We wanted to let the parents of our friends know that we wished to continue to be their children. I wanted them to know that they were not going to be alone, for some of us would be there to care for them. I remember I cried a lot at my friends' graves.

After the burial, each day I went to their homes to visit my friends' parents. Sometimes, I would help them to draw water from the deep well. Sometimes, I chopped wood. Whatever they asked me to do, I would do for them. I did not know that what I tried to do for them was a good way to help myself during grieving. I was trying to get rid of the fear and the guilt I carried within myself. As I recall those memories, I realize that I wanted to continue bringing the dreams of my friends into mine. I wanted to do whatever my two friends would like to do. In other words, I wanted their dream of love and of life to come true.

Later on in my vocation, these experiences help me to focus on the needs of people and to help them. It helps me do the best I can for the love of God and the love of people when I am doing the ministry of the church. I have always remembered my two former classmates. I lost touch with their families for many years after the war broke up our community. My father got a new assignment in South Vietnam. My family moved away and so did these families. I keep in my memory the mothers and my two friends. I still remember my friends because I want them to share their spirits with me in my ministry.

CHAPTER TWO

Quang Has a Vocation

How We Learned

The interest in going to school was very high among the youth of Vietnam. Because we grew up in a country at war, our future seemed uncertain. A good education seemed to be the only chance to take control of your future and perhaps obtain a better environment in which to live.

Children went to school from eight o'clock in the morning until noon. We walked home to have lunch and take a short nap. At two o'clock we returned to school for the afternoon session. We finished school at five o'clock. After school we walked to church to attend the rosary and the Eucharist. It took about ten minutes to walk from school to church. After Mass we were expected to walk straight home for shower and supper. That was the daily routine of school and church in my childhood.

Normally, most of the mothers went to church early in the morning. Some went to work in the city but most stayed home with their younger children. Sometimes they brought their babies to the field while they worked. Most of the fathers in the families I knew were in the military and often they were off to their posts at war. I grew up with my mother and my sisters. I saw many women, particularly my mother, who had to live with double duties in their responsibilities to their families. Often they functioned as both father and mother at the same time. They were protectors, educators, nurturers, moralists, and comforters as well as disciplinarians. They played an important role in my childhood. I associated strongly with my mother and my four older sisters. I often reflect on their abilities to love and to serve so well. Truly, indeed, they are my blessing. I learned so much about love, faith, hope, and life from their good examples.

Our clothing was very simple and none of us had many sets of clothing. A school uniform was one of them and it was important. In the parochial schools it was a white shirt and dark blue navy slacks for male students. Girls dressed in the traditional long white dress, the "ao dai."

Every parish in Vietnam seemed to have a parochial school. There were more parochial schools than public schools in the time of war. In order to go to public school you had to have an opportunity to stay in a city and have access to some sort of transportation. Most cities had one, perhaps two, public high schools; one was designated for boys and one for girls. Students could only enroll in public school if they passed the admission exams. They did not have to pay tuition. However, there was limited space so parents had to enroll their children in private or parochial school. They had to work hard to pay tuition for their children to attend parochial school. As matter of fact, children in poor families studied extremely hard in order to gain admission to the public schools.

My parents wanted my sisters and me to have an education directed by the nuns and the priests. I think they also hoped we wouldn't have to travel so far for school or deal with the roughness of the city. My parents told me that they felt much better if we attended the school of our parish community. We walked to school safely and studied in the atmosphere of the church's teaching. They believed we would receive both academic and religious education in the parochial school system. For me, it was not a problem where I went to school. As long as I had my friends to study with me, I was satisfied.

My parents worked hard to earn our living. They planned to cut their expenses in order to pay the required tuition. It was a great sacrifice on their part to provide a good education for their children. I knew many families in my parish community who had to give up their older children's education for the sake of the younger ones.

Normally, after they finished the ninth grade in private or parochial school, many girls had to stay home because they didn't have enough money to pay the tuition for high school. They stayed home to take care of their younger siblings, or they went to work to help their families. They began to learn different vocational fields.

My family didn't have to face that problem. In the end, all worked out very well for us. In the parochial school of our parish community, there was an award scholarship system to help the poor but good students. For example, if a student had excellent grades and was named among the top three in the class each month, then tuition for that month was waived. Fortunately, I was named to that top three consistently. I don't remember my parents having to pay tuition for me at all. My older sisters didn't have to give up school because they could use my tuition to pay for theirs. They went on to high school and they were happy. Even though we were called "trouble makers," my friends and I studied very hard because we wanted to relieve the burden our parents had to make ends meet. Students in public school also studied very hard because if they did not perform well, they would be expelled.

Most people in the villages of Central Vietnam worked as fishermen. They had boats and went to the open sea to fish. These parents worked hard to provide a better life for their children. They barely had enough money to pay for their children's education. These parents believed that education was one of the great ways, for some it was the only way, to take care of their future. They hoped their children would become teachers, doctors, or engineers, or work in one of branches of government. Monthly, if students did not achieve a satisfactory grade level, their parents would be notified. It was likely they would also receive a punishment from their parents. All of us, even though we had a little difficulty observing our daily disciplinary expectations and created many practical jokes, never forgot that we had to study and study hard. These challenges and demands helped me to develop a good respect and a strong commitment to study and hard work. They also helped me to appreciate the blessings I received from many loved ones in the family and in the community of the faithful.

Motivation

You might wonder how, as such a spoiled child, I could be motivated to join into the priesthood? Quite honor to you, I don't have an answer either. It seemed like a mystery for me to live in. After the fifth grade, the old pastor of my parish talked to my parents. I had served with him as an altar server since I was in the second grade. He told my parents, "Quang has a vocation."

My mom believed that God would let her know if this was true. She asked me if I would like to go to the seminary. In response, I said, "No way."

After a little while I was told by my mom, like it or not, that I would study at the minor seminary and again I said, "No way. I don't want it! I don't want to go there!"

I said this because, first of all, I always desired to stay home with my family, and secondly, because I didn't want to be in the seminary. For me, it was a weird idea to be a priest. I didn't have a good impression on the clergy or religious people at all. They seemed weird to me. On the other hand, I was excited because it seemed to provide adventures for me to discover. In addition to this excitement, I thought, by going to the seminary I would still be with my friends. There were four of us, in the group of altar servers, who were asked to consider enrolling in the minor seminary at the sixth grade.

In the diocese of Da Nang there was a high school seminary. If I went to school there I would have a greater chance to be with my friends and to see my parents and my sisters more often. However, according to the recommendation of the Bishop of Da Nang, Peter Marie Chi Ngoc Pham, I should be sent to the high school seminary at Hue, a city located farther north along the coast of Central Vietnam. The bishop said he thought I would have, by attending this seminary, a more effective educational and disciplinary program. I didn't know if this was true or not, but my parents and the bishop assured me it was. I became a little more trusting of my superiors and maybe my mother did, too. She had a hard time letting me study so far from home, but she gave in.

The bishop definitely wanted me to learn, in depth, the other religions of the country. In the city of Hue, the land of the Confucianism, there was also Buddhism and ancestor worship. He also believed the faculty was better. In the heart of Hue City, the ancient imperial land, were also a large number of Catholic religious orders with a variety of historical backgrounds and religious experiences. There were Jesuits, Redemptionists, Dominicans, Trappists, Sulpicians, Franciscans, and also numerous varieties of women's religious orders. I am not sure why there were so many religious orders established here in the land of Confucianism and Buddhism. Also, I wondered why there were so many religious orders when the population of the Catholics was only about four percent. Anyway, I went to a high school seminary that was about 120 kilometers from Da Nang. A new era of challenges, and the journey of faith for me to discover and to live had begun. It was August 23, 1966.

Later, my mother shared with me that the initial motivation she had for me to study in the seminary was twofold: first, to find out if God had called me into the priesthood or not, and secondly, so that I would observe and learn with better discipline. She hoped that the priests, sisters, and environment would help me to become a better person because she experienced how difficult it was to discipline me at home.

Before being accepted into the seminary at the sixth grade, students must have a complete physical exam and an academic test to see if they are able to handle the difficult curriculum. I passed all of them. I remember that weekend very well.

At least one thousand youngsters who had just finished the fifth grade went to take that defining academy examination. The scores on this exam determined the future for each boy—whether each would enter the seminary or not. From the one thousand taking the test, only one hundred and twenty of us were accepted to the seminary at Hue.

We were formed into two sixth grade classes, "A" and "B." Each class had sixty minor seminarians. I had joined the newest class of the Hoan-Thien Seminary. The name of the seminary was dedicated to two persons: Fr. Gioan (Hoan), a French missionary, and seminarian Thien, a Vietnamese student. Both were persecuted and received the crown of the martyrdom, in the Christian persecution period, on the same day. In 1986, Pope John Paul II canonized both of them in a group of 117 martyrs. It was a great day for the Mother Church and for the Church in Vietnam.

I thought it was a fun weekend for me. Everything was exciting. Everyone was so nice. The facility and its surroundings contained a deep quiet and a curiosity where one could engage in the discovery of the mystery of faith and life. Frankly, I was more attracted to life in the seminary than to becoming a priest.

Seminary

Even though it was a new, exciting adventure for me to study in the seminary, it was also a very difficult adjustment. There were only a few sisters who taught there. I always have fond memories of the women who were my first teachers and I enjoyed my classes with those sisters. They seemed very gifted by nature and very gentle in their teaching and guiding of their students. I appreciated them very much for their gifts. I believe it was a result of having grown up mostly with my mother, grandmother, and sisters. The women in my life loved me as well as encouraged me to become the best of myself for others. They are special for me.

These wonderful women definitely did a good job encouraging me, but they could not help me to establish a deep, strong self-discipline. I got my own way at home and was very spoiled. I rejected authority when it came to dealing with conflicts between what I thought or wanted to do and what was required. As a result of my stubbornness, I struggled with self-discipline up until I finished high school seminary.

Even though Hue is located at the center of the country, the attitude of the people in the royal city was very relaxed. They weren't considered among the economic elite, but they considered themselves high class in education and inherited the rich ancient traditions of the historical dynasties. They never seemed to hurry at all. The children walked to school or rode a bicycle as if they were having a "fun ride." There were very few cars on the street in the morning; many young men and women could be seen walking different directions along the streets, going to their schools. It was a lively picture of the life in the ancient imperial city.

After the school day, another scene of even more simple peace took place in the city and its streets. The students returning home from their schools created a lively life with laughing and talking as they walked slowly along streets. Beautifully dressed girls in their long, white "ao dai" and their traditional large hats, called "non," formed groups of three or four friends walking together. They seemed very happy. Boys walked with boys and girls walked with girls.

I still miss the lively and peaceful images of these mornings and evenings in Hue. The peaceful scenery was so lively, but quiet, as no one seemed in a hurry. That was the way of life outside of the seminary wall. However, in the midst of this peaceful spirit I still heard the sounds of bombs echoed from afar.

Actually, the people of Hue always seemed clever and quiet. They didn't talk very loud. Even when young girls were seen laughing together, if they met a stranger on their way, they would stop laughing and quiet down. On the contrary, the young men seemed always to make a lot of noise. I guess they were trying to impress those beautiful young ladies. As I recall those moments of my life, I realize those young men were trying to enjoy their lives as much as they could. Unfortunately, after high school, many would be called to join the military in a time of war. Therefore, toward the end of their high school education, they experienced a lot of anxiety and depression regarding their future. There were a lot of pressures during the senior year of high school. They needed to pass comprehensive exams to continue their education in college or they had to join the armed forces. To me it seemed regardless of what their wishes were, they just might end up in the battlefields.

In the seminary, we, the seminarians, were the ones responsible for taking care of about 14 acres of grounds. There were many types of flowers. We also had a wide variety of bonsai to be cared for around the chapel of the seminary.

The Blessed Sacrament Chapel was the center of the seminary life, where we celebrated Eucharist and nourished our spiritual life in prayer. It was built in an octagonal shape. All sides of the chapel connected with a modern roof that pointed toward the sky with the sign of love and life: the cross of Christ. Each side of the octagon had a door that connected with the bridge across the water pond to the main ground. On each side of the main gate of the chapel stood a very special bonsai plant. Both had been coaxed into the shape of a phoenix. Each, in their shape of adoration, showed the best of their beauty as the sign to worship the God of heaven and earth.

On the first Friday of each month we held a procession of the Blessed Sacrament around the chapel's seminary and its facility. We sang and prayed as we carried the Blessed Sacrament in procession to enter the chapel. We passed through the gate shaped with the adored phoenix, which reminded me of the image of the Ark of Covenant that the Jews placed in the temple. We entered into the House of God and offered prayer and thanksgiving. Each class in turn adored the Blessed Sacrament for an hour.

On the other side of the gate stood a set of bonsai trees coaxed into the shape of two dragons. The two dragons faced each other and held the sun in their arms. This second image signifies that we should all bow down before God's presence as the Sun of Justice who rises to rule the world. He is the Light of Truth, the Light of Hope, the Light of Faith, and the Way of God's Wisdom. The meaning of this symbol was so rich. I used to wander around the chapel working on meditations of God's love for the world, and for all, especially for myself.

The architecture of the seminary's facilities helped me to develop a sense of love for the artistic. Sometimes, I would design ordination cards, prayer cards, or print calligraphy of favorite quotations. Sometimes, I just painted. Often I used painting as a means to develop self-control, to gain the virtue of patience. Likely, I used painting to work an answer, or to focus on a certain issue and solve a problem. Painting has been a great resource to help me to pray or to write music. If I wanted to write a song about God's love, I might paint the Last Supper. While I was painting I might have feelings and develop a theme for a song. Or, if I ever had to help a certain person, I would allow myself some time to think about how I could help that person. I found myself doing something else to concentrate on the problem, and eventually, I would come up with an answer for the given circumstance. I found it was worthwhile to pray, to think, to discern before I passed judgment on someone.

Even now, most of the time I ask myself what makes people do this or say that. Could it be that they don't feel good or have some problem? They may have some reason that made them say something they didn't mean. What makes people do something to hurt someone else's feelings? I always sought reasons to forgive before drawing a conclusion. Even if I didn't have an opportunity to talk with someone who hurt me, I satisfied myself with a reason that allowed me to forgive rather than to hold him or her in my anger. As soon as I wanted to forgive, I didn't bother with the disappointment any longer. In doing artistic works such as painting, writing songs, and meditating on prayers, I found myself with peace in my heart. I began to understand the words of St. Martin de Tours, "I am a soldier of Christ. I cannot fight."

Music and the Arts

Composing music has been a great way for me to release pressure and to solve problems internally. I began to learn how to compose music when I was in junior high in the seminary. Music was a good technique for me to collect my thoughts and pray. Sometimes, I painted on a theme of a theological thought or just an expression in religious daily devotions. It helped me to enhance the methodology on reflections of the beauty that God created around us. Since we are created in God's image and live in the world, we are doing incorporated things to bring the whole world back to the Lord because we are part of that world.

Whenever I needed to relax, or in a moment of prayer, I often had a desire to paint or to compose. Philosophically, I loved to write songs because it was a good way to see the unification of the whole universal world and to be one with God, others, and the whole cosmic creation. I liked the notes of music, harmonized with each other to praise God.

Lately, I have been composing a lot of songs in the minor key. The minor key helps me express my feelings better and it is smoother. I grew up with experiences of loss and sadness in time of war. I saw people say goodbye to their loved ones. Deep down inside of my heart, and in my life, I saw brokenness take place in the lives of people. I felt that I was one of them. I found that the minor key of music had a greater impact in soothing my spirit. It helped me to grieve and to cope with the loss in my life. On the other hand, it is more soft and pleasant in tone and makes it easier to listen and pray. I composed hymnals in Vietnamese for liturgical worship and for spiritual exercises.

My family had always been a little worried when they saw me painting, because they recognized this as a sign that something was troubling me. When I had a situation I needed to work out I used to be quiet and silent for a while. Most of the time, I painted or wrote songs and spent that time thinking about what I would do or say in different situations. It was a different behavior from the normal daily life I used to interact with others.

I have written only a few songs in the major key. I did so when I felt joyful in my heart, or for the traditional celebrations of Christmas, New Year, and Easter. I am glad that I can express my prayer and feelings experienced throughout periods of my life. I found it was worthwhile for me to get in touch with my own feelings and struggles. By composing music I could balance myself easier.

Summer at Home

In the first year of the seminary, my friends and I were eager to go home for the summer. We waited and waited for those last days to pass before we could have summer vacation. I think it is a very common feeling for young students like us at "boarding school" to feel this way. It was so wonderful to finally go home for summer break. We said goodbye to each other and hoped that we could have a wonderful summer. There was another reason for us to say goodbye; we might not see each other again the next school year. Some went home for good because they didn't have good grades at the end of the school year, or, because they were poor and were unable to pay their tuition, room, and board. Others, depending on different circumstances, might have to return to help their families. Some of us had to return home because a family member had died. If their families needed them, they would not return to the seminary.

For me, I wished that I would not return to the seminary after summer at all. It was hard to live apart from my family. But, when I got home for a couple weeks, I found myself missing the life of the seminary. I came to realize I was becoming quite different from local people in the parish community. Life after going to the seminary was not the same anymore. Everyone said that I was growing up so fast, looked well, spoke funnier, was still polite, and seemed more prayerful. I didn't believe what they said. I was the same. Maybe I grew up a little bit, but people began to treat my friends and me differently.

Our former classmates from grade school began to treat us differently. They did not walk arm-in-arm with us or they did not put their arms around our shoulders as we used to do. This was the common social act of friendliness in our country. This was a sign that indicated we were friends, that we were buddies. I didn't know how to feel about it but accepted it as it was. Later on, my oldest sister pointed out to me that once I entered the seminary I was set aside, I was marked. People still "love you and wish to do the best for you," she said.

I had mixed feelings about this. In one way, the recognition was nice, but it was sad because I could not talk to them, buddy to buddy, any longer. There were certain boundaries they set up and I was not allowed to trespass. To be as we were, as we had been earlier, was no longer possible.

All honor to you, I think they were changing more than I was.

I tried to accept the reality and be happy. I reached out to friends, relaxed and enjoyed the summer with my family. My pastor treated me very well; he wanted me to stay in the rectory so I could be a chaperone for younger altar servers. It was the first summer vacation in 1967.

CHAPTER THREE

Seminary Life

The seminary was built at the end of the eighteenth or beginning of the nineteenth century. A French architect probably designed it, since it was funded and built by the "Les Missions De Paris." It was operated and administered by the Sulpicians. The altar of the chapel was right in the middle of the octagonal building. The younger students, the sixth graders, would always sit in the front and the seniors at the back. This arrangement was so nice because everyone was able to see, participate, and celebrate the Liturgy of the Hour and Eucharist. Every Sunday people from the surrounding communities came and celebrated the Eucharist with us. They came from many of the parishes around Hue City. They had a deep, deep affection for us. They liked to see us and how we worshipped. We had a very rich tradition and prayerful liturgy in the seminary. It was a peaceful and nourishing celebration of the Eucharist. This faith-filled environment helped me to feel more comfortable in developing the art of prayer. However, I still couldn't escape the feeling of being homesick. A lot of the time was spent thinking about home and how much I missed my loved ones.

At the north side of the chapel was a beautiful tower bell. It sounded peacefully with the tone of the Gregorian chant "Salve Regina." It rang three times daily. I loved the chant, but it didn't sound very good in the early morning because I wasn't awake from sleep yet. Otherwise, it was a very pleasurable sound of prayer. Before lights out at night, the sound of the bell was quite beautiful and peaceful. We joined in the spirit of thanksgiving at night prayer before we rested.

Many evenings, I took a walk around the facility after evening prayers and enjoyed the chapel bell's sound. We had about a half-hour to relax after dinner. During my walks I meditated on the meaning of the hymn with the sound of the chapel bells. It seemed that life was so peaceful, even though I knew there was war going on in some places. I prayed for peace in the country and for all people, including my father, involved in the war. May God protect them and keep them in peace. I wished that we didn't have to kill each other anymore.

The weather in the area was quite predictable. During the winter we had rain. It would not rain very hard, but did so every single day for a couple of months. It was a very soft rain. I loved walking in the soft rain through the "dew-fog." I know it isn't like this in America or in the western countries; it was not cold in Vietnam throughout the monsoon season. I never wondered how long I would wear my sweater. We just needed a light coat and that was good enough for the winter, although it could get cold. During the summer, the weather was hot, very hot. Basically the weather was either dry or wet. There were beautiful trees and plants all around the campus and city. Each season had beautiful fruit trees and different types of flowers blooming all year long.

The whole campus was about fifteen acres with a high cement wall all around. It was encompassed with eight soccer fields. We could not see anything outside and no one could see us. The walls were thick and made with concrete and solid rocks. I tried to "escape," sneak out, several times by standing on the shoulders of my friends to climb up and over the wall. I would jump from the top of the wall to the street and run into a nearby store and buy a package of candy, chocolate, or something we all thought we needed. As a matter of fact, we really didn't need anything. We just missed life outside the walls of the seminary. We would do some sort of silly thing like this to add a little excitement to the day. Of course, Quang was always nominated to carry out these "missions" for the class because I was quick and regarded as "stubborn."

Even though I always missed home, I came to like my fellow

classmates very much and began to appreciate the many differences, important roles, and identities we all had been called to. I didn't fully understand and appreciate this opportunity until the communists took over South Vietnam in 1975 and closed up the seminary in 1978. I was not allowed to study in the seminary any longer. How much I missed the life of my youth in the seminary!

On the weekend the seminarians' families were allowed to come and visit their children. However, my father and mother realized that this opportunity was not a good thing for me. Each visit was a wonderful experience for me to see my family, especially my younger sisters. While my parents had a conference with the priests, I walked my sisters around the facility and explained everything that they asked and wondered about. However, after my family went home, I was distressed and it took a long time for me to get back to the normal routine of life in the seminary.

I continued to want to go home and my parents knew my wish, but they encouraged me to put aside all emotion and focus on a life of prayer. They pointed out that I should be grateful for the opportunity to serve the Lord in the ministry of the poor. I had mixed feelings about what they said, but somehow I heeded their advice to remain in the seminary.

In my development as a priest, the image and excitement of "coming home" has been a very useful thought to me. I know how wonderful it can be to come home from the long journey of one's life. Spiritually, it is good for me to be home with the Lord, who is God of love and life. In the ministry of the priesthood of Christ, especially in the celebration of the Sacrament of Reconciliation, I am really happy to help people to come home. It is a great reward for me to see how one comes home to live with God and others in love. It is rewarding to see that depth of love build up one's life in faith and hope. It has been an effective way for me to show respect and honor to those who, with all their hearts, come home to live with their loved ones and with God. They are courageous people! To come back to the Church, to God's home, to the house of faith and prayer, is a great gift of wisdom that overcomes all obstacles in life to live in the fullness of God's grace and love.

For me, the Mother Church is a home where individuals can come to live and be nourished by the love of God that She has for all. I came to believe that God prepared me in a hard way to serve people, as I was not able to appreciate God's way when I was young. Now, later in my ministry, I feel much closer to home no matter where I am sent to serve, to bring God's love into the lives of people. I have a home where love is. It has been a wonderful feeling to help someone else feel at home. For me, love creates and yields strength, while strength in the form of power cannot create love.

Even though those regular weekend visits from family were not the pattern, my father would sometimes stop by to see me if he got a few days off from the war. I appreciated him very much, but it was not my father whom I missed so much. He was gone so much of the time when I was young and growing up. It was my mom whom I missed the most. My father was a military man and trained to be disciplined in the expression of his emotions. There was little emotion shown. Even though he loved me very much, he hardly ever expressed that feeling to me. When he visited me, I saw him as a gentleman who was full of energy and ready for anything. I appreciated and respected him for who he was and I didn't ask for more. He helped me to be a little stronger. In my culture we were trained that boys don't cry.

In the summertime, when I was home from school, my father would get a couple of days off from his duties and we would spend time with each other as a family. These good times never lasted long, however. We always had to say good-bye again.

Giving

While training and studying in the seminary in Vietnam and later here in the United States, I gradually overcame problems associated with submitting myself to the Church's authority. I accepted the challenges set before me in given situations. I learned how to do what was required of me. My focus shifted from "what" or "if" I am going to do something, to "how" I am going to do it and do it well.

In the seminary, I looked forward to Saturday afternoons because we seminarians would go to the remote villages to serve the poor as a part of our community service. I loved to give haircuts to those boys and girls. My friends and I learned to do this job very well. After all, we didn't want to make these children look foolish and feel ugly. We had some classes to learn how to be a barber from juniors and seniors in the seminary. I loved doing it for it was a very good way to spend time with the children in these rural villages and help them feel good about themselves. I felt good when I saw these children, in their new look, with big smiles on their faces. It helped them look good. I felt pretty good about doing those haircuts, even though I did feel sorry for the first boy whose hair I cut. I gave him a new look as a little soldier. He looked that way because his hair kept getting shorter and shorter as I tried to correct my mistakes. This happened even though I had been trained for about three hours on how to operate the hand-held clippers. Practice did help because I became faster and gave a more professional look. I didn't know that, when I came to this country and was in seminary, I would still be cutting hair for my friends at Conception Seminary College and St. Thomas Theological Seminary. I used to cut a lot of hair for the priests and seminarians, but none of them would do this for me. I had to go out for a haircut. (No hard feelings, my friends, I didn't trust your skill anyway! Ha!Ha!Ha!)

In the senior year of high school seminary we learned how to give vaccinations to the people in the villages so we could assist medical personnel in their works of charity. I became pretty good at this and could give shots so the kids didn't even know the needle was in their skin. They didn't even cry. I did this by clowning around. It was over before they knew what happened.

On weekends we went out to do apostolic works in the small villages and parishes nearby. We taught Catechism and prepared children for the Sacraments of Initiation (Baptism, Penance, Eucharist,

Confirmation). We were also introduced to a lot of sad situations. Sometimes, we had to collect dead bodies from streets or behind burning houses where battles had taken place a day or a week before. Mothers cried for the loss of their babies, and children cried over the bodies of their parents. There was mourning all over the villages, as the war went on and on. It was sad.

I kept thinking, I have to do something to make it better, to help someone. My friends and I didn't know what to do. If there was any small way that we could help these victims of violence and war, we did so. The thought and feeling that we might help these people to rebuild their lives made me feel more at ease. I thought if I could not prevent death at least I could give comfort to the mourners and share their grief with my prayer. Unfortunately, I rarely thought of the depression associated with death and the suffering it brought. It was devastating. It became a reality when I was a little older and lost some of my good friends and loved ones. We talked about it. We faced it. We knew that God cried with us, too.

During the week, we had a very set schedule for the day. We would wake up about six o'clock and be ready for Morning Prayer at seven o'clock. After Morning Prayer, about seven-thirty, we had breakfast. Classes began at eight o'clock and lasted until about eleven. Then all five hundred students went to the chapel for the celebration of the Holy Eucharist. After Mass we enjoyed lunch and a nap from about one to two o'clock. At two we went back to class until about five in the afternoon.

At five o'clock we took a break for physical education that was required. Most of the time we played soccer unless there was a heavy rain. Why soccer? This sport was probably a carry-over from the European system of education from the French missionaries. Actually, we could play basketball, volleyball, table tennis, or soccer. I liked to play volleyball, table tennis (ping-pong), and soccer, but I was too short to play basketball. Somehow, I was never able to have a good time playing basketball. But I could run very fast. I ran a lot and played pretty well in the soccer games for many years.

At six o'clock we cleaned up and went to Evening Prayer. We then had dinner followed by a fifteen-minute break for walking around. We returned to the study hall on the main floor of the seminary to do our homework. The younger ones studied under the supervision of the older students. The juniors and seniors spread themselves around the study hall, which held about one hundred twenty of us. They made sure we studied and didn't fool around. At about nine-thirty we went to the dormitory. At this time of the day there was a strict silence as we went to bed. We cleaned up and after our personal night prayer we retired for the day. There was no talking, yelling, or fooling around allowed in the dormitory. Of course, I was always in trouble for not observing this rule as I was looking for opportunities to play practical jokes on my friends.

At ten o'clock it was lights out. I used to cover my head with a blanket and continue to read and study using a little flashlight. I used to memorize my notes and assigned readings to be ready for the next school day. This was true, especially, when there were poems that we were required to know and recite.

I liked to be ready when our teachers expected us to learn something by heart. We were required to stand in front of the class for these recitations. If you were able to do it from beginning to end with no hesitation, then you would know for sure that you would have a good grade. Frankly, the only thing that really excited me and made me happy at that time was to be with this large group of friends my own age. We continued to challenge each other to complete our studies with excellent grades. I really enjoyed that the most. Each month we had a report card and the top ten received a reward. The top three were granted free tuition for that month. I always received both each month. I must have had a hundred of them. Getting these rewards became part of the routine for me at school. I didn't know that by receiving these rewards I helped my family a lot in reducing their stress. They had to pay for my tuition, room, and board. All I knew was that I had to be in the top three. It was fun and exciting! What a mystery of God's love and providence for me!

My prayer life was forming as a young person. Sometimes, I prayed well, but most of the time, I really created trouble. During the first year of the minor seminary I really missed home badly. I couldn't just let go of all the good times that I loved so much. I missed the tender care of my grandmother, mother, and sisters. I was now living in an environment that was all boys and they could be really rude to one another. I managed to pass through the first year, but I didn't want to stay in the seminary. However, I kept thinking of my family's sacrifices for me and I didn't want to hurt their feelings. They were proud of the fact that I was studying for the priesthood. I even thought that if I left the seminary I would put my parents in a difficult spot with my pastor because he was my sponsor as godfather for the seminary. Most of all, I was afraid that my parents and family would think I was good for nothing if I just gave up. It was so difficult and frustrating for me to decide whether to go on with my studies or simply return home. About ninety percent of that time I just wanted to go home because I did not like the disciplined life imposed on me by the seminary. What a baby!

In 1969, students stayed at the seminary from the beginning of the school year until the end. There were no Christmas holidays, no New Year holidays, and no Easter break time with our families. Why? It was expensive buying tickets, but mostly it wasn't safe on the roads. The faculty of the seminary tried to eliminate the risk in traveling at the time of war. Later on, we had vacation during the school year when it was possible to travel. For the three months of summer we were allowed to go home. During these summer months we were under the supervision of the local parish priest. So most of the time I found myself reporting to someone.

The priest in the local parish gave us particular attention. For example, in church we were to sit in the sanctuary during all of the services. At our church we had several seminarians at the college level and one or two who were assigned to the parish for their year of internship. There were also about thirty of us who were at the high school level. All the young men sat on one side of the sanctuary and all of the sisters and novices sat on the other side. The sisters were teachers, nuns in residence who did the pastoral care and helped train the novices. The novices were young women in training for the consecrated life. We had many young women in that vocation. What a beautiful life they choose to live. The pastor, an old faithful priest, always said to us, "We are called so we need to behave and respect the blessing that the people as the church are bestowing on us."

I didn't like to sit in the sanctuary, but I really treasured the spirit of love that I had with my religious sisters and brothers. We had good times in the family of faith and love. We sang at Masses and did summer ministry for the youth in the parish. The whole parish community loved us and we loved them, too.

Culturally, the Catholic Church in Vietnam has some differences with the Church in the United States, although the structure of the religion is the same. Normally, the left-hand side of the church is reserved for women, and the right-hand side is reserved for men. If I went to church with my mother or my sisters I was not allowed to sit with them. This was true of all families. Boys sat with their fathers and girls with their mothers. It was a little strange when we walked into church. In the sanctuary it was the same. That was the way I grew up. I don't know why they had that kind of arrangement, but I can see it so clearly as I share this observation with you. Even nowadays it is still practiced in different parts of Vietnam. I guess it is a part of the cultural observations that establish a people's identity. Perhaps, they were avoiding any distractions when people prayed or celebrated the Eucharist. As a young kid I did not care about that, I sneaked around anyway. It didn't matter to me where I sat. The priest would just say, "He is very liberal and stubborn," and that was it. I didn't take this custom very seriously at all before I went to the seminary.

Even though I had problems with the self-discipline, I did pay attention to my schoolwork. I paid very careful attention to education and tried to be successful by completing every task they required of me. Unfortunately, I didn't pay much attention to what people thought of me. This concern only came into my being after I finished high school seminary; then I paid a little more attention to self-discipline. As a high school seminarian I knew that I had to study hard and do well academically. A drive to be competent was part of my personality.

During the first couple of years I was miserable and created a lot of trouble. I determined that if I created enough difficulty or problems with the church authorities, they would kick me out of the seminary. In that way I could tell my parents, and my pastor, "They don't want me. They don't think I have a vocation." With this reasoning, I thought I would release my parents from the embarrassment of facing the priest and their neighbors. I began to create more and more trouble at the seminary.

Tricks

In the eighth grade I got tired of one hundred twenty of us being on the second floor. We were in the same dorm with the sixth and seventh grades. It was possible to go from the second floor through the third floor and up onto the roof for fresh air, but this was not allowed during the day when we were tightly scheduled. Every day, after a long day of study, prayer, work, and play, we would be very tired. Once we got to the dormitory at night we would rush to the toilet to finish up for bed. This was a communal toilet, a trough along one wall of the second floor. The first students to the toilet were the first ones to get into bed. We were a bunch of kids and we were not very polite about waiting our turn. Regardless of the restriction on pushing and shoving a number of the bigger guys were always first at the trough. One day I was just sick and tired of this part of the routine and decided to have a little fun at others' expense.

Early in the day I got into the dormitory, which was strictly forbidden. It was not permitted for any seminarian to return to the dorm unless you were really sick. Anyone found in the dorm had better have a very good reason. Permission from the chaplain was necessary to go there, but I went anyway.

I went up to the second floor of our dorm and I prepared a trick on the other students. Previously, I had figured out how to hitch the positive and negative electricity to the metal trough of the urinal. The trough was long enough for about twenty boys to stand up to it at one time. It was angled at about fifteen degrees to make is easier to clean.

When nighttime came we returned to our dorm and the routine repeated. We were supposed to be absolutely silent. It didn't happen that night. When the first twenty big boys ran to the urinals there were very loud shouts and screams of pain. The electricity, 220 twenty volts, was quite a shock to them. I didn't know that I could have killed them with such a high voltage. All I remember was that I thought it was so funny. I didn't think about the outcome.

Later, the boys told me that it stopped their actions abruptly. The first bunch at the urinal rushed out of the toilets and out of doors. They thought they had seen a ghost. It was so funny to me at that time. Some of my buddies looked at each other and smiled; they knew that Quang did this to those big boys for what they did to the little ones. Everyone seemed to forget what the rules were.

Very soon, the chaplain showed up and demanded to know what all the noise was about. What was the cause of all this disorder? He walked into the toilet area to investigate. I don't know if he tried it or not, but he soon returned saying to the students, "Bring Quang to me." My reputation had been established in the seminary as a devil being born into the world. The chaplain knew who did it.

When I was brought into the presence of the chaplain he asked me, "Did you do that?"

I said, "Yes."

I had to kneel down facing the wall for the rest of the night. That was my penance for breaking the rules and doing harm to my fellow students. About five o'clock the chaplain came and woke me up. He sent me to the kitchen for my community service as part of fulfilling my penance. I had to help the sisters—"Lovers of the Cross," who cooked for the seminary—make breakfast. I was not allowed to go to chapel for Morning Prayer, for I had set myself apart from the community by doing wrong things.

I liked hanging around the kitchen with the sisters. They worked hard and I could help them. During the school year I had been sent to the kitchen on many other occasions when I misbehaved and the sisters knew me very well. They wondered why I kept doing practical jokes to others.

They asked me to mix the powered milk for breakfast. I boiled the water and mixed it with the powder milk. It required quite a large volume to serve five hundred seminarians for breakfast. I had to stir it all by hand because we had no machines and it was quite a heavy task. I had to stir and stir and stir milk in the big container. The sisters told me that if there were enough bubbles on the surface of the container it was ready to serve. While I was stirring I noticed that the kitchen was next to the laundry room. I stopped work for a moment and slipped into the laundry room. I got a cup of laundry soap to mix with the milk. I stirred it all up and it looked good. All you could see was the foam that came up. It is supposed to be that way anyway. I told the sisters that the milk was ready and they agreed.

After Morning Prayer everyone came to the refectory for breakfast. They had milk, cheese and egg sandwiches. Everyone seemed to enjoy it, but for the rest of the day they had diarrhea. They had to cancel classes for the entire day.

Of course, once again, the chaplain figured it out because I was the only one who didn't have diarrhea. And, of course, he asked again, "What did you do this time?" And, of course, like every single time I got in trouble, I told him the truth. My purpose at that time was to get the faculty to kick me out of the seminary. I attempted in every way to get myself expelled, but it didn't work. The bishop of Da Nang had warned them about my menace, but that I would be a good and smart student for the priesthood. I didn't understand what made him tell the faculty that. Only now, as an adult do I realize why. God chose the weak and made them strong.

The morning routine at the dorm was always the same. When we woke up, the president of our class would roll out of bed and lead us in prayer while the chapel bell was ringing. In the ninth grade I was elected the president of my class, believe it or not, and when the bell rang I got out of bed and screamed at the top of my lungs, "In the name of the Father and the Son and the Holy Spirit."

Everyone responded, "Amen." I continued, "Oh Lord, come to my assistance." Then, every student would roll out of bed and kneel on the floor. They were suppose to respond, "Oh Lord make haste to help us." We would then say the Glory Be. After the wake up prayer we would rush into the restrooms to shower and get ready for the day.

As president of the class, I would be the last one to leave the dorm, making sure all students went to the chapel. If anyone got sick I would report it to the chaplain so they could be moved into the infirmary.

Every Monday morning we had a lecture and a ceremony in front of the seminary in which we honored and saluted the flags of the country. Following the ceremony the rector of the seminary or the dean of students or dean of studies gave the lecture of the week. Sometimes it was one of the chaplains or one of the faculty members who addressed the whole student body. Most of the time we had to be in line with our class to listen and to behave well. While we were in line the rule was, "Don't create any trouble."

The ceremony would normally take about a half-hour. Afterwards we would start our normal classes. One Monday I got so bored listening to the dean of students, I sneaked behind the line of my friends. I used a paperclip as a needle to poke someone's behind. Oh boy! They jumped up and created a disorder. The whole of my class had to kneel for the rest of the lecture. I was a terrible guy for my classmates. Generally, they liked me a lot because I always helped them in their studies, but not when I created trouble.

I loved the priests who taught in the seminary. Fr. Pierre Gauthier taught me in French literature. Fr. Santiago and Fr. Loc taught me music and instruments. I had Fr. Petit Jean for mathematics and Fr. Ossalango for history. Fr. Paolo Duvan taught me Latin.

These priests came from the Missionary of Paris. The group of local priests in the Archdiocese of Hue taught me science, religion, language, arts, and liturgy.

Each class was held for about an hour and then we would take a five-minute break and move to another class. The schedule was pretty heavy and hectic. Most of the time we were required to study very hard. This was a part of the training a seminarian received to become a priest. They should be knowledgeable and willing to study. Many of the course requirements didn't make a lot of sense to me then.

Each quarter we had final exams. From the final exam results at the end of the school year we found out about half of the group would be sent home because they didn't receive good grades, or meet the health requirements necessary to stay at the seminary. Each year when I returned to the seminary after summer vacation, I found out I had lost a few more friends. This was especially true during high school. On the other hand, each year a few more seminarians were added from dioceses around the country. These were young men who had been selected by their spiritual directors. They recommended who had a vocation and who did not.

Each year I hoped I would be one of the guys sent home. I kept waiting, but they wouldn't let me go. I kept praying that God would give me a sign to know whether or not He wanted me to be in the priesthood. My spiritual director assured me that he would tell me the truth about my vocation, but in the meantime I would have to continue to pray and to study. I couldn't allow myself to fail academically to achieve my goal of leaving the seminary.

By the time we got to our senior year there were only twenty-eight of the original one hundred twenty students left. The twenty-eight of us had been together for almost six years. There was a wide variety of strengths and skills among the young men in that group. Four years later when I finished seminary college there were only twelve of us left.

The final interruption of our studies was caused by the fall of Saigon on April 30, 1975. Soon after that we were forced to go home.

We were evacuated from the seminary and forced to return to our families. In the end, there were only five from that class of one hundred twenty who eventually became priests. A friend of mine, Fr. Paul Tam Minh Nguyen, is in Sydney, Australia. Another friend, Msgr. Francis Dung Minh Cao, is in Rome, Italy. Two friends, Frs. Thao Doan and Hieu Nguyen, were ordained in Vietnam and are taking care of people in the very poor, remote areas. They call this place "The New Development Area." They are deep in the jungle with ethnic groups of people in the barren soil areas. I was ordained in Denver, Colorado, in 1990 for the Archdiocese of Denver.

Boy Scouts

In the senior year of the high school seminary I had several interesting experiences with scouting. Boy Scouts and Girl Scouts came from different religious communities, getting together to help people who needed assistance rebuilding their lives. Most were Buddhist scouts from several different communities. We were brought together for a common purpose—to help build homes for the poor. We didn't worry about whether anyone was Catholic, or Buddhist or practiced ancestor worship. All we could see were Boy Scouts and Girl Scouts and when we greeted each other we just honored the spirit of the servant. We were here to serve the needy. That was how we related to each other. We were servants and leaders. We recognized in each other the goodness of a decent human being. We didn't ask each other, "What religion are you?"

The first thing we would do was salute each other using scouting ritual. We greeted each other with inquiries about what area or what troop we came from. We didn't ask, "What temple or church do you belong to?"

Most of the time we were very warmly enthusiastic in our welcomes to one another. It was an enriching experience for each scout and for me.

Scouting helped us to become knowledgeable in ways to serve and to communicate with others. We shared our entertainment skills to build up the spirit of people whom we were sent to serve. Normally, we gathered children together to sing songs, tell stories, and play guitars.

Most of the songs we would teach the children to sing were folklore songs that described the history of Vietnam. The songs were about the love of the country. They were about the beauty of the rice field and the peacefulness of the family in the evening before sunset. One of my favorite songs was about a shepherd who sat on a water buffalo playing a bamboo flute while the buffalo returned home from the fields. It was a peaceful scenario. It seemed all creation and its creatures lived and moved in peace of heart and mind.

The buffalo was the property of the family and entrusted to the care of the children. The buffalo spent the day in the fields working. In the evening the children would lead the buffalo home and make sure they got feed from the green grass in the pasture. As they lead the buffalo they made sure they didn't walk into rice fields that belonged to someone else. The children sang and talked with one another. The buffalo walked peacefully side by side. It was a beautiful scenario, describing peace. Even though the children would be acting silly sometimes, the scenery was still very peaceful. Another beautiful thing was that after they got home they would take a shower at the well or take a bath in the river and say to each other, "Let's go to church." They made sure they went to church to pray.

The people in the community lived close to each other and knew each other pretty well. They called each other by name and invited, "Go to church."

Every family made sure the children went to church first, and afterward they would go home and have their dinner together. Dinner was the most important meal of the day for the whole family. Of course, dinner was followed by homework, evening prayer with their family, and then to bed.

Even in the middle of the war the spirit of faith of the people would not stop growing. There were peaceful scenarios. People were not wealthy in material things, but I think they were rich in spirit because of the love they had for each other and the togetherness they enjoyed. Families tried to stay together no matter what. I was so happy to be a part of their lives. Eventually, life became much more complicated. Severe problems took place while demands on humanity increased rapidly. We couldn't help people alone, and that was when the participation of all scouts was a tremendous help. I treasured these memories of helping people in the time of war and of need. Together, we built houses, gave haircuts, provided basic medical supplies, and most of all, helped children to continue their education.

Later on in my priesthood when I find too much stress in a given situation or there seems to be a lot of complaints or demands, I try to remember the hardships of the time of old so I don't become discouraged or depressed. If I survived those situations before, there is no reason for me to fail to love and serve people now. I remember when we had so little to share with people, and we made it work for all. How much more we have now compared to what people had before. With a little effort from everyone, we can rebuild the whole world.

CHAPTER FOUR

Forgotten People

Each year we had to stay at the seminary and study for a continuous nine months, even though the school year seemed longer because of uncertain political circumstances that brought many anxieties to us. Many of us worried about the safety of our families. On top of this, the demands of high academic achievement required a great deal of time and commitment. Many of us felt a lot of pressure. Despite all of this, I have to admit the setting and environment of the seminary were perfect for me. The spirit of beauty and peacefulness in the seminary became a great place for my prayer life. It was a wonderful place for me to go through the process of training in self-discipline and for the priesthood. Even though I was quite a troublemaker at first, I could not deny that this setting, as well as the spirit of prayer life, compared to the normal life of the people on the "outside" of the seminary, was very attractive to me. I lived very well in the spirit of thanksgiving for God's blessing that had been given to me. I grew to be more grateful and didn't take God's blessing for granted. I began to pay respect to others.

I remember the New Year's Eve of 1968, the "Year of the Monkey." There was a horrendous attack on the city of Hue by North Vietnamese soldiers. This battle definitely created a sense of fear and ugliness of war. It caused a great loss for everyone in the country and it brought a deep sense of sadness into our lives. It was a tremendous experience of hatred and corruption. There were serious conflicts in politics and war all over the country at that time. As a result of these evil forces many people had to leave their homes in fear and in sadness. Many fled to the seminary to seek safety. They came for protection, seeking refuge in the house of God. We took in everyone who came, thanks to the goodness of Archbishop Phillip Dien Kim Nguyen, the Archbishop of Hue, who gave us permission to help people in the time of crisis.

The seminary survived the attack. Just a few rockets blew up on the roof of one building. The damage was minimal. In the beginning of 1968, in the midst of the New Year celebration, the attack took place and several North Vietnamese soldiers were killed on the top of the building and inside the property of the seminary. One part of the building was destroyed. This involved only one wing of the building and it was restored afterward.

Many people came from Dong Hoi, Quang Tri, and even from the city of Hue. In the time of disorder and evacuation, the faculty, staff, and students did their best to take care of people. We created different kinds of tents and shelters to accommodate the large number of people. There were trailers set up on the soccer fields for temporary housing because most of the facility on the main floor was full of people. We used study halls, classrooms, chapel, gymnasium, dormitory, and meeting halls as shelter for the refugees who had been directed to our compound. It was amazing and hectic. With many extra people with us, we ran out of supplies of food and sanitation in a couple of days.

"What are we going to do?" I asked my rector.

He said, "God will provide!" Truly indeed, the supplies arrived soon after from the military personnel and from other charity organizations. In the hectic situation I prayed that everyone would be safe from harm and from the rockets and bullets. After a very long day of working, sitting against the wall of the chapel with my classmates, still hearing sounds of explosives from afar, children crying, people's prayers offered to their God, I closed my eyes to rest. A radio that announced bad news on the Tet offensive made me have bitterness in my heart. It should be the time of traditional celebration of the new springtime for all, not for the sadness that took place in the beginning of the year. Tet would not be celebrated properly if the coming of the New Year was not greeted by the crackling of countless firecrackers to scare the evil spirits away. This 1968 New Year was greeted with death and gunshots.

Tet is the most important festival day of the Vietnamese. It is the first day of the lunar calendar year. It occurs at the beginning of the spring equinox. Springtime is of great significance for the agricultural nation of Vietnam. It is a celebration of the return of spring as it symbolizes a new beginning and the rebirth in the religious perspective. This is a time when people truly open their hearts to everyone, friend or foe. This is a time for paying debts, correcting faults, forgiving the errors of others, letting go of past difficulties, and making a new beginning as well as new friends from old adversaries. People make an effort to wear brand new clothes. They sweep and clean the entire house, especially the family altar. They repaint the house and decorate their homes with many different kinds of flowers such as plum, peach, and yellow apricot flowers. Likewise, they prepare traditional dishes to celebrate with their families and friends. The spirit of the New Year is in the air and in the heart of the people.

The Vietnamese people believe that by ridding all thoughts of evil one contributes to the general concourse of the family, community, and of the universe. Everyone makes an effort to come home from wherever they work and live for the New Year celebration. During the first three days of the New Year people invite the deceased to take part in the life of their descendants. The first day is reserved for family and paying respects to the ancestors. People gather together at the house of the firstborn and offer incense, food, and drink as a sign of respect and thanksgiving to God and their ancestors. After this ritual, the grandparents and parents sit in their chairs, under the family altar, to receive the respect of their children and grandchildren. Traditionally, the older generations prepare themselves to have plenty of red envelopes, as the sign of a prosperity blessing and a good happiness wish, to impart upon the younger generations. They put new money in a red envelope to give to their children and grandchildren. Beginning with the firstborn, to the youngest, each one takes a turn and comes forward to pay respect to their grandparents and parents. Each receives a red envelope as a prosperity blessing and a good happiness wish as they begin the new life in the spirit of the New Year. Then, they share the very first meal of the year with each other. In the afternoon of the first day of New Year the nieces and nephews come to the house of their relatives to pay respect to their family's elder uncles and aunts. The descendants ask for their ancestors' blessing and protection.

The second day is the day to honor the teachers. Individuals come to their teachers' homes and express their appreciation for teachers who imparted wisdom, knowledge, and intelligence to them as students. Normally, all students happily gather together to pay respect to their teachers. Sometimes, at the teacher's home, younger students meet the former graduated ones. Even though these former students graduated many years ago and hold different public offices, they still remember and appreciate their teachers. It is good to see them together to pay respect and to express the spirit of appreciation to their teachers in the most profound way.

The third day is reserved for visiting friends. This is a day of conversation and reminiscing, usually over games, food, and traditional beverages. This is the most merry and noisy day. The spirit of celebration of the new life—new beginning, to the future with great hope for peace, good health, prosperity, and happiness—is the dream of everyone in Vietnam.

In the midst of all the tragedies in the beginning of the New Year of 1968, our faculty had students keep up our spiritual prayer during the day and our service schedule for the refugees. We gathered together in each dormitory and celebrated the Eucharist with the people. Wherever people were, so was the Eucharist for we had enough priests in the seminary to offer Mass. We created different groups to gather wherever we could so people did not have to get lost in the hectic traffic on the seminary property.

Those days of fear and sadness that I experienced as a young seminarian have had a powerful impact on my life in the priesthood.

My friends and I learned to accommodate the needs of the people and lead them to know that God is love and life. We tried to help all the people who lost their homes and their loved ones. I experienced many different memories regarding the grief that each individual felt for their loss. Each of us has experienced the loss of things, environment, career, possessions, or loved ones. For me, the loss of loved ones is the most difficult experience for people to have and to cope with in their suffering—to overcome the grief and accept the reality that their loved one has gone. It was hard for me to believe that during the two weeks of helping people in the New Year of 1968, we were calling people refugees right in their own homeland. It didn't seem possible then, and even now it seems a quite strange thing for me to understand. All I could see was the ugliness of war and its consequences of suffering that people endured.

During the two weeks that people were at the seminary it was difficult for us to maintain and clean up the seminary facility. It became a very important task for us to keep up the entire facility for safety and health reasons. We asked the scouts and the military troops to help us clean up the facility and provide food and water. They did a good job helping us wherever they could. It became the routine for my class, each day after Morning Prayer, to go to different sections of the facility, the gymnasium, classrooms, and study halls to clean up. Some groups worked in the kitchen cooking.

One morning, a couple of days after the people had been with us, I sensed an awful smell while I was cleaning. I followed the smell to the corner of the classroom I was in. There I found a young woman holding her baby in her arms. She had wrapped her baby in a bath towel. She was swaying, softly singing a little folklore song for her baby. Ordinarily, this scene would have been a most pleasant sight to experience. Many mothers in Vietnamese families used to sing little country songs so that their babies would go to sleep. But, this young mother kept repeating the same words over and over as if she didn't know what she was singing. Her eyes were closed as her mouth mumbled the words. I believed she was out of her senses. I discovered the towel wrapped around the baby was saturated with yellow water. The deadly smell came from that towel.

It was determined that the baby had been dead for at least couple of days. The mother could not believe her baby was dead. She just kept holding the baby close to her heart and pretending her child was still alive. A stray bullet took the life of her child during the evacuation from the Tet attack. We had a tough time convincing her to let go of her baby so we could prepare a funeral service and burial for her child. It was a painful experience for her and for us all.

Witnessing the tremendous loss of her baby to that mother, I realized how painful the death of a loved one could be. The death of her baby was completely unacceptable and beyond her belief. It was so painful. She could not accept the fact that her baby had died. She simply lost her mind for a little while. She didn't know what she was doing or saying. She didn't know how to express her feelings. She behaved completely as though her baby were alive. She laughed and talked to her baby as though it were alive. She was breast feeding her baby, laughing and smiling at her. Then she would drop on her knees and hold her face in her hands and cry and cry. It was so emotional. It was terrible. It made me feel awful and lost. I didn't know how to react to her emotions. I was numbed and didn't know what to say to her. I didn't know how to comfort her loss. All I knew was, deep down inside my heart, to be silent and experience her pain. I knew that God was with her, too.

I helped her to clean up the spot where she was sitting and living the past couple of days. Other people in the classroom tried to help her and give her comfort as well. They were all shocked. I appreciated the comfort they gave to her, but I felt sad and disappointed when I heard them say to her, "Please don't cry," "God loves you," or "God will take care of you." I had been taught that God is Love, Truth, Way, and Life, and I knew the truth in those common statements that people said. I knew from the bottom of my heart they were right in their words of comfort to her, but I would have preferred that they say nothing, that they just be there with her and say no words. I knew that it is very hard to understand and to accept God's will. It is so true and profound to say that God's love for us is true, great, and everlasting, but it is extremely hard to accept.

After she fell asleep I went away to continue my work for the day, but I kept thinking how would I react if I were in her position. At first, just like that young mother, I could not accept the situation either. I wasn't sure how to analyze the feelings or how to put it in words at all. I just wanted to tell the people in the classroom, to ask those "good people" please not say that "God loves you" to her, because her baby wasn't with her any longer and she could not see God's love for her in her time of despair. All she wanted was her baby. She might feel overwhelmed to experience the sadness of life without her baby. Her future seemed lost. Maybe she knew and accepted her suffering better than I could. But, I kept being silent. I knew the people said what I would like to say to her. I prayed for her and asked God to keep her in love and in faith.

For me, the baby girl was the source of the love in her life. That child gave her the will to live in the struggles of life and gave her the strength to go on with life in a time of war. I didn't ask her where her husband was but I overheard that her husband was in the military. Maybe he was in the battlefield at the moment of his child's death and his wife's mourning. I could not imagine the moment they would meet again. How painful it would be! No doubt she had seen a lot of different disasters take place in her life, but she had to have kept hope for a better future. She would have kept hope for her child and now her baby was gone. It seemed to me that her hope was gone as well. Many people lose hope because they lose their loved ones. It was tremendously painful for the young mother whose baby was beautiful - healthy, and suddenly dead because of the war. What an ugliness of war! When would peace take place on earth? How it could happen?

I kept thinking if God really loved the young woman, He shouldn't have taken her baby away. In my heart, I knew that God didn't take the baby away. He did not take away the hope and the joy from her life. War and selfishness of heart had done that ugliness. Give us your heart, O Lord.

During the time of sadness, I kept seeing the conflict between faith and actual human conditions. I didn't want to see those horrible things happen to anyone. From a theological point of view, I didn't know how to answer the questions that young mother might have. Deep down in my heart, I knew that God would take care of her (through our goodness) no matter what. Eventually, I believed that Christ even died for her and for all. Christ died for all of us so that we may have life, the life that has no end. The power of death cannot dominate us, but that is in the life to come. At this very moment and in every single day of my life I still struggle to open my mind and my heart to accept God's will. The journey of faith began as I tried to understand and forgive those bad things that happen to good, innocent people.

Through these tough experiences, as seminarians, we were able to gain a deeper understanding of pastoral care. I found that I would never be able to satisfy or bring hope and love to the people completely. Only God is able to do so. I am only a servant of God. On one hand, I trembled in fear and became depressed seeing the bad things that were happening. On the other hand, my experiences with these suffering people increased my faith. I felt good helping my classmates and other people serve the Church and continue Christ's mission by bringing peace into the disorder of everyone's lives. In our lives, there was much suffering, death, and sickness that needed to be taken care of. Many poor people struggled with power and oppression. Many different things, good and bad, took place each day. I learned to trust and to love God more each day. I learned that, through individuals' consent to do God's will and to give with all their effort, God's peace would find a room in people's hearts. God would then complete the works of redemption for humankind, and to restore His goodness and holiness in the hearts of all.

During those days of tragedy at the seminary I kept thinking and praying with the words of the Prayer of St. Francis of Assisi. It convinced me that God would make each of us an instrument, a channel of peace. God could use me to bring hope, comfort, love, and healing to broken hearts. I wanted to help, at least to share with others, a portion of God's goodness. I wanted to bring God's healing into those places where people had endured suffering. These experiences definitely became a part of my personal resolution to listen to God's Word and to nurture God's Love in my vocation.

The difficulties would come and go while the refugees stayed at the seminary. When there was a cease-fire in the refugees' home area, they would return to their own village and rebuild their homes once again. They temporarily left their homes for safety, but they would always return to rebuild. For over twenty years of war this happened over and over again in the lives of the poor. Still they did not give up their homes or their land. In their home and their land they were reminded of the spirit of their forefathers, who shed their blood to protect the land of their ancestors. It was given to them as a heritage of the family. The land held the life of their ancestors who once lived and fought for their freedom and values. Culturally, the family-oriented Vietnamese could not live far from the tomb of their ancestors. They would never willingly abandon their homes, which were their identity and honor.

The refugees at the seminary exhibited a tremendous spirit of life and courage. They were proud to be who they were. Even those who were fearful of oppression and war were willing to return to their land and rebuild their homes over and over again. They used to tell me, "Only the rich and the famous are afraid to lose their wealth. We, the poor, have nothing to lose. We will remain with the land our ancestors entrusted to us."

They told me the truth that as long as they lived on the land of their forefathers they would have a better opportunity to take care of their ancestors' tombs. This thought helped them to feel that their loved ones would continue to protect them, and their ancestors' spirit would never leave them unaided in their lives. Traditionally, in the lives of people in Vietnam, the spirit of communion with the living and the dead remained strong among the practice of religions. These attitudes and behaviors were shaped by the customs and beliefs of ancestor worship. Truly they had the choice to go home or to relocate to a new living area, but most chose to go home to their forefathers' land.

When the seminary was flooded with refugees we prepared whatever we had for breakfast, lunch, and dinner, and shared it with them. Most of the food supplies came from our own cache, but we also received donations from a variety of charitable groups such as Catholic Caritas, Inc., the Red Cross, and other religious communities in the country. We seemed to have a lot of medical supplies from Germany and France. They supplied us with powdered milk, sandwiches, rice, vegetables, and canned food so that we could feed the people who were with us temporarily. The menu was the same for lunch, a bowl of rice and a sandwich made with peanut butter, cheese, or jelly. The refugees helped us out in whatever way they could. They did some food preparation and cleaning right along side the young seminarians.

While serving lunch one day at the soup kitchen, we ran out of food before the last person was served. There stood a little girl. We were out of everything except for my sack lunch, which had a butter sandwich in it. I could not disappoint this little girl. Her eyes looked at me, full of hope that she was going to get something. I didn't even think twice. That sack lunch had a sandwich and a little can of fruit cocktail. I had it because the lovely sisters in the kitchen were still taking care of me. They knew I would never remember to pack my lunch.

As soon as I gave the girl my lunch she was completely silent. She didn't say a word. I wondered what she had on her mind. Her eyes suddenly opened wide and brightened up her face. She mumbled some words to indicate that she was happy and satisfied even though she didn't know what was in the bag. I didn't do a big favor for her at all. All I knew was that I was happy to see this little girl had something to eat. Her smile at me was a true blessing. It made me realize that many times I took blessings for granted. As young seminarians we had not yet had to worry about where our next meal would come from. I knew that I could go back to the kitchen and ask for an apple from the lovely sisters.

This small incident with the little girl helped me to appreciate all good things I had been receiving from others. I realized that true happiness took place in my life when I opened my heart to the needs of others. It didn't mean that we were satisfied and happy only when we got all that we wanted in life. The true happiness is a reward for those who share from the heart with the needy. It is a moment when we recognize the goodness of others. It is a moment when we return what love has been given to us. To love and to serve in true happiness is when someone, from the goodness of the heart and from the blessing of the Lord, shares with the less fortunate. I thanked God for that opportunity. I came to realize, eventually, that when we made someone else happy it was a true thanksgiving to God and to all who nourished us and taught us. It is an honor to give from the heart.

Later on, living and serving in the United States, I have learned as Mother Teresa of Calcutta has taught, "Do small things with great love." Now it completely makes sense to me. I am grateful that I have had many opportunities to practice this virtue of wisdom and to recognize that it is possible to have happiness even in moments of disaster and in the depths of suffering and loss. Perhaps it is more visible and in some ways easier to exercise this great gift in the ministry of people in moments of grief and loss. Truly indeed, we can recognize the Lord's blessings to us through the goodness of others. From this point of view, I see it is better to give than to receive.

We had a group of medical doctors and nurses from Germany who had come to the hospital to serve. They came to town and served on a big boat in the river. It was a real hospital, a very big hospital. It was considered very, very expensive and a very good institution. When people were admitted into the hospital, which was administered by a group of German volunteer doctors and nurses, it always increased their hope that they were going to get well one hun-

71

dred percent. That particular group always gave the impression to the poor that they were so very talented and gifted. They were professional in their skills and practices. They were a beautiful gift and blessing to the Vietnamese people.

It was true that God offered us a glimpse of heaven in our everyday life, even in the time of despair, if we gave ourselves a moment to recognize it and celebrate it. We should recognize this taste of heaven because the Lord always offers us comfort and nourishment. God comes to us in many different ways through the goodness of people around us and changes us to be the Eucharistic People. Even during those days that were tough and hectic I began to look at the given situations and see that the Lord our God was always with us. Always!

When the war was not raging near us we would go out into the communities. We helped rebuild and repaint homes that were damaged by rockets and bombs. We also taught the local people how to read and write. We tried to provide health information to help them upgrade their living conditions. Sometimes we would teach the girls and boys to do artistic things or show them how to sew clothes with sewing machines. On top of all the skills we taught people, we also learned from them to become storytellers. They had many stories to tell us. They gave us their knowledge on the gifts of natural herbs and how these were used in the lives of the poor. I found these natural remedies very interesting.

At the seminary, we tried to provide the children with classes every day after breakfast. Normally, we would go off campus and teach kindergarten and even the higher grades in the faith communities. It was good for all of us to serve people in a variety of aspects. There were many opportunities for us to help someone less fortunate than us. I could see the eagerness in the children to learn. They really wanted to know about the things around them. I pondered on what made them desire to learn. They made me think about who I was. I pondered on where I was, with everything provided for me, and that I didn't see its blessing but still created troubles in order to get the seminary to kick me out. I felt ashamed as I compared myself to the children who were less fortunate than me. They wanted to learn as much as they could. They showed me that I shouldn't take God's blessing for granted. They had suffered a tremendous loss and faced many difficulties in life. They were homeless and poor. They were away from the only home they had known and still they were eager to learn. For the first time in my life I felt ashamed of myself and of my behavior.

In my heart I talked to myself and resolved to become a better person. I determined to do better even though I knew I would not be able to change overnight. I believed that I would never give up any opportunity to study, to learn, or to gain insight from a deeper understanding of the situations of life. I would learn by opening wide my eyes to see, and my mind to observe how people reacted to the realities of life, as well as from books. During good times or bad, I believed that everyone, everything, could become my teacher. So bad things happened and I experienced how people helped me. I began to learn and to appreciate my own fortune. I began to show appreciation for the blessings I had received. I was so very fortunate to have my family, teachers, the Church, and the community I lived in. It made me feel that I could participate rather than just belong. I decided that to serve people I would try to do ministry together with people.

Many of us joined with a Boy Scouts program to learn survival skills and to help poor villagers around us. We tried to live and be active by bringing the goodness of the Lord our God into the lives of these forgotten and unfortunate people. We did common services in different villages with humility.

We tried to build houses with simple construction materials. Basically, we went into the woods and cut bamboo trees for the house structure. The roof material was hay from the field. It was amazing to me how the whole house connected together with coconut strings and bamboo nails. It was still a home for the poor as long as they had each other. The military in the area were kind enough to help us by providing materials. What we needed we requested and they would help us out. They would bring a whole load of bamboo trees for us. Then we would use the skills we learned in Boy Scouts to create a house for a family. We used ropes made out of coconut trees. Nowadays, some of the poor families are still building their houses with those simple materials. We made roofs out of hay or palm branches. There were really no homeless people in Vietnam for long.

There was no need to seek any government assistance or permission to build a house in the countryside. We could build houses anywhere we wanted in the field or around the surrounding villages. There were no building codes to meet unless you were in the cities. It was also possible to build in the city if you could find a piece of land. A permit would be required, but this was usually a simple procedure, and then a little shelter could be put up. There were troubles and difficulties to obtain permission to build a house in the backyard, but most of the time people just added to the original house. I am sure that there were homeless in the city, but I didn't see anyone sleeping in the streets of Hue. Everyone could have a home, not only the poor villagers, but also the young people. Many young people, who had lost their families because of the war, could still have a home. It was amazing the things that everyone could do for each other in times of despair.

There were a lot of depressed individuals all over the country because of the uncertainties of war. No one knew if they would survive until tomorrow. Many young people turned to drugs to relieve their concerns and depression. They would use heroin and alcohol together. We saw it on the streets. The Archbishop of Hue tried to gather those young men and women and put them into homes where they could live their lives with dignity. They were offered some education and opportunities to develop some useful, employable skills. Many of these young people learned to sew clothing or make shoes. There were times when it was possible to learn carpentry. Most of the women did pretty well in the community home. They felt less pressure in their lives, because they were not required to enlist in the military unless they wanted to. Many of the young men would eventually end up in the military. Still, I could see the positive outcome of the efforts to train these young men and women. These homes were offered to them as a place of hope. It worked well for the youth.

As young seminarians in our junior and senior years, we were sent to community houses, to be as brothers to less fortunate young people. The seminarians played a vital role in working as volunteers with the youth groups. We learned leadership and management skills. We worked well with these young men and women. It was surprising and rewarding to us. Even though we were young we were respected and the people listened to what we had to say. We were often accepted as the people with authority when we went into the communities to do good works. Even the elders trusted us and listened to our suggestions and observations. We were allowed to teach in schools and hold temporary vocational classes for the youth. We had clothes, notebooks, pens, magazines, and canned foods donated to us from different charitable organizations that we could hand out to the needy.

I did the best I could on these assignments and always learned from these experiences. Many of those lessons helped prepare me for positions of leadership. They helped me meet the needs of others and taught me to serve people with the zeal of love for Christ, who lives in the lives of people. Furthermore, these lessons were helpful when we escaped from Vietnam by boat.

I had a lot of fun learning these things and practicing my skills in seminary. In the end I realized that I was worth something to someone else. Even though the work we did was not highly skilled, it was very practical work with practical application for the people. We found that, at the heart of ministry, we were able to reach out to another human being as we connected ourselves to the Body of Christ. The gift of being present in the lives of the poor and the needy was a true gift of the Holy Spirit, who gives life in the Church for the world. This was a profound revelation and an explanation to us on the Mystery of the Incarnation of the Son of God into the world. We got a true sense and meaning of the living community. Christ is alive.

Most of the time, we didn't know what would happen to these young men and women if they would stay in the city or went back home to their villages. Many of them wanted to go back to their villages, so we helped them return to their homes. For those who wanted to re-establish themselves in new living areas, we worked with other charities to build houses for them. I found these tasks satisfying because they gave me a deeper understanding of my vocation. Its purpose made me feel valuable and connected to the many parts of the Body of Christ. This experience added excitement and joy to the field of ministry. It seemed like a new idea and a new opportunity to bring the "Good News" into the world in its anxiety. It planted the seed of the Word of God into the hearts of people—into the field—and waited to be nourished by the grace of God until it yielded fruit. I didn't preach the Gospel or teach catechism classes yet. That came later. I was really just out there, being one with the forgotten people. The religion and theology classes would come later in the seminary college. What I was doing was not only a result of my training in the seminary, but also came from a heart with a sincere love of God and of people. Every weekend we spent with the poor, we experienced an immediate reward for our service and ministry. We shared our true humanity meeting with those less fortunate than we. It was a great experience.

Boy Scout activities also involved camping trips and community service. We had troops, leaders, and Eagle Scouts. The Boy Scouts gained a lot of respect in the society because of their honor, sincerity, and dedication to serve in the community. Truly, in community service, we did get help from different troops and were honored because we had the common scout uniform. I was glad that I was able to join them. I had a good time learning and doing service. Participation in scouting activities allowed me to see that I was not really alone in loving and serving others.

We had a lot of different friendships with other troops. Sometimes, we worked with high school novices (religious sisters and brothers) in different ministries. We had opportunities to talk and work with these young women and men who came from other religious orders and convents. These scout troops were also a mixture of religious backgrounds. It was good for us to be with each other in these apostolic services. We saw that we could give help and bring hope to people who had lost their homes and loved ones.

For example, just a little skill in nursing allowed us to vaccinate people with help from the Red Cross and the Caritas Agencies. We went into the deeper jungle areas in small groups. Because of our help, the Red Cross could do more services effectively. We filled in for their limited personnel while they had more needy people to serve. In the small villages we continued our practice of educational and medical assistance. We became servants of the people and of our Lord. I have to confess that at that moment I only wanted to be away from the seminary for a while and have a good time, but when I met and helped people it made me happy. A true sense of the gospels or the "Good News" was at work in me.

Still, the idea of becoming a priest was seldom in my mind. Religious belief and conviction did not motivate me to do the things I did. I was still a self-centered youth who wanted to do good things for people for the good feeling it gave me. It made me feel good because it is better to give rather than to receive. Furthermore, I saw that being a seminarian had advantages to serve and gave me a special identity. It was better for me to participate than to belong. I had fun, I had joy, when I participated in those ministries. It was a double blessing to harmonize the gifts of the natural law with the rhythms of my heart. I became a little more mature, a little more disciplined. I was proud and pleased with those years of service during my high school seminary. I learned a lot of things about human anthropology and I didn't even recognize that I was in love with the vocation at that time.

CHAPTER FIVE

More Forgotten People

When I was in the seminary college during the school year of 1974-1975, I made a decision that I was not going to continue with the vocation to the priesthood. It occurred to me that I would rather go home and live the life of the sacrament of marriage.

There are several reasons why I chose this route. First of all, due to the cultural perspective, I wanted to honor my grandparents and my parents. I am the only boy in my immediate family. My father is the first born also. I was expected to be the leader of my generation. I thought it would be an honor and a responsibility to carry on the last name of the family and to make it prosper. That was my responsibility and it was also a means of honoring all of my ancestors. I also realized this path of living would bring prosperity for me. Secondly, after studying in the seminary and working in the different ministries I wanted to have an opportunity to develop a real career and financial security for my family.

Perhaps, above all other reasons I might have thought God would not want me to be a priest because of my practical jokes on others. I thought, perhaps I should not proceed because of my manners and lack of discipline. I was a stubborn one and had tendencies to think independently from the authority. I didn't care much about the honor of being a religious person nor having those social expectations either. I just figured that God had not called me to the priesthood and that other priests and the Archbishop had been wrong to indicate I had a vocation. I thought to myself, "Oh well, after having served the Church in different ministries, I think I now have a chance to go back to the family life." I thought I wanted to explore a different perspective of life. With these convictions and a decision in mind, I approached Archbishop Phillip Dien Kim Nguyen, and asked him if I might return to my family for good. He didn't say a word. He was silent. He asked me to pray hard for a week or two, then, we would talk.

It soon became apparent that he was still convinced that I had a priestly vocation. I disagreed with him and continued to deny it. I was not easily persuaded and tried to tell him that I did not have a vocation, but he said, "Yes, you do."

Our discussion went back and forth for quite some time. He said yes. I said no. Yes and No. Finally, he said, "Why don't you just go ahead and take a year off and explore your thoughts as you work in a different area of ministry? Work at something new that you have yet to experience."

My task during that year was to continue to examine and discern whether God called me into the priesthood or called me to live the family life. Finally, I said, "Okay, I accept your advice and challenge. I like to be challenged anyway."

This time I was not to work with the poor or help the victims of war or to do any kind of charity work with the homeless because I already had had these experiences. I had worked with street people, gang members, and prostitutes. I had worked with young people and tried to help them learn a skill.

The Archbishop's final words were, "Don't worry! I have a place for you to go to work and to discern your vocation." So it was.

So the 1974-1975 school year was to be a year of internship for me. On the day that I was supposed to report to my supervisor for the new ministry, I was picked up by a boat and then taken to an island on the open sea. My supervisor was the pastor of Lang-Co Parish. After we greeted each other, he sent me to the port for my designated ministry. We would see each other at weekly supervision. The parish was a fishing village located at the foot of the Hai-Van mountain pass. This location was between Da Nang and Hue. The port near the mountain pass was also called Hai-Van. This word describes the meeting between heaven and earth. "Hai" means the ocean and the water and "Van" means the clouds in the sky. It was a beautiful pass.

I kept my appointment and got on the boat. Other travelers including a missionary team were bringing food, clothes, and medicines to our destination. We rode for about one hour and a half straight out to the open sea. I finally saw some small islands and then residence buildings. It was the Hai-Van Leper Colony. What a big shock that was! I thought to myself out loud, "Leprosy! What am I going to do with the lepers?"

The people at the pier were waiting to welcome us and help us to transport supplies. I could see them a distance away and thought, "Oh my Lord, what can I do for them? How should I greet them? Are they contagious?"

I didn't see any sisters with habits or any other religious men at the pier. They might be busy with their schedules. Everyone could be infected with the leprosy, I supposed. The folks on the pier were in the early stages of the disease as they were still able to walk around and lend a helping hand to their community. Most of them were volunteers. I had heard of the leper colony and knew that the Daughters of St. Paul ran it. But now I saw the lepers with my own eyes. I was scared. I was afraid. My mind buzzed. I didn't know much about Hansen's disease, but I thought it was the most terrible disease on earth. I tried to control my emotions and be polite, but the closer our boat came to the dock the more I realized I was terrified and a little bit sick to my stomach.

I had goose bumps. I didn't know if I should shake hands, if they had one, or if I should just bow when greeting them. It all happened so fast. When we arrived, the people just jumped all over to welcome me. One patted me on the shoulder. Someone else took my hand and held it firmly. Another person shook my hand while they said all sorts of welcoming greetings. They were so warm and seemed so happy to see me.

I just didn't know how to react to the whole situation. I just said to myself, "Okay! It will be fine."

I didn't know whether I should be happy to be with lepers, whether I should be terrified or sad. I had never felt this way before.

I kept in mind that this was a good challenge and I had asked for it. It might truly be the beginning of my journey of faith to discern God's call for me after all. I had seen many people in many different situations, and I had always tried to help them in their need. I believed that I had the ability to serve others and knew that when I did help them I felt good in my heart. I gained some confidence from these thoughts and experiences, and I needed a feeling of confidence to function effectively in life. But, at the leprosy colony I was literally scared. I had never felt so terrified. I had never felt so afraid of people. It felt strange to feel fear of these "forgotten people." I should not be afraid of them at all.

Fortunately, the immediate situation did create a sense of excitement in my heart. It was totally new to me. After a deep breath I followed the guide to my residence, located at the end of the island separated from the lepers' dormitories. There, I shared a house with two religious brothers; one was a Franciscan and the other a Dominican. They had come to minister to the lepers and worked in the camp's clinic.

They were very kind to me as I told them that I was there to discern my vocation. They understood. They smiled. I met two new friends, Brother Hoa, O.F.M. and Brother Bao, O.P.

There were two sections of this isolated island in the middle of the ocean. One section was for the children's residences and the other for the adults. Some individuals in camp were married to each other and had children. The children were kept separate from their parents in the hope they would not contract the disease.

On that first day, after a restless night, I woke up to the sound of the church's bell. I went with my friends to the church, located in the center of the camp next to the clinic.

I walked into the adult camp and the first person I saw didn't have a nose. Other people were missing all or a part of an arm. Still others had lost individual fingers, a whole hand, or a whole foot. I wondered what they missed in their lives as a result of these disfigurements. I didn't know what to feel about them other than pity. The situation was overwhelming for me. My feelings at that time were terrifying. I was reluctant to talk to them because I didn't know what to say. I didn't want to hurt their feelings if I said something that was offensive to them. The whole situation continued to overwhelm me and yet I felt a deep sense of excitement.

The priest assigned to the regular ministry of these people did not live on the island. He came once a week to offer the Sunday Mass and officiate other sacraments. He took time to do a weekly supervision for me as well. Brothers Hoa and Bao took turns with Communion Services for the weekdays. The Sisters of Daughters of St. Paul staffed the administration of the colony.

I didn't see the priest in the first week. During that week, I helped lepers to bathe and bandaged the sores of those unable to do this for themselves. I helped them to go to church, clinic, or the dormitory and fed them in the dining hall. A daily routine was soon established for me and I was involved in all types of cleaning and helping in their needs. I didn't know when the feeling of "being terrified" was gone out of my mind and heart. I soon felt comfortable with them. They taught me how to love and serve these forgotten people with humility, gentleness, compassion, and understanding. They reminded me how blessed I was.

During the first few days I learned that there are two types of leprosy. Those suffering from one type had a lot of sores on the body that did not heal. The sores produced a very foul odor. The second type caused the skin and underlying tissue to become very dry. As a result an appendage would eventually drop off. There was no odor with this type.

The islands were very beautiful. It was like a bit of heaven with no sound or sights of war. In my spare time I walked around and explored the hills and shores. The ocean was clear, blue, and beautiful. The sand on the beach was half-yellow and half-white. It was so beautiful as it glittered in the different lights of day and night. There were many coconut trees, wildflowers, and thick vegetation. I thought of how beautiful it was there and of all the suffering that occurred there. In a sense, it was a small view of all life: in the smallest creature there is a fullness of creation. I often reflected on the many people who were suffering, not only from the ravages of war and displacement, but from diseases of all sorts, spiritually and mentally as well as physically.

One evening after dinner I said my evening prayer that was my routine, then took a walk. As I was walking on the beach, I suddenly heard the sound of music. It was classical piano music, beautifully executed. Full of amazement I followed the heavenly sound to a chapel on a hill. It was the chapel of the Sisters of the Daughters of St. Paul. Opening the door of the chapel, I walked in and there was one of the sisters in her full habit playing Chopin. I thought to myself, "Wow, how beautiful she is!"

I thought to myself that at last I have seen something normal and yet abnormal at the same time. Quietly, I took a seat at the back of the chapel and listened to the beautiful music, gathering myself together. I hoped that I hadn't interrupted this beautiful moment.

I viewed the sister in profile in the sanctuary. It was a lovely picture. She was so beautiful. The spot of light from the ceiling was softly focused on her and her surroundings. What a gorgeous sight it was! I felt that God was saying something directly to me. I couldn't figure out any meaning at that time. I wondered if she knew I was there or not, but she didn't stop playing. I tried to sit still and not breathe. After she had finished playing she walked to the back of the chapel and greeted me. She said, "You must be Brother Quang. I have heard that you would come to work with us for a year."

I said, "Yes, I am."

We sat down and talked. She played more music, which I really enjoyed. I told her, at first, I was just so terrified working in the adult camp with all the horrific signs of illness. She smiled and said nothing. Later that evening she asked me if I would like to work with her in the children's camp. I told her that I didn't know that there was a child's camp. I also let her know that I was very grateful for the opportunity. Her name was Sister Teresa. I never learned her Vietnamese name. Teresa was her religious name. The sisters do what Abraham, Saul, and Peter did in the time of old: they receive new names when they start their new life in the Church.

The next day she came and got me from the adults' center and led me to the children's residences. For the rest of the year I worked there and also in the adults' center. The leprosy colony became a new school for me to apply in depth what I had learned in the seminary's courses. During this period I learned to put into the practice of daily life the training I had received in music, service, the camp, leprosy, sadness, perseverance, and commitment in the religious life. It began to stir up within me a sense of joy and a sense of being alive in the midst of struggle and loss.

Sister Teresa and I used to play and sing a lot of music in the education of the children. She played piano while I directed the children's choir. We took turns playing the piano and directing the choir.

There were around two hundred children in the residency. Most of them were one or two years of age, with the eldest in grade nine. They were beautiful, fresh, and bright. None of them showed signs of having the disease—yet. If there had been internal damage at work it was not known to me. I didn't know how or when the disease could occur in the life of a child and I did not want to know. I just wanted to be with them and relate to them for they were little children who deserved to live with all human dignity. They were wonderful.

During the early part of my discernment at the colony, I learned that in addition to being a nun, Sister Teresa was trained as a medical doctor. She had returned from New Zealand about a week before I arrived. She was about twenty-six years old, but looked younger than her age. She looked like she had just graduated from high school. Her precious presence made me feel that the leper colony was a better place than anywhere in the world. I was in awe and wondered, "What makes Sister Teresa—young, beautiful, with all her many talents and gifts—become a nun?"

I kept asking myself this question and I could find no answer. Finally, one afternoon during the break time I decided to ask her what made her decide to be a nun.

Break time was around three o'clock in the afternoon. The snack for the children included a little piece of toast or a small baked potato. Maybe a small hot cup of chocolate or lemonade would be served. While we were serving the snack, I asked Sister Teresa the question, "Sister, so what makes you, being that you are so beautiful, highly educated, with all your gifts and talents, want to become a nun?"

She didn't answer my question. She just looked at me and smiled. I loved her smile. She had the face of an angel. The way she worked with the children was so good. She truly embraced them with her heart. It was so beautiful to see a beautiful lady surrounded by all the children.

She was the most gentle person I ever met. The way she interacted with others was so peaceful. Her smile brought life to all she touched. It seemed as though she was the sister or the mother to all those forgotten children. It really touched my heart. I loved to watch her hold one child in her arm and put her hand on the head of another. Those children loved her so much.

For a while, she just smiled and ignored my question. Then one day, after I had asked her the same question again, she answered me, "If you really want to know why I am to be a nun, I'll tell you. Let's take a walk during break time and I will share with you." At break time of that day we took a walk. She led me into the cemetery of the colony. I had not yet walked in that direction and wondered where she was taking me. Soon we came to a spot where she pointed at one of the tombs and said, "There lay my parents."

I could not believe what she had just told me. This beautiful woman, this sincere and faith-filled nun, this medical doctor, this great pianist, this lover of the poor was a child of a leprous couple. I was totally astonished. I was mute. I tasted bitterness on my tongue. On the way back to the children's camp, I could not find a word to talk to her. I was in awe, silent. I began to understand what made her the most compassionate person in the whole world. She was a blessing from God to me. Oh! How much I loved her! I was deeply moved by her suffering and her courage. Her saying "yes" to God in the most humble way of life, to love and to serve the poor, was the most sincere thanksgiving prayer to God.

I began to understand her prayer of the day, "To You, God of Love, I offer my all, my love, what love has made." I had goose bumps. What a beautiful prayer! I had no word to describe my love and my appreciation for the beautiful Sister Teresa. All I can do is to continue her works of love in my daily life. I thank God for her model of God's love for the poor.

As our friendship grew, her life story was revealed to me. Sister Teresa had been born on the island and grew up there. She understood and received firsthand all the goodness of the sisters who worked there and the goodness of the loving people who were infected by the disease. They lived in the community of faith and love. The small community of the leper was a home for herself and her people. It was a small Kingdom of God on earth. It was a heavenly home for those who needed help and protection.

I knew because of this beautiful sister, I had been privileged to see and taste the real meaning of love and life. There was no competition or jealousy among the people, only love. They just continue to love and serve God by loving and serving each other on their small island. I knew this because they had many good leaders as Christ-like as Sister Teresa. They were blessed in their lives, for their eyes had seen the goodness of God.

I had seen lepers in the streets on the mainland. It was evident especially after the fall of Saigon in 1975. These poor people could be seen crawling on the street begging. The war's turmoil had made the needs of so many become so great. It was an extremely sad sight to see because people are afraid of lepers.

Sister Teresa told me that since she was born and raised in the camp she wanted to do the best she could to comfort others. It was a natural blessing for her to do something for these forgotten people. She had received a lot of help when she was young and it was so special for the Daughters of St. Paul to accept her into their religious order. She taught me it was good to pay back with love what love has made. It was a special blessing for her to be accepted by these sisters.

When she was in the sixth grade they sent her away to school to study for their religious order. She loved the religious life very much. She desired so much to do something for these forgotten people. She wanted to be with them because she felt she was one of them. She didn't know that, through her love and faith-filled example, she was the one to help me to understand the meaning of the theology of Christology. Her Christ-like manner was truly indeed a sign of God's love for me.

The Sisters of the Daughters of St. Paul received financial assistance from the Church and a number of different charities, both nationally and internationally. Their help came from Rome, Germany, Switzerland, and France.

The buildings of the leper colony were made of brick and had sheet metal roofs. They were very simple. Although they were lightly made they were sturdy enough to handle the six months of rain that occurred each year. Normally, in the monsoon season, there were thunderstorms with heavy rain but it lasted only about an hour. There were a few wood buildings, too. I think the choice of materials had to do with the amount of funds the administrators received from the supporting organizations.

These were the most wonderful Samaritan shelters I had ever seen. It was wonderful not because of the building itself but it was a home for the suffering and the lost. These sisters were like angels sent to provide safety and security for the people. This community of love opened to accept any person suffering from Hansen's disease. They formed a family of faith and love to live with dignity as children of God.

I thought a lot about what Sister Teresa shared with me of her vocation. Her insightful conviction and her faith had a great impact on my vocation of the priesthood. What a great answer she had for me! It was full of explanation on the Mystery of the Incarnation of the Son of God, who because of love became a human being to live, to die, and to raise us up into the fullness of life. I questioned why Jesus became a human being rather than a super human deity. He could have used His power to deliver people from harm and suffering. He could save us all from disaster and from the power of death. Why had Jesus chosen the hard way to save us?

I began to understand the meaning of the Son of God as a truly human being. He became who we are—without sin—so that we could become who He is. He joined into the common suffering of humanity in order to show us the way to overcome death and lead us to true happiness that we were and are constantly seeking.

Sister Teresa said, "I just want to do something for them because I am one of them."

She told me that she wanted to love those forgotten people very much. Her response to God's call was more than a sense of belonging: she participated. It was a tremendous example of the mystery of God's love. I learned of God's love through Sister Teresa's services to the poor and I treasure it in my heart. I could see that she worked with lepers gently and truly did identify herself as one of them. She was a lover of Christ for the poor rather than to be a winner, as the world would like her to be. For the rest of the year I was at the leper colony I reflected on her statement of proclamation, "Because I am one of them."

In addition to the sturdy buildings there were a number of bamboo shelters. Many of these were built in the style of a gazebo and had no sides or had sides only about halfway up. The living was very, very clean. The residents of the island took turns in cleaning their environment. It was their home. Those residents who were still able to work in the field planted vegetables year-round. Others planted lots of flowers along the paths and around buildings. These flowers were blooming all year long just like any tropical island.

Children of parents who had leprosy might or might not get the disease. I am not certain how the disease is transferred from person to person. The sisters were careful and used gloves when they worked with infected wounds. During the time I was there some people from the camp were able to reintegrate with their families on the mainland, but most of them chose to stay with their friends and help the community. Usually there were about four hundred residents.

The camp existed until 1979. The Communist government then took the island and turned it into a resort. It was a sad day for all the lepers and the sisters. They had to transfer to other small communities on the mainland. Many returned to their homes in the cities and ended up living on the streets, or at cemeteries. They no longer had a home with the Daughters of St. Paul because they no longer had the support of the new government.

Later, with the help of the sisters, the lepers gathered together into small communities in different places, isolated from the world. There were other villages where lepers congregated on the mainland but they were in the deepest parts of the jungle.

During that year of further discernment for my vocation a lot of different things happened that assisted me in making a decision about my education, vocation, and direction. I continued to wonder if God wanted me to be a priest or wanted me to live in the sacrament of marriage and have a family like so many of my friends had done. One incident that helped me make my decision occurred soon after I had arrived at the leper colony.

One of the assignments Brother Hoa and I volunteered to do together was to prepare the Lenten celebration. I remember we arranged all of the necessary liturgical items to celebrate the Lenten season in the community. I think most of the people of the camp were Catholic. Some people had no religion or were Buddhists. Many became Catholic during their stay. Regardless of their religion, everyone on the island seemed attracted to the celebrations in the church with the sisters. The church was a wonderful place to gather together. It was a simple, small structure. The fourteen sisters, who also ministered to the residents of the camp, served all of its needs. The sisters had just a small house with a chapel located away from the dormitories.

Brother Hoa came from a central Franciscan province. He also had an artistic talent and so as part of our effort to prepare for the forty days of Lent we carved a crucifix. We had a lot of time to do this task as a gift to the community. In order to make the crucifix we had to chop down a tree. There were a few wild oak trees that were dead. We selected a tree that was very old and large so the crucifix would be life size.

Both Br. Hoa and I decided it would be a good idea to carve Jesus as a leper. He was carved with some missing fingers and infected wounds. The main part of the body of Jesus was carved deeply and looked wounded. On Good Friday a guest priest, my supervisor, from the city came to celebrate the liturgy of the Passion and Veneration of the Cross for us. We were excited and so grateful that a priest would come to celebrate with us.

After the services the priest became very mad and disturbed. To our surprise he was very upset with us. He had noticed during the veneration of the cross that we had changed the traditional look of Jesus. Because of this he thought we had not paid proper respect to the Son of God. He said, "How dare you?" followed by many other comments. We were scolded very harshly.

My Franciscan brother told the priest, "Quang and I thought Jesus loved us so much that He would become one of us in this community. We thought it would be very appropriate to present that Jesus looked like one of us."

The priest said, "In that context, yes." Still, he was not impressed with our efforts. I didn't take much notice of the priest's rage. It wasn't important to me. I took his explanation, but in this community of lepers, I still liked the idea of representing Jesus in this way. If Jesus truly loved the people in the colony I believed he would have said, "Yes," to becoming one of us. These thoughts helped me to recognize the dignity of these human beings even though their families and friends had forgotten many of them. They had been forced to live on this remote island, even though it was a beautiful place and a house of love. I felt more in love with these desperate people every day. I grew closer and closer to them.

I didn't know when the feelings of terror disappeared from my heart, but they did. I think it was after I met Sister Teresa and experienced the way she loved and served the lepers. These sisters were not afraid to love them. The love they poured out on these people was so tremendous that it overcame all fears. I truly admired these wonderful women.

I soon began to feel the same as they did for these people. I was no longer afraid. I willingly lived among them, getting to know them and enjoying them. I listened to their stories, memories of previous lives and how they ended up with this community. Their conversion experiences were full of insightful wisdom. Every day I listened to their stories of love, life, faith, and hope. Their stories began with: "When I was young…when I was in the city…when I was in school…when I was in love…"

I got to know these folks as individuals and to appreciate who they had been and who they were. They taught me how important it is for each of us to live in the present with the spirit of appreciation for the gifts we have for one another. When we are together it is not so important what we are going to do, but how we celebrate it with one another. It is good to recognize the individual blessing as we are called to build the living Mystical Body of Christ.

I began to see the disfigured lepers in a different way. Regardless what their bodies looked like, they wanted to be in the group, to be a part of the body as we celebrated together. Each person reached out to others and to be the missing parts for one another. Some patients even brought others to the celebration of the Eucharist on mats so they could be part of the group and receive spiritual nourishment. They did not excuse themselves from activities in the community by claiming too much physical pain. I realized there were many kinds of physical suffering as well as psychological pain that these forgotten people had to endure. However, they convinced me that they were willing to share what they had to help each other. In many silent nights, deep down inside of my heart, I heard the voice of Jesus call me to be his own, "be my hands, be my heart, be my love, be my peace…"

Even though my Franciscan brother and I got a negative recommendation from the priest after the carved crucifix incident, it was all a very positive experience for us. The priest was a very traditional man. We liked the man. He had a point in his thinking that we should only represent Jesus in the traditional manner: He felt the lepers were normal human beings and he didn't want us to remind them of their illness. That was his intention. I didn't pay too much attention to his comment. I thought we both made sense. I needed to see the Lord Jesus, the perfect image of the eternal Father, expressing His love for these forgotten people totally. The carved leprous crucifix was an external visual representation of that love. I did not mean to express a heresy of God's love for these people.

That Good Friday in 1975 began to change my life in some degree. It was only one month after Easter that year that I returned to the city. I had made up my mind. It was nearly time for me to submit my answer to the Archbishop of Hue regarding whether I would go back to the seminary or go home to my family. On that Good Friday in 1975, after I had finished working through the services at the leper colony, I knew I should go on with my studies for the priesthood. In a sense, I knew that no matter what happened I would like to become one of the poor. I knew that no matter where I would be in the future I still wanted to be a priest, to live and to share with others in the journey of faith toward love and life. I hoped that I had the courage and perseverance to become one with all people. We are the people of God, the people that God loves with all His heart. I believe that God trusts and depends on each of us, all of us, as sinners to continue to bring His love to others.

I am not going to worry about whether people go to heaven any more. I don't think that is the main mission of the priest. I want to assist in making sure that heaven exists in the hearts of people now and every single day of their lives. If they believe in Jesus' death and resurrection for their own sakes because of love they should recognize that there is heaven in their life, in their hearts, in the ministries and services to one another, in their families, in different relationships, in the communities, and in the parishes, as spouses, parents, children, or brothers and sisters in the family of faith and love. Then, I think we are truly blessed and saved.

All of us are needed. We are to learn how to celebrate our life, with God's grace, every single day rather than to live through one boring day after another. Every single day, in good times or in bad times, I believe that through the love of God, heaven already exists for us and in us. When we say, "the Kingdom of God," we declare and confirm the truth that Jesus established on earth. He already did it. Now Jesus needs us, not because we are worthy but because he loves us and believes us, to help one another to recognize the true existence of the Kingdom of God on earth. How? I remember the words Jesus said, "I will be with you always," so we are going to make it (confession of faith in Christ) yield fruit in words and deeds as Jesus has done and showed us how.

In the different ministries and charities I worked with in the past, I began to recognize the presence of the Kingdom of God. It is right here wherever we are. That was why I began to share with others that no matter where I am now and will be in the future, or to whom the Lord sends me to serve, I just want to become one of them. I wanted to share in their daily struggles and walk with them in their journey of faith toward love and life. There have always been difficulties in daily life but I no longer lose hope because I know the destination and the reward that God promises us every single day is his presence in the Eucharist and in the lives of people. When we totally open ourselves and become one with other people and with their difficulties, we taste the Kingdom of God here on earth. When we help others here on earth we get a glimpse of heaven. We can help one another to recognize that we live in the kingdom of heaven now.

Sister Teresa kept the crucifix that we made in the community church as a souvenir. Br. Hoa and I wanted to give it to her and dedicated it to the leper camp. Before I left I asked Sister Teresa to become my spiritual director. She was a tremendous blessing for me. Her advice to me was very simple and sincere but it was full of wisdom. There was nothing but a more intellectual and a faith-filled reflection that she gave to me through her witness to the love of the Gospel. What I wanted to know, I had already experienced in her actions and her loving attitude that she had toward the suffering people. So, I asked her to keep the crucifix as a souvenir of our friendship. She knew how stubborn and proud I was. She humbled me with her words: "If you want to live in the truth of happiness, then be a lover of Christ, and do not be a winner as the world expects."

One of the inspirational incidents that I will never forget occurred with Sister Teresa during a preparation for the Christmas celebration of 1974. We traded the duties of playing the piano and directing the children's choir. One of the tasks we needed to prepare for the children was the telling of a Christmas story that included singing Christmas carols. We wanted to celebrate with the children the story of God's love for them and for us.

I never wanted to sing. I had always managed it so that Sister Teresa would do any of the necessary singing. She had a beautiful voice.

She didn't know that I had had an unfortunate experience in the sixth grade as I entered the minor seminary. At that time, the choirmaster told me that I should become an altar server instead of a singer. He may have been joking, but it really impressed upon me that I didn't have a voice to sing. I believed his words and never questioned myself about it. It didn't bother me at all. So, I never had the desire or courage to sing for others after that experience. Sister Teresa eventually started to ask me to sing and I found it was extremely difficult to refuse her request. I never told her the complete story.

I simply said to her that I didn't know how to sing. I didn't know that I could. I couldn't stand the humiliation that I might have to endure. What if I stood in front of the people and messed the whole program up. Finally, she agreed to sing and I would play the piano. It was an agreement between us.

The time for the Christmas concert drew near. Sister Teresa got the flu and completely lost her voice. It was so bad that she could only use hand signals and write on a piece of paper to tell me that I would be the one to do the necessary singing. I had no choice. Oh my heaven! What a terrible fear I had to face! I shouted back at her that I was not going to sing no matter what. I begged her. I would do anything she asked me to do just don't make me sing. Instead of singing I offered to play an instrumental solo. I wanted to leave out the verses that required an adult voice. I just couldn't face the humiliation if I messed up. I didn't have any confidence I could sing at all.

She wrote on a note, "The whole program will fall apart if you don't do this for the children and for us."

We needed to do the Christmas program because everyone had been anticipating it. Most of all, we needed to carry out what we had promised to the children. We could not let these children feel sad. She kept handing me the note that said, "We need to fulfill our promise. I have lost my voice so you need to sing."

She wondered why I made this entire simple task so difficult. I didn't have the courage tell her the truth of my fear. I was so afraid. I couldn't even sleep for a couple of nights because I was so nervous. I was never nervous when I had to play an instrument. I had a phobia about opening my mouth and singing. Now, I am no longer nervous about singing in church, but then, solo? Me? Quang? No way! And I meant it!

Somehow, with her persistent sweetness, she managed to convince me I would and could sing. I kept trying to think of a way to get out of it. How could I find someone else to do this? How could I find the confidence to do this? Finally, I thought that maybe in the middle of a colony of lepers, in the middle of nowhere, I could sing. If I screwed up who would ever know? Anyway, the audience might not know the song, the words or the tune. Perhaps if I did screw up they would be kind and realize that I did try to sing for them. I kept that idea in mind. I kept thinking that people would have mercy on me and treat me with compassion and understanding.

I tried to learn the songs and get familiar with the lyrics and melodies. On December 23, when we began the Christmas festival, there was also a Christmas party. The sisters had gathered a few gifts for the children. The children's choir and I gathered together and the Christmas carols began. For my part, I stood up straight and closed my eyes, trying very hard to not forget my part. I knew I would become frightened looking at all the peoples in the church. All of their eyes fixed on me. They seemed very nice and gentle.

Then, there I was. I opened my mouth and sang and sang and sang. I just wanted to finish my part. I did the best I could. All honor to you, right after singing the Christmas carols, for the first time in my life, I had a real kiss from a nun. Oh brother! She said to me, "You sing beautifully." She gave me a big hug and a wonderful kiss.

I was shocked and said, "Sister, what did you do that for?" She smiled and said, "Well, I mean it. I just wanted to give you a kiss because you have done a marvelous job."

I thought she was just being nice but many people came to me and spoke the same kind words about my singing. They said that I had a wonderful voice. In my disbelief all I could respond was, "I DO?" I wondered why the priest, the choirmaster in the seminary, told me that I should become an altar server. I was going to ask him when I returned to the seminary. I just wanted to know.

From Christmas through the Lenten season Sister Teresa and I sang quite a lot together. Sometimes it was with the children's choir sometimes it was a duet at Mass playing the piano and the guitar together. Sometimes we even sang with the adult choir. The way that the liturgical music was celebrated in the Mass was very beautiful and I found a new appreciation and love of the liturgy. The enthusiasm of these parishioners was evident in their songs of prayer and praise.

They really sang with their hearts to God. I think they really sought refuge in the God they trusted and believed in.

These wonderful people helped me to fall in love with liturgical music. I had learned a little bit about music theory from practicing piano but I didn't have a real appreciation for it until then. There were people singing without lips, people clapping hands with several fingers missing. It was really astonishing to see someone bringing just his or her elbows together, keeping time to the music. It was a wonderful scene that brought a tear to my eyes. Whatever they had left in themselves they expressed totally in the spirit of singing and giving thanks and praise to God. These people taught me so much about life and how to express our prayer to the loving God. I learned a lot about the beauty of human beings during my discernment at Hai-Van leper colony. Since then, whenever I have an opportunity to work with children in the choir and hear their voices in the wrong key or they mess up the notes, I always have a smile on my face for them. I recall those experiences with Sister Teresa. At least they have more courage to sing than I did at their age.

Sister Teresa's favorite song to sing and play on the guitar was the Fleur du Cactus (Flower of Cactus). It was on an album by the singing nun Sister Sourire. The lyrics have a sweet sentiment: "My little sister, the flower of the cactus, you have chosen to flower, to blossom in the house of the Lord, all of your life. You have been chosen by the Lord to blossom in the house of God forever in paradise." I think I could remember it by heart even now.

We sang in both French and Vietnamese. Occasionally we sang in Latin at Mass. Sometimes, I noticed people worshipping in tears. I wondered how, in their desperate situations, the music helped them to pray, to live on, and have positive feelings about themselves. Something had to be present to help them view life so positively.

I wondered, "What if I was one of them?" I wouldn't know how to feel about it or how to react. I learned more about humility and trusting in God's providence every single day. I learned by being there even though I was fortunate not to have the disease. The way these people expressed their faith in their daily lives was a strong lesson. They had been forgotten by their loved ones. Many of them had been separated from their families for a long period of time. Perhaps their families didn't even know about the camp's existence.

This all helped me recognize the beauty of God's creation. Even these suffering souls continued to reveal God's goodness. These people revealed God's beauty in the way they expressed themselves in the virtues of worship, prayer, and their services to one another.

People without hands, ears, or eyes were able to work together beautifully in the community. The sickness could not stop their life and love. I saw a man who had lost both legs. He was still able to see so he rode on the back of a man who had lost his sight. They kept walking together. They were willing to be the missing parts for each other. The whole experience looked like a fairy tale. I saw real love in real life as a lesson that my grandmother and my mom had also taught me. I could not believe it could happen in the real world. It expressed, in a unique way, what I could see for myself.

These people leaned on one another to help each other get from one place to another. They went to church, to home, and to the garden. They worked in the garden, helping one another plant vegetables and flowers. In the spirit of this loving community I did not have to wait to die to see heaven. I had already experienced the life of heaven in the middle of this community filled with faith, love, and life. I experienced such goodness in a community of individuals who had been neglected and forgotten by so many. They were lovers of Christ for one another. To the world they seemed to be losers, burdensome for many, but, in God's eyes, they were the winners of God's kingdom for they had seen God's presence in their midst. They were a sign of God's love for each other.

CHAPTER SIX

Reformed and Renewed

Sometimes physical illness and its suffering is shown in silent mourning. The cry in silence exhibits tremendous suffering as a feeling of losing oneself. These people lost their former identities. Many expressed their pain and loss by screaming loudly in response to their hopelessness and loneliness. In time, they turned inward to accept the reality even if this acceptance was expressed in a negative way.

Others looked around and saw people in worse condition than themselves. This gave them the encouragement to accept reality and to lift themselves up from depression and self-pity.

These people were very advanced in their philosophy about their condition. Their reflection on their own mortality was full of wisdom. They had accepted that they were going to die and they pretty much knew what would cause their death. They had a better sense of celebrating their lives than a normal healthy individual might have. They were able to comprehend and accept who they were. Their faith transcended their failing bodies.

When outsiders looked at them as a group of lepers all they could see was that the amount of suffering these people endured far exceeded what normal people might experience. They no longer seemed to control their lives. I had a lot of mixed feelings. I didn't know whether I should express my sincere sympathy for them or just be with them. The disease affected them in many different ways. Some loved words of comfort; some never wanted pity. It didn't matter if they lost their eyes, their ears, or their arms they were still able to express their love when they gathered together. Sometimes they would want to do something as simple as sending you a kiss; and they would kiss their shoulder and throw it toward you because they no longer had arms. Some communicated with each other maneuvering and twisting their tongues and making some sounds. They had learned many different ways to communicate. It was an amazing thing to see and to learn. It took awhile to understand what they wanted to say.

Some babies were born with the disease. They were never able to learn to walk, so they hitched along on their bottom. They sat on a little piece of plywood for protection from the mud and hard ground. They walked by using their hands to push forward. It looked so painful, but they were still able to express joy, suffering, and mourning along with everyone else. It taught me to be a good listener to their silent mourning. Physically, the people were trying to express themselves with what they had left. Surprisingly, the more serious their condition, the more beauty their spirit revealed. It was expressed in the warmth of the human gestures they offered to one another. It made me appreciate more that I was able to hold a child in my arms. It is such a gift to be able to shake hands or hug another human being. It is definitely a gift to talk to another person. I can hear their cries; I can see their suffering and bind their suffering more closely to my ministry. All these experiences helped me become more compassionate when I encountered the many situations of life, death, and hope.

In the past, in fear, I had helped other charities collect dead bodies in time of war. After all these encounters with the lepers, upon my return to the seminary I never felt terrified of the suffering people or the conditions of their bodies. During the war we were not able to retrieve some bodies for several days or a week. They were bloated and smelly. There were times when we would go to retrieve bodies and find the children were still clinging, crying, and crawling on the bodies of their dead parents. This was pretty revolting and required a strong stomach. Sometimes, I could not eat for a couple of days. After my experiences at the leper colony I was able to accept the reality of death and its ugliness. No matter how awful it was I was able to stay calm. I was able to care for the victims' bodies with dignity. I was not afraid of these situations anymore.

My duties at the leper colony were truly a great challenge and that was what I was seeking in my youth. It seemed that whatever I did not want, God gave me. As a result I have developed quite a sense of humor, sometimes even a weird sense of humor. I didn't always recognize God's challenges and now I realize that God trained me in a hard way. He trained me in a difficult way of life. I am glad that God led me into the depth of sorrow, that God wanted me to bring peace to the forgotten ones. I learned that with God's grace we can bring joy into desperate situations. Only in God, can we find the truth of life.

In the summer of 1975 I left the colony of lepers. On the way back to the seminary, I visited the Archbishop of Hue. I personally wanted to thank him for the opportunity to discern God's call for me. I had learned a great lesson from the colony experience. I wanted to tell him that I had quite a good time with a busy schedule caring for those forgotten people. I wanted to tell the Archbishop personally that I had found the call that God wanted me to go on to the life of service as a priest.

He just smiled and looked at me and said, "I knew that."

I asked, "How do you know that?"

He said, "Well, because I see that you put your prayer into works. You are always eager to do something good and you want to take the joy of people and make it your own joy. In other words, you can cry with people and you can laugh with people. This virtue is the first characteristic of a call to the priesthood."

Later, when I studied the priestly formation in theology, I saw that the roles, duties, and responsibilities of a priest, or of a faithful one in the church, are deeply rooted in faith, hope, and love in Christ. It began to make sense to me. I believe that we are a priestly people who are called to be one in the mystical Body of Christ just as you and I responded to our baptismal call to glorify the love that God has for each of us. Even though we are not worthy servants of God, God loves and chooses each of us to proclaim His holiness in our life's vocations. The Archbishop said to me, "You have that natural gift, Quang. You didn't earn it. God gave it to you. You have it in your own heart."

I didn't understand his comments completely, but I trusted in his words and prayed that God would bring my sincere desire to completion. When? How? I didn't know the answer but I knew that I had to begin my journey of faith trusting in the words that Jesus promised to his disciples: "I will be with you until the end of time." The Archbishop knew and told me that I had a vocation: "Because not many people have that gift. The gift is that you open yourself to embrace and share the wounds of the people. This gift gives people comfort and they accept you as Christ's servant."

I didn't fully understand his comments about me. Somewhat, as I reflected on his comments, I could see the meaning of Christ's followers. I found myself laughing in joy when I helped children sing and play. I felt peace when I helped the lepers in their need. I realized that I liked to help not only people in the leper colony, but others in the small villages as well. When someone needed my assistance, if I was capable to help, I would do so. Helping people was my call to participate in the Church ministry. If there was a need, I tried to meet it. It was a voluntary desire from the heart to respond to God's call for me.

The Archbishop of Hue looked at me and said that he was glad we had been able to work things out. He guaranteed me that the experiences at the leper colony were just the beginning. He kindly reminded me as he said, "That is just the beginning, Quang."

Each and every day I feel there are challenges that God offers us to grow in His grace and develop trust in His providence. God's providence is good and true. When I have to let things go I do not know what I am going to do next. I trust that God will provide protection and guide me into His Way. The only one thing that I need to do is to open my mind and heart and allow myself to listen and recognize the true Word of God, who calls me to follow Jesus to love and to serve.

I was with my family for a month after I returned from the leper colony. It was the first time that I did not participate with the youth ministry projects. I returned to the seminary a month before classes started for the fall quarter. I spent time in the library and in the chapel reading and praying before the other students returned. I used this quiet time to read different subjects such as philosophy, psychology, theology, and different topics of pastoral care. I spent time in silent prayer. It was what Jesus would invite his disciples to do after they had done their work, to find a place to rest and pray.

I thought how nice this was, for the first time in my life, to spend a month in the seminary by myself. It was quiet and peaceful. It was then that I made up my mind; it was probably the first time in my whole life that I made a decision by myself. It was not based on my parents' influence, or on the pressure of family's honor to motivate my decision. I made up my own mind to continue in the formation for the priesthood. At that moment, the life, the love, the faith, the spirit of Sister Theresa who helped me to discern my vocation came back to live in my mind and heart. It created a wonderful, warm feeling in my heart, and knew that I had made the right decision.

I spent the whole month quietly in the seminary. I went to daily Mass and had the rest of the day to myself. It was the first time I was totally free from regulations, so I created my own agenda for the day. I took time to thank God and prayed for those people who took to heart their services to become role models for me and my future ministry. From that time on I was in peace, even though in 1974 war was in all of the country. It was a disturbing situation and yet I found peace. I found peace not from outside, but in my heart. I remembered the words of Jesus, "Your treasure is where your heart is."

I appreciated these holy words. I thought then, "It is true."

If my heart is at peace then I am not going to worry about how hectic the day may be, or how busy I am; I won't be distracted by other activities. I learned to trust in God's providence and to love

God more each day. Not to love God as an intellectual concept, but from my real experience to touch the real person of Jesus when I reached out to the poor and forgotten people. I placed myself as one of them.

I thought of the dreams of those forgotten people. Their dreams were the same dreams Jesus had for others and for myself. I think Jesus would love to have a loving hug and trust from each of us. He would love to hear words of compassion and understanding. I was reminded that before I left for the leper colony, I had high expectations for myself. I had expected to learn a great lesson from an intellectual point of view, but Jesus taught me simply to love, to trust, and to have faith in Him. I was at ease with people, but I was tough on myself. I did not have much patience with myself. However, I did gain peace and I saw that in life's situations the most important thing is to have faith in God and to love God by loving others. I realized that in the common experiences of life, in the poorest situations of life, I had found the richness and strength of God. It began with me. Even in my own weaknesses and limitations as a human being I was able to do good for people. In God's goodness and holiness, how much more He desires to do for each one of us.

During that month of silence at the seminary I rediscovered the reason I love God: God loves me first. God is so real. He is not only present in the person of Jesus, the dead figure on that crucifix, but He is risen and alive. He is alive in every single person I encounter.

In my journey of faith, I came to love and serve children at orphanages, people who have lost loved ones, and people who have not yet discovered who God is or where God lives. I have learned, I have touched, and I have studied with the poor. Who of these were famous? They had no voice in society at all. They were forgotten. In Vietnam, many people did not know about the existence of the leper colony.

I said to myself, "Trusting in God is not really easy. It is absolutely hard!"

Only when I allow God to replace my heart with His can I find peace. In other words, if I allow myself to feel what Jesus would feel and allow myself to do what Jesus would do, then, I can discover God: the God of truth, love, and life. God is the Lord of compassion and understanding, full of love and rich in mercy. When I pray, celebrate the Eucharist and other sacraments, then it all makes sense. In the lives of the suffering, the poor, the sinners, and the faithful ones, I see myself in the family of God.

Sister Theresa's love and faith were really important to me. What impressed me was the love she had for me and I had for her. I did fall in love with her, not in the sense of a romantic love, but as a grateful, spiritual love. The way she lived, served, and worked with people was God's blessing to me. She enjoyed her work. She lived to serve those forgotten people with love. She paid attention and gave her loving efforts to care for the people. When I watched her as she assisted the sick, whether they were men, women, or children, she offered her services with love, patience, and compassion. She gave as a medical doctor, a sister, a friend, a healer, and a teacher. Whatever she did for them she did with a deep love of God. It made her so beautiful. There were not many people who knew her because she lived her entire life at the camp after she returned from New Zealand. She was born among the poor. She grew up and worked among the poor and she died with them. She was such a beautiful blessing. She was such a role model to love and cherish. I hope that in the priesthood, as Sister Teresa advised me, in celebrating sacraments for people, or meditating the works of God, I bring God's love into people's lives with my ministry. I promised her I would do that if God chose me to be a priest. I keep Sister Teresa's words in my heart. I hope some day I will be able to look at people and say, "These are my people and I want to live among them, struggle with them and endure with them. Maybe then I will die among them."

Two years after I was ordained into the priesthood, Sister Teresa passed away in 1992. She remained in Vietnam and I went to the United States, but we sent letters to each other. Her letters always came on time, as I needed her spiritual direction. I still remember her greatest impact on me was her decision to become the poorest among the poor. I hope we can begin to see how poor we are in Jesus and how rich Jesus is for us.

The image of poor and rich in the eyes of God is completely opposite to the worldly point of view. I hope that in the development of our spirituality, no matter how hard it is to serve and to love people, we do so because we love God in return. Because I love God, therefore, I love others. I cannot deny that there are difficulties, suffering, conflicts, and challenges in life, but there is also God's grace. I shall not be afraid. This thought encourages me in time of doubt and fear. I gain a deeper understanding of God's love for me through prayer and support of the People of God. I have come to know many good people, who, through their conviction of Christ's love for them, become the testimony of the true living Christ in their works of faith and love. Thanks, God, for sending them to my life.

After the summer of 1974, I went on with my philosophy and prepared to study theology in the major seminary. Prior to March 29, 1975, my studies were going very well. In fact I was really enjoying my studies because I knew what the purpose of my priesthood would be. I wanted to have a deeper understanding of my studies in order to handle people's feelings in their utmost tragedies and difficulties. I had only one focus in mind for the priesthood: to be a person of prayer. I wanted to share people's suffering. It became a blessing for me to understand their suffering intellectually and emotionally. I also wanted to be present with them physically to comfort them. In that way, whether I spoke intellectually or with real emotion from my heart then I would still be who I am.

The war became more intense and widespread after March 29, 1975. I remember January 28, 1973, when the peace treaty between the north and the south of Vietnam was signed in Paris. They exchanged prisoners of war and this event was witnessed by the United Nations. I thought the whole country might achieve peace, but it was not meant to be. The reality was that politically, both sides kept fighting and the peace agreement failed. Instead of keeping peace, the Communists attacked South Vietnam.

Hue was taken by the Communists at the end of March 1975. During that time we were very nervous and scared. We didn't know how to react or how to plan for the future. My friends and I wondered whether or not we should remain in the seminary to go on with our studies or go home to our families who were waiting for us and deeply concerned for our safety. On the one hand, we wanted to go home. On the other, we wanted to remain in the seminary. The entire country was in total disorder.

Before the fall of Saigon, we were under the control of the North Vietnamese military. They were everywhere in the seminary. I had heard a lot about the north Communist soldiers since I was very young. I had seen on television that these men were only about fourteen, fifteen and sixteen years old. Moreover, in addition to the previous descriptions, they were described as devils. The faculty of the seminary instructed us to be careful when speaking to these men. For the first few days we wondered among ourselves, "Who are they? What are they going to do with us? Are they going to hurt us? Are we going to be in trouble with them? Are they Christians?"

They began to control the daily schedule. We felt uncomfortable and nervous. Our gift of freedom was taken away. They watched us day and night. The troop leaders were always menacing and angry in their manner. We were living in fear.

Later, when we lived together in the seminary campus, some of these young men showed me their rosaries. They always had them in their pockets, but they were not able to expose them to the public due to their restricted regulations. One of these young soldiers told me, "You know, I came from a Catholic family, too."

Before he was sent to battle in the south, his mother handed him this rosary that was given to her on the day of her wedding. She asked the Blessed Virgin Mary to protect him and always keep him safe. I was stunned. I asked myself, "What would God do in this situation? How would God answer a mother's prayer for her son? If a northern mother had a son in the battle, she prayed for his safety; the same intention offered to God that a southern mother would offer when sending her son to defend freedom and protect the country. How could it be? To whom would God grant his peace?" I didn't know the answer.

It was a sick and evil war. It was sad that brothers and sisters killed each other. He would have liked to have gone to Mass with us, but he didn't dare. He loved to walk around the chapel and listen to the liturgical songs and prayers. Because of the philosophy of Communism they are forced to declare that they don't believe in God or anything else, except Lenin's theory and Marxism. There is no God for them. The fact was there were many inner conflicts between faith and reason among the northern soldiers because many of them came from Catholic families. I was lucky that I was able to get to know some of the North Vietnamese soldiers.

We tried to continue with some of our old routines. We studied in the morning and after lunch went to the fields. We dug up the soccer fields and turned them into potato fields.

During that time living conditions were very frustrating. Our desire to study interfered with our concerns about our families in the south and in Saigon. We didn't know what was happening to them. We tried to keep up our spiritual life and prayer. We knew the classroom time was coming to an end.

The Communists controlled all of us and gathered us twice a day. One of the sessions was after lunch when they gave us work to do in the fields. In the evening session, after our prayers and religious instruction, we were gathered together and forced to listen to lectures on Communism. The topics were on how to love our country by supporting Communism, and on philosophies of Karl Marx and Lenin. Every night we heard the same lectures given by an officer who did not even know how to read. He had learned the lecture by heart. He said it smoothly and sounded like a recording machine repeating, repeating, and repeating the same words. I guess that was how they tried to clear what was inside of our minds.

The brainwashing was a heavy pressure for us. Psychologically speaking, it drove me crazy! One evening I was sitting next to the Archbishop of Hue. I said, "Archbishop, I am so tired to hear this stuff, I can't handle it anymore." If I had to hear this lecture one more time about the wonderful theories of Communism and how we were all sinners against Vietnam because we did not fight against capitalism, I would go mad. The officer went on to tell us how wrong we were for studying under the influence of the missionaries and worshipping God under the influence of Catholicism, which was a foreign religion in our country. There was no God but the Communists. It was driving me absolutely cuckoo. I was afraid that one day, under such pressure, I would blow up and protest against these Communists and I would be killed.

The Archbishop looked at me and said softly, "I wish I was able to tell you more, but remember the verses of the scripture that Jesus told to his apostles and followers. You have eyes to see but you don't see, you have ears to hear, but you don't hear because you have hardened your hearts. You want to hear according to your own desire. You want to see what you would like to see and therefore you miss seeing the truth.

"Now," the Archbishop said to me, "I want you to use your ears wisely. That means you hear but you have heard nothing and you see but you have seen nothing."

I took his advice seriously enough so that when we heard the lectures about Communism I used a notebook to write poems or compose children's music for class.

The second part of the evening gathering was the "self-examination." It sounded like self-confession. We took turns telling others that we did not honor the teachings of Communism.

I had to stand up and say something like, "Today I did not live in dignity according to the way of life as a Communist. I did not serve others well enough or I did not hard enough in the field because I was lazy. I will try harder to be a good citizen of my country." In fact, I did not think about Communism and I didn't think about the teachings of Uncle Ho. You know who Uncle Ho was? That was Ho Chi

Minh, the leader and founder of the Vietnamese Communists.

My friends and I just kept saying to each other, "This is all crap!"

It really drove us insane. When my turn came up I must have something negative about myself to share with the group whether I liked it or not, whether it is true or not. I had to play along with the game that the Communists forced us to play. For us, it was a game of survival. But this was the terrible game, and it went on for about a month.

The fall of Saigon occurred on April 30, 1975. The hope that so many of us had to be freed by the South Vietnamese military collapsed. We thought and hoped that we would be freed from the dominion and capture by the north. Our hope was gone. It was over. I ran to the chapel and fell on my knees before the sanctuary, looking at the crucifix. I had never seen Jesus look so sad. I thought of the country, South Vietnam, now under the rule of the northern military and its Communism. The people of Vietnam would severely suffer. I could not believe that the Communist took over the whole country. The fear and sadness made me look at the person of Christ on that crucifix with tears. Jesus looked more wounded and miserable than ever. I wondered how long God would allow us to be in this miserable situation.

I didn't get angry with God or blame Him for our circumstances of fear and failure. I just wondered, "Why? WHY? Why did it fall? Why did the armed forces of South Vietnam fail to regain the freedom of its people?"

Many people had dedicated their lives to serve and protect the freedom so that we could live with human dignity. I believed in the system in South Vietnam that promoted freedom, where each person could live according to his or her dignity. Maybe it didn't work well, but it was good enough for me personally and I could see that it did work. Suddenly it just came to an end and failed bitterly.

In the seminary chapel I reflected on the fall of Saigon—just like when her enemies attacked Jerusalem and destroyed her. It was a sad day.

What am I to do? How is my family? Are they safe? Are any of our friends safe? In fact from March 29 to April 4, 1975, we had lived with the Communists and with their system they brutally controlled our minds. They controlled and erased our system of thinking and our perceptive. Continuously, we put ourselves under the restriction of their rule. One time, when one of my friends refused to follow their orders, thirty of us were confined in one room for two days. The room was so small that we could only take turns sitting down to stretch out our legs. We were really packed together. We were not afraid that they tried to punish us. We were treated this way because we were rebellious and opposed to their control of our religious practice. Therefore, we were in trouble most of the time.

The Archbishop of Hue and the faculty and staff of the seminary had to use their wisdom to get us out of the situation. Afterwards we had to promise that we would listen to the orders of the new government and the voice of the court of people that is always correct. I couldn't understand all that was going on and I questioned it often. I could not find an answer for the problems that took place during that time.

It could drive you crazy, literally. In fact, two of my classmates, who had experienced the thirty-in-a-room routine about ten times, went out of their minds and were declared to have mental illness. Two young seminarians, wonderful people, ended up mentally ill because of this stupid system of Communism. In our anxiety the Communists were laughing at us.

I looked at my friends and didn't know what to say. I just cried silently. Those tears were not only shed because I took pity on them but because of anger at our enemies. When you become so angry and cannot say a word publicly, you can easily lose your mind. I couldn't express my emotions in words or actions, but at least I could cry. I thanked God for that ability to cry, not publicly but privately.

A lot of different things happened during that month. We came to an end of our unknown future when Saigon fell. The staff and the board of directors of the seminary gave us a choice: we could stay at the seminary and go on with our studies or we could go home to our families. They did not know for sure if the Communists would allow us to go on with our studies. They said they would notify us about what would happen in the future. I made a decision to go home to see if my family and my parents were all right. I found out that my father would be taken away to be reeducated for fifteen days. That was the promise when the Communists took him. Each person was to pack food and clothing for fifteen days. The promise was a lie. My father did not return until thirteen years later. He was lucky he survived the cruel treatment he had to endure.

Within two weeks I wanted to return to the seminary even though my mom was begging me to stay. She wanted me to stay with the family for the summer and wait for further information and direction from the seminary. I needed to be home to help my mother and my family. I had a tough time making a decision.

After making arrangements with my mother and my sisters, I went back to the seminary to continue with the formation of the priesthood. After all these difficult experiences things did not improve.

I promised my mother that I would not be away long. I just wanted to find out what the future was for my religious study and my vocation. When I returned to the seminary, I found that only about sixty of the five hundred seminarians had returned. We decided to go on with our studies the best we could during the summer of 1975.

We hoped that the church would be able to ordain the older seminarians in the theology program as soon as possible, so that there would be enough priests to go around to all of the parishes. In fact, the Archbishop of Hue ordained a lot of priests who were in the fourth year of theology. They had been scheduled to be ordained that summer anyway. The ordination was quickly done. We were so glad for them.

We did not know that for the next fifteen years, after the ordination class of 1975, the Church in Vietnam would not ordain any priests. The new Communist government controlled the Church in

Vietnam. They had the final word about who could be ordained and who could not. Those of us who had a good background but whose families had anyone connected to the previous government didn't have a chance to be ordained into the priesthood. The only way one could be ordained was in secret by the bishop, but these priests could not publicly do their ministry at all. They worked underground for the faithful.

My friends and I went on with our studies. It was an intensive time and we had many interruptions in our schedule of the day because of the interference by the new government.

Then in the summer of 1976 the Communist really took over the seminary. This time they took it all. The seminary facility was turned into military housing for the soldiers' families. Even before they took over completely, some of the soldiers brought women, some wives, probably some who were not their wives, to live in the seminary. They did their laundry and hung it from the balconies and windows of the dormitory. It looked pretty ugly. They renewed their life styles from the jungle and even brought their dogs, pigs, chickens, and ducks with them. It was the most ugly thing I ever saw. They turned the seminary completely into a military base.

Chapter Seven

Into the Jungle

The Communists had taken over the seminary. In my opinion, they tried to drive us crazy and make us give up our vocation. They tried to make us return to our families. I don't think they directly tried to force us out of the seminary, but indirectly they did so by making us feel so uncomfortable. However, the Archbishop strongly indicated that no matter what happened we were going to keep the seminary. Still, my friends and I could not help but make plans to escape.

After the fall of Saigon on April 30, 1975, we were stuck in the seminary. It was very difficult for us to get official passes to travel from Central to South Vietnam. For almost two years, we were stuck together in the community of the seminary. We worked hard, hoping the future would brighten up for us.

In early February of 1977, we began to prepare for the New Year celebration. We planned to take advantage of all the excitement among the people who traditionally prepare for the New Year's festivities to escape from Vietnam. While the soldiers and the local police were shopping and planning gatherings with their families and friends, we were planning our escape.

There were six of us: Dung, Liem, Khoa, Tam, Khanh, and myself. All of these young men were from families established in Central Vietnam. Their families lived in and around the city of Hue. I was the only one from South Vietnam, from Saigon. They and their families had a variety of connections with different individuals who, for a price, would be willing to lend their assistance to six escapees.

Some of these guides had been in the military service in Khe-

Sanh, near Quang Tri, the ancient province north of Hue. There was a big and bloody battle there in 1972. These people assured us that if we were capable of walking for a week, they could get us across the border of Laos and then into Thailand to seek refugee status.

The six of us thought that this was a good time to make an effort to escape. It did not appear to us that the military or the police were paying the usual amount of attention to our behavior and whereabouts. Who would have thought that we, university students and seminarians, were likely to escape?

One afternoon after we had been working in the camp, the former soccer field, we made our escape. After we had worked for about an hour, the guards took a break to smoke, we signaled to one another, went to an agreed upon spot and climbed over the big high wall that surrounded the seminary. We were off to meet the people who had organized this march to Laos. These people had prepared fake documents, which would allow us to travel.

We traveled by bus to the province of Quang-Tri. When we arrived we hid at the home of the parents of Dung. We rested there for two days. We told neighbors and friends in the village that we had permission to visit the family of Dung. Those individuals who had prepared for our escape told us when and where to meet for the next leg of our journey.

When we met our organizers we were surprised to find that there were also other men, women, and children in our small group. The final group totaled about thirty individuals. The families of the organizers were with us also. We had paid about three hundred dollars each for the privilege of going on this outrageous attempt. Poor children! Of course, we did not blame them at all, but we began to doubt the safety of the group. After a discussion with the guide we all decided to do the best we could to escape together.

The guide knew the necessary areas of the jungle because of his background in the secret service before 1975 and by chopping wood in the jungle after 1975. Now, we had to pay him well to become our guide and not turn us in to the Communists for a reward.

The organizers had prepared dried food to take with us for the entire trip. Originally, the guide estimated that we needed to prepare food for a journey of ten days or two weeks to cross the Laotian border and on into Thailand. We got to the province of Khe-Sanh.

The area was so heavily populated with military personnel that it was unfavorable for us to walk. During the day the military soldiers patrolled trails in the jungle. They had many secret checkpoints and we did not know the location of any of them. Because of this we were forced to hide during the daytime and walk at night. Sometimes the guides would disappear for a while, then come back with information as to whether or not we could walk during the daytime. We relied totally on two guides who had had some experience walking in the jungle. They told us when and how to proceed. The anxiety was heavy in our hearts.

Many difficulties took place on this trip. One of the most serious challenges was keeping the children quiet. It was difficult even for adults to keep quiet during the day. The darkness gave us some comfort but even then, as we walked in the jungle, there were plants with thorns that would tear at our clothing and skin. Snakes hung from the vines and crawled along the ground. There were poisonous plants, tigers, and other types of mountain animals.

Each night as we traveled there were multiple incidents in which a child would cry out from being scratched or just being scared. Their mother or father would have to hold their hand over the child's mouth to muffle the sound and then we would all wait for a while before proceeding. Those poor women and men felt so guilty and feared that because of their child we would all be caught. No one wanted to be blamed for that happening.

We six young friends hung together, but still tried to help out the others as much as we could. There was no place to run to in the dark. I remember at that time I stayed pretty calm. We walked with a backpack containing dry food and several containers of water. We just hoped that the water from the jungle streams where we refilled these containers was suitable to drink. We had no choice.

Once in a while, during the day, one of our guides worked his way ahead and marked a way for us to follow at night. He used all of his instinct and experience to lead us. At night we held on to the backpack of the person in front of us. That was how we had to travel. We didn't make it very far on any given night. We continued to hide during the daylight and tried to observe carefully and remember the way we had traveled.

We walked night after night. It was comforting when occasionally there would be a space in the thick jungle and we would see the moon and stars. This light was not good enough for us to see the trail, but it made us more visible to each other.

The guide kept telling us, "Follow the person in front of you. Just follow the footsteps of one another." At first I thought, "This is ridiculous. If there were only adults we could run faster. If we didn't have to take care of so many we could travel faster and it would be safer."

My friends and I felt trapped by the number in the group, but we knew we had to do the best we could to make a successful escape for everyone. Those were the facts and we tried to do the best we could to help each other. So in the darkness of night, one by one, we tried to watch the person in front of us. We could not help but get a little spread out along the trail. Sometimes, it was the cry of a child that guided us to the person in front of us. We walked and we rested, hiding in the bushes. Occasionally, we were able to locate a cave to rest in. We didn't make very good progress toward the border of Laos.

On the tenth day we became aware that our guides didn't really know where they were going. I kept seeing them look at the map and the compass. They talked back and forth. We began to worry for we knew that we had not made good progress and we were about to run out of food. Otherwise, everything was working out just fine.

It was frightening when the guides said we had to stop and hide ourselves for a couple of days due to the military searching in front of us. We had to wait for this searching to end before we could continue the walk. We moved into the deep jungle and settled down to camp. It was then we started to do some hunting. Once again, the Boy Scouts' survival skills came in handy. We made traps with vines and bamboo sticks. We tried to locate animal trails and make traps involving slipknots on vine ropes. We covered the ropes with leaves and waited. We caught rabbits, mountain cats, and even a deer. Basically, whatever living creatures moved, such as snakes, rabbits, or fish in the stream, became our food.

Now, we had a problem. How did we cook? We knew cooking the meat was not possible because the smoke and associated food smells would have been an easy signal for the patrols. So we skinned the animals and sliced the meat very thinly. We then placed the meat on rocks in the sun and made something like beef jerky. That was all we were able to do. No fires were allowed at any time. Even the people who smoked had to cover their cigarettes with their hand and only allow themselves a few puffs at a time.

We were stuck in the jungle for another week. By now, we had enough dried meat for the journey. The original plan called for ten days or two weeks, but in the end we wandered in the jungle for almost a month.

Eventually, we managed to cross the Ho Chi Minh Trail, but by the time we got close to the border between Laos and Thailand, we were captured.

After we were caught we were brought back to the military patrol base located in the woods. The guides were also arrested and put in prison with us. They treated us very badly. Thank God no one died. We were very tired and skinny. We looked so ugly for having not shaved for a month, but that did not matter. What mattered was what would happen to us next. Everyone looked depressed and fearful.

A few days later, we were dragged back to Quang Tri Province and put in jail. The life in prison was horrible. Each day seemed like an eternity. We lost our freedom. The guards treated us worse than animals. We had to do forced labor in the field. We cleaned up after the soldiers. Once again, after working hard in the field, we had to listen to Communist political lectures about how to become a good citizen of Vietnam.

We stayed in prison for about a month. During that time we

searched for a guard who, for a price, would help us to get out. The men were held in one cell and the women and children in another cell. We were not able to see each other or communicate. The cell was about fifteen feet square with seventeen men in it. We could lie down to sleep for a while, but it was very difficult to get any decent sleep because there were so many mosquitoes and we were constantly being bitten. The temperatures were hot and the humidity was high. Our skin was always sticky. It was not like a prison in America. It was a living hell.

We were fed one bowl of rice and a couple of cans of water a day. We were interrogated repeatedly and when they didn't like our answers we were hit with the butts of their pistols many times. They wanted to find out who was the leader of the group. They wanted to know how we had walked to the border. They wanted to find our trail and to stop others. Maybe they wanted to make more money. It was also possible that they themselves wanted to escape.

After a month in prison we were able to make a deal with the guard. He would let us go with papers signed by their troop leader. The papers said that we had been reeducated with better understanding of Communism. The papers read something like this, "We, the prison leaders, are ready to testify that these men are capable to love and serve the country of (Socialist) Communist Vietnam."

The condition for our release was that we were to report back to our supervisors in the seminary. The seminary priests knew that we had planned an escape, but they didn't have a clue about any of the details of our plans. I was afraid the priests might be in some kind of trouble because of what we had done. Fortunately, the Communists had just recently taken over the whole country; they were not yet well organized. Somehow, they had not threatened the priests and administrators of the seminary. The Communist officers seemed to accept the fact the priests did not have any involvement in our escape and that it was an effort of our own planning.

We returned to Hue from Quang Tri province in a small cabin on a train. We were released after we paid two hundred dollars for the six of us. It was fortunate that while we had been in the seminary our families and close friends had given us valuable gifts. We had gold necklace chains, rings, and eyeglass frames made of gold. We used these items to reach an equivalent of two hundred dollars. This was how we returned to the seminary after more than two months. It was now April 21, 1977.

While we were in prison we were forced to listen to Communist lectures. These were memorized lectures given by people who did not know how to read or write. How did we know they could not read and write? The day they released us from the prison, they held the paper, reading to us the statement, upside down. The same lectures were repeated again and again. Every single day we heard the same lectures. That really became a horrible torment. It was very abusive to one's mind to listen to those lectures over and over again.

We had had some experience with brainwashing when we were at the seminary in 1975, so I knew how to survive those punishments. For the last two years at the seminary we had been forced to listen to essentially the same lectures regarding Communist doctrines. I had learned to let it pass through my ears and let it go easily. Sometimes we were required to participate in discussions and to praise the Communist's principles and the revolutionist theories in Vietnam. We had learned it all so that we could talk about it and play along with their game.

That was the first time I had been in prison. Still, we were so lucky and we thanked God all of the time. We had had quite an adventure and we knew that it might have ended much differently, much more tragically. It had been a very dangerous situation for us. Still, we were uncertain how to feel about our failed attempt to escape. The priests always loved us and helped us to reenter the community of the seminary, even though it was much changed from when we first came as young men.

None of us ever talked about our escape experience because we feared that even in the close-knit community of the seminary there might be someone who was a secret agent for the Communists. We called this kind of person an "antenna-receiver." There were always attempts by the Communists to infiltrate organizations and gain information about the participants. The seminary was not immune to this type of attack. The Communists may have used our dearest friends against us by threatening to harm their families if they did not report what they heard any of the six of us saying. So we kept quiet. Still, once in a while, late at night, when we had nightmares as a result of our prison experience, we would carefully and quietly talk to one another. As time went on we worked out codes and quietly communicated with one another during our daily devotions and routines. In time, we were planning to escape again. This time, however, we were going to do it on our own, without other people accompanying us. That was the talk.

CHAPTER EIGHT

Guns in the Lake

In April of 1977 we returned from prison (the first time) to the seminary. About a month later the government decided to close the seminary. In fact, all the seminaries in the country were to be closed immediately.

It was a dirty trick and it was done very forcefully. Previously, they threw some guns into the fishing lake around the chapel. Then, suddenly, the police and army soldiers gathered around the lake and sent someone down to gather up the guns. This was how they managed to accuse us of holding guns for a revolution. It gave them a good political reason to kick us out of the seminary completely. Their accusations were based on evidence that we were holding weapons illegally and were planning a resistance. We were a group of young men who were ripe for military service. We had no way to defend for the truth. We had no choice but to turn the seminary over to the new government. It was a sad day for the Church of Vietnam. We all had a few days to pack our personal items and return to our families.

The Archbishop of Hue spoke to us before he sent us home. It was for our safety that the Archbishop spoke to us. He said, "I strictly order you not to try to escape the country because we are entitled as seminarians to study for the Church and to love and to serve the Church. In union with the Holy Father and the universal Church, we are the People of God in Vietnam. The Church will live within the country of Vietnam. As a good citizen of Vietnam we have to uphold our honor and follow the structure of the new government and its laws so that we may together build our country for the future…."

Privately, he encouraged each of us to be faithful to the Church.

He also said, "From now on, be prepared, because this time may be an opportunity for you to be a martyr for the Church. It may be an opportunity to testify to the strong faith that you have. I encourage you to love the Church and to endure in your suffering."

His words reminded me of a chapter of the Gospel of St. John (21: 15-19), when Jesus appeared to Peter and the apostles. After He was resurrected from the dead, Jesus asks Peter, "Simon, do you love me?" Peter says, "Lord you know that I love you." Jesus replied, "Then take care of my lambs, my sheep." Three times Peter confessed his love for Jesus, and three times he received the new responsibilities. Jesus said, "When you are young you can go wherever you want but when you are older you stretch out your arms and let the other people lead you, even if you don't want to go." This is how Jesus told Peter that he would have to die to testify for his faith.

The Archbishop of Hue, Phillip Dien Kim Nguyen, told us that many difficulties were waiting ahead of us and that our faith would be challenged and put to the test. He assured us that we shouldn't be afraid of the fire. As certain as the sun rises, the Lord would deliver us from all harm. He wished that each one of us, as we returned to our families, would continue our studies the best that we could with our local pastors. We needed to depend on the local priests for further instruction in theology. He hoped we would continue to participate in the pastoral care for local communities.

He continued, "I don't know when or how you are going to be ordained into the priesthood, but the priesthood of Christ is to love and serve God and others. Whether you function as a priest or in the laity it is time for you to have faith and put into practice what you have learned and believe. I do encourage you, if you have an opportunity to escape from Vietnam, please do so. One day you may return to rebuild the Mother Church in Vietnam. The Church needs your help. The future of the Vietnamese Church is in your hands."

All of us were in tears as we said good-bye to our beloved Archbishop. I always admired his wisdom and his gentleness. He knew each of us by name. He knew our strengths and weaknesses.

He was so willing to be there to support us. I knew he was a person of prayer and, in a sense, I loved him as I loved my father. It was so sad that we had to be separated. We didn't know when we would ever be together again. It was a sad day, May 15, 1977. In tears and in sadness I departed the seminary, my home.

We had no choice but to return to our families to live for good. We had the proper papers to present to guards at checkpoints on the way home. I had papers that authorized me to travel from Hue to Saigon. I was to travel by bus and have the papers with me. On the way to Saigon, I decided to stop by Da Nang to see my sister.

One of my sisters was living in Da Nang, and because her husband had worked in the air force before 1975, they were stuck there with her husband's family. I suggested to the other five friends in my group, "Let's go down to my sister's and see if we can stay there." It was my idea that perhaps we could plan an escape from Da Nang to Hong Kong by boat.

During the previous years of seminary, for several summers, I had worked in a parish in Da Nang. A lot of my friends in the parish were fisherman. They had had similar experiences with the particular idea of escaping by boat. They even knew of some people who had successfully escaped via this route.

With that intention in mind, my friends and I arrived at my sister's home. We told her our plan to escape and she said she would try to help us. This was the sister who was just older than I. Her name was Lien.

We got in touch with some of the parishioners who knew me before. The six of us were healthy, strong young men. The owner of the fishing boat and the organizers of the escape realized that we would be helpful for the trip. Because of our youth, trustworthiness, wit and strength, we might be needed. We were allowed to join the party free of charge. In exchange for room in the boat, we would help to drive the boat. We all agreed on the settlement. We worked in the fishing factory for a couple of months and waited for an opportunity to depart from Vietnam.

Finally, a connection was made with one of my former parishioners. He was willing to help us out. He had done the trip twice before. He had taken people to Hong Kong and returned to Vietnam as a routine part of his fishing trips. What made him to do that kind of business? Why didn't he remain in Hong Kong? He wanted to make more money before he took his entire family out of Vietnam. He wanted to make sure it was all well planned before he risked the lives of his family members. Also, he had to wait for his two sons to return from the reeducation program.

We were prepared to attempt the escape, but it failed because the boat we were to take was captured just before we were supposed to get on for our escape to Hong Kong. We were scared because we had taken a small boat called a "taxi" out and to meet our vessel. We were concerned that when we turned around to come back to land we would be captured by the patrols. We figured that if we were caught we would end up in jail again. Lucky for us, our guides were good and experienced. They told us that if we were stopped by the patrols all we needed to say was that we had been out fishing. The pilot of the taxi-boat had a permit to go out to sea to fish for a day. It was fortunate that we were not stopped and did not have to use this explanation at all.

After this failure to escape to Hong Kong we were all very disappointed. I did not want to be a burden to my sisters, my parents, especially to my mother, if I returned home in Saigon. They would worry very much for my safety. I didn't end up in a small local prison but I was still in the large prison of Vietnam. The idea and the hunger for freedom were still very strong in my heart. The desire to obtain freedom was ever on my mind.

Before we said good-bye to one another we agreed, the six of us, to keep in touch and to meet in one month in Saigon. These very dear friends of mine were going to gather together and attempt to escape one more time. They returned to their families in different cities of Central Vietnam and I went home to Saigon in South Vietnam. I said to my friends, "Come to my parents' home and we will work it out with several different parishes and plan to escape again. Hopefully, we can rely on the help of the people who love us and are willing to hide us." Again, we planned to escape together as we departed from each other.

We were now into the early months of 1978 and at the time my family was stuck in the south. It took me a couple of days to get home to the suburban area of Saigon. I reflected about what really happened in the last few months. What had I learned from all these experiences? What was it that God wanted me to do? What will happen next? I looked out the window of the bus, the road was left behind me; the trees and fields passed by quickly. I hoped that the oppression of the country and persecution of the Church soon passed. God's will be done! I believed that.

Finally, I got home and was welcomed by my family. Everyone seemed to release the heavy anxiety in their hearts after they learned that I was all right.

I worked to gather information while waiting for my friends to join me. Quietly, I collected the rhythm of the weather in the different seasons and how it would affect our escape from the southern ports. I found some of the possibilities. The month of the meeting came and passed, but no one came. No one showed up! I was worried that something bad had happened to them. Somehow, they had become involved with helping their families wherever they lived. Of course, I was disappointed that none of them could join me. However, I understood. I wrote to them and told them that I was working to prepare for the new opportunity.

CHAPTER NINE

At Home

In June of 1978 I arrived home. I thought, "Maybe this is an opportune time to challenge myself in keeping my vocation."

What would happen in the future, I had no idea at all. At least I was still able to keep my vocation and still wanted to become a priest, even though I could not see how I would ever be able to continue my study due to the oppression by the Communists. The best I could do was to get in touch with the local priest just as Archbishop Phillip had instructed us to do. My parents lived in a totally different district of the Church from where the seminary was located. I, of course, had the proof that I was a seminarian that had been released by the government and voluntarily returned to live with my family. I lived in peace for about two weeks.

Of course the former house of my parents was taken away by the new government, and my father ended up in reeducation camp because of his military background in South Vietnam. The former soldiers of South Vietnam had been accused of being murderers. The families of the ex-officers of the previous government, who were murderers, had no right to stay in the homes built by the blood and tears of the people.

That accusation was a lie. Everyone knew it was not true, but they had no voice to protest those false accusations because they feared for their relative's safety. My family was driven away from the house where we lived for many years. My mother took the family and moved to Long Thanh, a suburb of Saigon. It was only about thirty-five miles away. We went to the house of her mother to live for a while.

A few months later, I found out that my father had relatives living only about six miles away from Long Thanh. We moved to their village, Phuoc Ly, temporarily, to avoid any further difficulties with the local officers. I farmed with my relatives and secretly planned my next escape.

My relatives helped my family build a small house. However, the number of Communist soldiers in the area was very great. They divided themselves into small groups and billeted with the local residents. Whether we liked it or not, they were in our new home, and we had to feed them. For about two weeks I passively lived in silence. I tried to say nothing and do nothing even though I was quite upset.

I presented myself at the local office to get an approval for my residence with my mother and sisters. Two weeks later, the police came to the house and ordered me to report to the local district because I had been selected to serve the country in the military. I had been called to report to the local office to fulfill my duty as a Vietnamese citizen and I ended up on a list to become a Communist soldier.

I didn't want to do this, but if I didn't do as they ordered, my family would be in trouble. I kept thinking, how could I get out of the whole messy situation? I didn't want to join the military and then be sent to Cambodia to fight and to kill or to get killed. I would feel honored to serve the country and the people if it was to protect freedom for the common good. I would never want to fight as a Communist. It seemed to me that the only way that I could prevent my family from having further problems with the local Communist officers was to go to the military base at the appointed time and present myself. Then, I would run away from the military base and find a way to hide. Otherwise, I would be sent away to basic training, then off to Cambodia to fight the Khmer Rouge. In great anxiety and depression, I kept scheming as the date to report approached.

I talked to some of my new friends and relatives. We belonged to the same parish community and some of them had also received the order to report to the military. I had to find a way to disqualify myself from this outrageous service. Before one enters the military service, one must go through the physical examination. One way I thought I could affect the results of my exam was to chew a lot of tobacco before my exam so that my heart would beat very fast. Perhaps that would be a good way for me to show them I was not in good enough shape to join the military.

That was what I did on the day of the physical examination. However, it didn't work, even though I managed to get my heart racing very fast. My heart was beating so fast I felt I had been running a marathon for a hundred miles.

They asked, "What happened to you? How come your heart is beating so fast?"

All I said was, "I don't know." I was playing a game with them and giving it a good shot.

They said, "We could work it out for you. Even though you may not be able to fight in battle, you will still be able to cook and do a little light work." Once again, I decided to escape.

Later that day, we were gathered together in the camp. I found a number of my friends who didn't want to become a Communist soldier, and quietly we planned an escape from the base. One rainy evening we dug up the ground under the fence. We sneaked out and ran through the minefields, hoping to get into the woods and find our way home. It took a little time but we made it. I don't think the guards searched for us for long. I think the Communists thought since they had control of South Vietnam no one could escape. Sooner or later, they would catch us. But for now, I had to find my way home and hide.

I had prayed hard for our success. With the guidance of the Holy Spirit, through intercession of the Blessed Virgin Mary and the saints, I prayed that my patron saint, St. Peter, would deliver us from harm and bring us safely home. I thought and believed that from their intercessions God would listen and deliver us from harm. I told my friends if God wanted me to become a priest to serve His people, He had to be with me.

Finally, we made it into the woods. The woods in the south were not the same as the deep jungle near Khe-Sanh, Central Vietnam. We were there for about five days. We wanted to make sure that the military police had stopped searching.

The reason I had to report in the first place was to prevent my family from being in trouble with the local officers. After I checked in at the military base, my family could say they did not know of my whereabouts. My family could say that I had reported as I was ordered, "He went to present himself. We don't know where he is." My purpose was to prevent my family from having any problems after my escape from the post.

After walking in the woods for several days, I finally found a way home and approached the back door of the house early in the morning. My mom woke up to open the door for me. She was glad to see me, but she was also very frightened that I would be in trouble. She whispered in my ear and signaled for me to be silent for fear to wake up the soldiers in the backyard. Quietly, I climbed up to the attic of the house. No one would think that I was hiding there. No one knew there was an attic in the house except my mother and me. It was not a place to live in because it was so small and close to the roof of the house. No one would believe that I was there.

I told my mother that I wanted to hide in the attic. I thought that during the day I would be very quiet up there, reading by myself. During the night I could sneak down to take a shower and get something to eat. I would need to be very quiet because the soldiers were still in and out of our house. They took over one room and all of my sisters and my mother were in another room.

I didn't know why these soldiers had to live with the village's residents. The reason they told to all residents was that the people created the soldiers for the people; therefore, the residents had the duty to feed them and to shelter them so they could continue to protect the people. It was a very unpleasant situation. There was always someone watching you. We couldn't talk to each other freely at all. The sense of fear was always in the air. One could not breathe.

Every day the local police or the military police stopped by the house and questioned my mother and my sisters. "Where is your son?" "Where is your brother?"

My relatives and my sisters were threatened to tell the truth about where I was hiding and how I was planning to escape. They were being interrogated by these evil men over and over again. I heard all of these questions so many times while I was in the attic. From the attic I could hear everything in the main room of the house. When they came the neighbor's dog barked and in my fear of being captured I would hold my breath tightly. I heard their voices and I knew that they had come once again looking for me. I didn't really think they could hear my breathing but the will for survival just made me freeze. It seemed that my nervous breathing was like a rock band's drum in their ears.

I listened to their many threatening statements about what they would do to my family. They said they would do many miserable things to my parents, my sisters, and my grandmother. They not only threatened them, they also made it sound like revenge and punishment. They said, "If you point out where he is hiding and you tell the truth, then your husband will be home soon."

This created a tremendous emotional disturbance for me. I felt so angry with them. I thought, "You are a bunch of liars." I felt so helpless and most of the time I felt so depressed.

My spirit was in bad shape. I felt hopeless, helpless, and powerless. I did not know how to balance my mental state at that time. I wished that I had the miraculous power to turn myself into a small mosquito and fly away. This was not an easy time in my life at all. But, in order to survive, I spent nearly a year in my mother's attic.

I had hid myself for almost a year, until the middle of 1979. It was not so bad in the winter. It rains a lot in the winter and the temperatures were mild in the day. It was a little cool at night and I wrapped myself in a blanket. During the summertime it was like being cooked alive. I was living in an oven at 120 degrees. Vietnam has only two seasons, rainy and dry. There are six months of continuous rain and six months of hot, burning sun. It was so hot in the summer I could only dress and live in my shorts.

Eventually, even my mom knew it was not a fit place to live, but she had no other choice. I had no other choice but stay in the attic. All day long, day after day, I had to kill time. I read anything that came to my hands. After I had read all the books I had with me, I had nothing else to read except all the newspapers published by the local government. They were filled with boring nonsense and Communist writings. I never read that stuff. I had heard enough at the seminary after 1975 such as, "Love your country. Serve your country. You have to become a member of the Communist Party to show to others that you are a good citizen of Vietnam. How many years have those capitalists dominated our country? It is time to rebuild our country with freedom…" I was just sick and tired of it. I needed something else to do so I asked for paper and pencils to draw. Later on I learned how to paint, to compose music, and even to sew clothes by hand.

All honor to you, I almost went nuts. I almost became mentally ill. Toward the end of 1978 the soldiers no longer stayed in the village. However, I was still afraid that the local officers would send someone to capture me. I lived in the attic for a couple more months to make sure that I was safe in my home.

The year of 1978 was a bad time for everyone in the whole country. Many people had to work very hard in the rice paddy, vending on the streets, and chopping wood in the jungle to buy food for their families. The harvest was not good. Everyone seemed to get poorer each day. My mother was so concerned for the whole family. I saw her worried face each night. She had many anxieties and worries for the well being of my father and for all of us. She looked much older. I knew my mother was physically getting weaker. Early in May of 1979, the Feast day of St. Joseph the Worker, patron of the Church, I made my usual trip down from the attic to have a shower and food. I said to my mother, "Mom, I cannot live under these conditions any longer. I am almost mentally ill. I need to do something to help our family. I don't know what to do. I don't know what to say. I don't know what to think. I am trapped in my own prison that I have built for myself."

She was silent, then whispered in my ear, "The whole country of Vietnam is a prison now. So where can you go? You have to face reality and be a strong person. Accept the reality and face it, work it out with your faith."

I asked her, "What do you want me to do, Mom? I cannot serve the people publicly in the ministry, even though the local priests need help. They need help but I cannot show my face. I cannot do anything to help myself or anyone."

My mom said, "Why don't you go into the woods and work there a little while? Maybe conditions will change and they will forget about you. You can chop wood with your cousins to earn a living. It will help you to release your inner anger. Come back when things get better. We will try to bring food into the woods to help you to survive."

This didn't sound very good because they had to bring food to me. The road from home to the woods was not safe. What if something happened to them on the road? I would never be able to forgive myself. The distance between the woods and my home was too far. It took at least a day by bike. I didn't want to create any more troubles or difficulties for my family. I said to my mother, "I'll think about it. Maybe I will try to escape to the jungle and get to the border of Cambodia. I need to study some routes on the map." With that intention in mind I tried to live in peace for a while in the attic.

Where would I be able to go? How would I get legal documents to travel on the road? Do my friends still want to escape with me? I hoped and prayed for the opportunity to get away from this living hell. I pondered many questions but I had no clear answers at all.

I decided I needed to cross the border into Cambodia, to get to Thailand, and then seek asylum there as a refugee. First I had to have permits to travel from place to place. I found a large eraser and drew a seal of the local office on its surface. With a little knife, I made a seal to ink the permit paper to travel in the area.

With that fake permit in hand, I headed to the woods. I met my older cousins who were working there. They helped me to chop wood and sell it to different dealers for money. I sent money home to help my family and bought food in the nearby villages. My family didn't have to transport food for me. I felt much better chopping wood and earning money to help my family. On top of that, I felt much better working in the woods. It released the anger and frustration out of my heart. The police would not come near the woods. I felt much safer in the deep of the woods.

Each day I worked hard, and carried wood to the dealer and cashed it for money. It was not an easy job but it worked for me. It was better than to remain in the attic. I made new friends and found some other young seminarians who ended up in the jungle like me. I began to quickly establish a new circle of former seminarians. We were able to quickly establish a deep sense of trust among us because of our shared background in our religious vocation. We were always concerned about secret agents or betrayers, but we had to trust someone if we were to get out of the country. So the third escape took shape and it would depart from the south of Vietnam toward the border of Cambodia. This time, we agreed to form small groups of four to escape and to support each other.

We formed four small groups to depart an hour apart. In this way we could look after one another in the jungle. But, after only one day of walking, we were stopped by military patrols. They captured the first group on sight. My friends screamed to signal the rest of us that they were captured. We heard their screams and were able to flee. I couldn't return to chopping wood because the patrols, sooner or later, would come and search for us. I had no other choice but to return to the attic of my home. I felt so helpless, powerless, and empty. My mother and my sisters couldn't find words to comfort my distress. All they could say was, "Do not let your heart be troubled. God will show the way for you to follow."

I tried to believe that their words someday would come true. I remember that I was so disappointed in myself, and I was angry with

God. Day after day, I fell into a deeper depression, as I remained hiding in the attic.

CHAPTER TEN

Return to the Attic

One night, after a long day of hiding in the attic and steaming myself in the hot, humid, scorching heat, I sneaked down from the attic to eat something. I quietly woke my mom up to ask her if she would allow me to escape again. First, I had to find out if she had any money left. My mother didn't want me to escape again because she said that if anything happened to me, she would become a failure person in her husband's eyes. She wouldn't be able to explain to my father what happened to me. On the other hand, my mother wanted me to end all these tragedies by getting married like my friends. They were no longer running away in fear because the Communists would leave them alone after they married. Usually, married men devoted themselves to taking care of their families. The Communists believed that, after getting married, young men would not have time to join other men in a revolution.

I was the only son in the family. Traditionally, I had an obligation and a responsibility to carry on the family name. As I was the only son in the family, my sisters were taught that they must help me so that I might live and carry on the family name. It is extremely important in the culture of Vietnam for the family name to be carried on to the future generations. I knew what my responsibility was to my family's tradition, but I didn't want to marry at all. So, after a lot of discussion back and forth, I pointed out to my mother that if I stayed home I would not have an opportunity to be with the family anyway as I was always in hiding from the Communists. I said to my mother, "Even if I stay home I don't want to get married because I cannot live with the Communists. I cannot pretend that everything would be fine. This is not my vocation. Besides, if I cannot even take care of myself, how can I take care of others?"

My mother said, "Well after a little while you will fall in love with someone. You will be able to give your love and life to her. I know you will find someone to love you and care for you, and you will love her and you will do the same for her."

Honestly, I was not thinking about getting married. I did not want to bring the people that I loved and cared for into threatening and insecure situations as I had created for my mother and my family. I would rather handle this difficulty by myself than get anyone else involved in these hectic problems with me. They didn't have to do that for me. They didn't deserve to suffer for me. No doubt, my mother's words to me would come true. However, I still believed that God's will would be done.

At the end of our conversation my mother said, "Well, if you have already made up your mind, I can only pray to God that He will help you."

I was not in a prayerful mode at that time. I knew that God was near and willing to answer my prayers. However, I was consumed only with the desire to escape from my attic prison. I had to go away from this "living hell."

Everyday, my mother and sisters shared with me bad things were happening in the parish community. They told me what the local Communist officers had done to the priests and how they controlled the exercises of religious devotion in the community. Everyone was living in fear, hungry for food, and in the highest anxiety for the future. The more I heard of these lamentations the more I decided to escape out of the country. How could I get away? How could I escape? It was the only thing I could think of and I prayed all day long, "How? How? How?" I knew that it had to happen soon.

My mother told me she still had some jewelry that her parents had given her on her wedding day. My father had given her his wedding ring on the day he was taken away to the reeducation camp as he said, "You keep this ring, as you may need it in the near future." I knew these gifts were tremendously important to my mother. They were priceless to her. I couldn't sell these to others to pay for my escape.

My mother said, "Don't worry. I will find a way to gather at least a hundred dollars so that you can make a deposit to hold a seat in the boat. We can work for the rest later." As I am writing this story, I recall that at that time, I was a very selfish person. I just wanted to get out of the country. I didn't care how much it cost. I just said to my family, "Please, get me out of here!" I could not stand it anymore. I was ready to give it all up.

During the next few days, as I remained in the attic, my older sisters tried to book a trip for me. They talked to my relatives and their friends to arrange for me to escape. While I was waiting, I tried to recall the appearance of the seal of the local police that I used to make the fake traveling papers. This time I didn't have a large eraser to carve a seal, so I used a potato cut in half. I sat there in the attic, and little by little, I carved the seal. Then, using red ink I made my own permit papers for traveling. I attempted to go as far south as possible. That was all the way to Ca-Mau. It would be closer to the boarder of Thailand, with just a little trip across to the Gulf of Thailand to get to the land.

I was using the contractors my older sisters met in the church's activities. These people promised me a good deal. They told me that for one person it would be three hundred dollars. They would lower the cost if I were willing to work on the boat during the trip. Of course, I took their offer without any hesitation. I believed I could work hard to repay their kindness. I didn't have any friends at that time because of the year that I had spent in isolation. Many of my previous friends from the seminary had settled into their new routines of life. Some had married and had family responsibilities. They were stuck. I decided to escape by myself.

With the fake traveling permission papers I got into Ca-Mau and stayed for a couple of days. I hid in the boat owner's house for four days. We were waiting for a good time to escape. Finally, when the time was right we got into the "taxi" to go to the "mother boat" waiting for us at the appointed place near the open sea.

Unfortunately, the local police caught us at the dock. I had fallen into a trap. Locals had made a trap for the owner of the boat and for me. I lost the last hundred dollars and was forced to get away before I was caught. I got into the deep water and followed the current to the other side of the river. We had agreed before boarding that if something happened, we had to run away by ourselves. We couldn't wait for each other. Otherwise, we would be caught as a group.

Upon reaching to the other side of the river, I had to run. I don't think a sprinter could run that fast. I was so lucky that I was alone and not responsible for anyone else. Besides, I didn't know anyone else. The only choice was to run as fast as you could. To stay behind was to end up in prison and conditions in prison were horrifying.

So I took off and ran. I ran as fast as I could. I hid in bushes, behind bamboo trees and water coconut trees, trying to find my way back to the family of the owner of the boat. I had to trust them, as there was nowhere else for me to go. I had to find out if they had betrayed me. I wanted that money back. After four days in the bushes I worked my way back. I had to hide for another week in their home. I was trying to figure out how to get the one hundred dollars back. This was just a waste of time. We both had been the victims of the betrayal. I came to know that when people are poor they would do anything to survive and even betray others.

On the other hand, to coordinate an escape out of Vietnam by boat was a hot business in 1979. People took this opportunity to become rich. Everyone talked about it. They talked and gave others private tours to show their boat and to assure business. The more they talked about the "season of escaping" the more traps they made for innocent people. The owner of the boat promised to include me in the next escape. He would contact me as soon as he could for he needed my help.

I had to borrow money from the family that I had stayed with. I made my own traveling papers again using the potato seal and the red ink. I crossed my heart as I promised them that I would somehow repay the money that I had borrowed.

I bought a bus ticket and rode the bus home. Sitting on the old bus with other passengers, my whole heart was filled with bitter feelings. I was depressed and resentful. My whole being was consumed with anger and frustration. I came to a sense that I did not care to live any longer in this desperate situation. Looking out the window of the bus I saw the sunrise and I said to myself, "There is another day just about to begin and another life begins. If there is another life beginning it has to be my life. I cannot lose hope. I have many things to do."

I promised myself to put my spiritual life back together. I couldn't allow these difficulties to take away my trust and hope in God. I felt much better, even though I did not know what to do next. I crossed the checkpoints with no further problems, and at last I returned home safely.

After the last attempt to escape, I decided that the best approach was to escape with trustworthy friends. I must once again get a group of friends together and make another attempt to escape. It was important to have just a small circle of friends who can trust each other. I was convinced that this was the best way to escape. Unfortunately, at this time, the whole country was in the throes of a great famine and an epidemic of infectious skin irritation. Everyone sold anything they had to buy food and medicine. Due to the lack of money, the local police could be bribed with very little money. My mother sold all the classical music records my father had left to buy food and to pay the local police for my temporary freedom. Because of this bribery, I didn't have to hide in the attic anymore. I was allowed to work in the rice paddies or chop wood in the field near the river. I decided to collect money to buy a small boat to go to the different woods located along the river. The river led to the open sea where the wood was transported to the city to sell. I earned enough money to feed my family. The job was difficult because I had to live in the small boat and endure mosquitoes and unstable weather.

Each week I worked in the woods located along the river for five days then on the weekend, when I came home, I helped my parish community direct the choir. I couldn't help the priest in the ministry of pastoral care at all for I feared that he would get in trouble if he publicly acknowledged my presence in the community as a seminarian. With his approval I worked quietly by myself to bring communion to the sick and the homebound. I felt much better–spiritually and physically. I wanted to serve people as a Eucharistic minister because by serving them I felt closer to Christ. Also, I liked the job of chopping wood so that I could get to know different escape routes. Each week I went to different woods further along the river. I remembered all the details of places to hide. Each week I came closer to the open sea. Day after day, looking to the open sea from the woods, my hope grew and I gained more confidence in myself. I believed that, with God's grace, I should have freedom at last.

It didn't take long for me to start the next plan of escape. Being able to work in the woods and participate in the choir, I got to know other young men. We tried to make several different connections to escape by boat. The owner of the boat from Ca-Mau, from the previous escape, offered me another opportunity to work with him so that we could get out of the country. We also came to know the owner of another boat in the local area who wanted us to work for him to prepare an escape, too. I decided to work for the local boat owner because it gave me more opportunity to travel and contact people. He took care of the business of contacting people to buy a seat on the boat. Of course, people had to pay money up front to guarantee a seat on the boat. It was a risky business for we had no means of protection. We operated based on people that we trusted. If they didn't honor their promise to help us to escape, to whom could we complain; where could we go to seek protection?

The local police could be bought with money. My mother wanted me to stay home as long as possible, so she kept paying the local police for my temporary freedom. I knew that we were just using each other. I didn't trust them and they didn't trust me. It was a game. Each party waited for an opportunity to get its goal. I wanted to escape and they wanted to capture me. Until then, I would be all right. I could go to work and I could go to church as long as I didn't do anything publicly against the Communists. I assisted the priest in services by giving communion and visiting the sick or the poor of the parish. I was all right for a while. It was only for a while... The fourth attempt was scheduled to board everyone at night at Vung Tau and depart to the open sea.

Fourth attempt

I had more time to make connections and preparations for the next escape, but the more I spent time on it the more opportunity they had to make a trap, for my friends and me. There was a lot of money being made by the local police and there were a lot of hearts being broken. The owner of the boat made arrangements to transport women and children to the boat by local canoes. The young men and I were to swim to the big boat. The plan was to make the boat less conspicuous. The boat went ahead of us to the "hot spot." We swam along the river to avoid being caught by the local police or local patrols. Each time we came to a checkpoint, we went deep under the water to pass across. We swam and we rested along the river's bank. It took us about eight hours to get to the meeting place. On the night we were supposed to gather together to get aboard, the local police were waiting for us. They were shooting at us. One man was hit and killed. The responsible person, the local owner of the boat, didn't show up. I was in the engine room waiting to start the motor and I was captured. I didn't have a chance to break away and ended up in the local prison.

We were sent to the prison of Ben-Da, Vung Tau. All the women and children were searched thoroughly by the guards and police. The searchers took whatever they found on these women and children. These guards made big bucks when they stopped our little boat. Luckily, after a couple of days, the women and children were released. I was happy that they got out of prison.

The men of the boat were left there for about two months. We met other men who had tried to escape like us. They were also caught and ended up in the prison. Daily, we were forced to work in the labor camp. We walked for a couple of hours from prison to a field located on a jungle beach* and worked there until late in the evening. In the midst of all these difficulties, the relationship between China and Vietnam deteriorated. They prepared to fight each other. The Vietnamese were afraid that the Chinese would attack on Vietnam's border, or that they might attack the whole country from the sea. We were forced to plant trees and construct bamboo traps. The bamboo trees were chopped down, sharpened and stuck into the ground. It was a lethal trapping system. There was another type of harmful trap that we were forced to make and to set up. The prison guards provided us with big nails and plywood. We nailed the nails into the pieces of plywood, placed them on the ground and covered them with soil.

I didn't see any Chinese attacks from the open sea. There was no enemy to die from these traps, but several prisoners were wounded from the traps that they were forced to make. The high tide made the surface of the booby-trapped field look exactly like the other areas. It was easy to step on these traps for the soil was soft as mud.

One night, I couldn't sleep because of the mosquito bites. I talked with my friends to plan an attempt to break away from the prison. Once again, I had reached my limit and had to risk my life for freedom. I crawled around on the muddy floor and whispered to seven of my friends that I intended to escape. I had a plan and told each of them, if they wanted to join me, to look for me tomorrow in the field. I said to them, "Just look at me. I will give you a signal."

*Editors' note: In Vietnam, the coastal jungle can encroach into tidal areas, with trees and vegetation growing on soil that is submerged during high tide. When such an area is forested, the cleared land forms a "jungle beach" that is exposed during low tide, but appears as part of the sea at high tide.

At break time the next day, we asked the guards for permission to go into the bushes to relieve ourselves. I knew how to get away. I had observed that after lunch and a smoke the guards would take a nap. They had set up a system where the prisoners watched each other. If someone was missing the remaining prisoners were all in trouble. This was a typical method for controlling the behavior of prisoners in the Vietnamese Communist system. Still, my friends and I agreed that we could not let these threats keep us behind bars for good. That day, we took our break as usual, and upon my signal, we quietly got into the water and moved along the jungle beach to another branch of the river. We ran into the thick jungle to hide. The guards could not find our footprints to follow us. The seven of us gathered in a hiding place in the jungle. After an hour, search parties were sent out to hunt for us in a certain diameter from the field and prison, but we were not found. We heard their screaming from afar. We had to move away from their search area as fast as we could. We hid in the jungle for a few more days. Each day we moved farther away from the labor field as we waited to see if they would tire of chasing us and no longer asked the other woodchoppers about us. I knew the area well enough to lead my friends near the riverbank so that we couldn't get lost. I knew the gathering areas where many of the woodchoppers landed their boats at night. If we could find them we could buy food and water from them. If we could meet people from the parish community who worked as woodchoppers in this area, we should be able to ask them to bring us safely home. As I planned, we met a group of people from our parish community. They fed us and we helped them to chop wood. They were kind enough to assign each of us to their friends' boats and allow us to accompany them to the city. We now looked like real woodchoppers and they brought us home.

Finally, I was able to return to my favorite place, home. Of course, it was necessary for me to also return to the attic for a while. The residents in the village knew what happened to me, but they didn't say a word to the local police. I began to go back to work as a woodchopper. About a month later I was trying to make contact with my friends again. My friends and others were saying to each other, "Yes, we need to escape and the effort to escape is well worth it. It is important to trust."

Once again, my poor mother and older sisters were trying to save money for me to use for the next attempt. My mother was selling everything that she could find so that I could get a place on a boat. She knew that I could not accept to live with the Communists. Once again, I had to try to escape.

Fifth attempt

The designated place for departure was again Vung Tau. We planned to board the boat only a few people at a time from each taxi. I was hiding with a family in a small fishing village and other families did the same for my friends. We hid for a day and a night before boarding the boat. The boat was hidden in inlets that were full of water only at high tide. The advisers said to us, "Let us wait for a couple days. We have plenty of gasoline. As soon as we gather everyone and have gathered all the food and the necessary water, we will leave."

Food and water arrived by the little taxis. At night, when the tide was out, we spread out in the jungle to sleep. There were woodchoppers who might see us and report a large gathering of people hidden in the jungle. This would net them some reward and recognition with the Communists. Or, they might want to escape with us. We might then face the problem of overloading the boat's capacity to safely cross the ocean.

The next day the same routine was repeated. During the day we hid on the boat and moved to another place to hide, picking up more people and more money for the organizers. This went on for three days. On the third day when we woke up we didn't see the boat anywhere. There were twenty-six of us at that designated spot of the jungle. We looked at each other and asked, "What is going on?" All of us wanted to know when we would get on the boat and truly begin the escape.

150

The owner of the boat made a little map showing where the people were stationed throughout the jungle and then the boat went away. They TOOK OFF! They made a trap for us. They led us to believe that we were on our way to escape when we got on the boat. Then, they told us to hide in the jungle until everyone was gathered, but they dumped us. They never came back. Of course, they had our money. Losing money was one issue, but being betrayed was another serious issue we had to live with.

I went looking around to find the boat with a friend of mine. After almost half-day of searching, we had to return with the bad news. We couldn't find the boat anywhere. The women and children began to cry. The men were cursing. Everyone was so disappointed and felt so angry. We didn't know what to do, or what to say. We didn't know how to return to the city, how to reenter the city without getting caught. There were patrols, guards, and checkpoints all along the rivers looking for people like us.

I was so stunned. How many times did I trust people to have them take my money and, in return, betray me? I was sad. This was a real dilemma for us to solve. The most anxiety we had at that time was, "How do we return home safely from the jungle?"

We knew that if we were not careful we would get caught. Then, we would be in deeper trouble. That very night my friends and I discussed at length a solution for our problem. We agreed that we had to try to make a deal with the woodchoppers in the jungle to bring us home. We approached them and explained what had happened to us. We told them the truth: that we had planned to escape out of the country, but that the owner of the boat betrayed us. We said to them, "We have nothing left! We had no money with us." We had no valuable items to use to bargain with them. We offered to work and carry wood for them so that a few people at a time could leave the jungle and return home. We could pay them when we got home. At first, the woodchoppers were so afraid to do what we asked. They were afraid to be caught at the checkpoints. They placed conditions on us. First, they asked us to pay the fine if the police caught them. Second, the women and children had to stay in the small middle room of the boat

151

at all times. They would pack dried wood around the emptied spot to hide them as they pretended to carry dried wood only. Finally, we got a deal for the women and children to be transported home. Those of us remaining would be the last ones to leave. I didn't see those people again. I don't know if they escaped again or not. However, I think everyone was safely returned to his or her home within a week. Sometimes, I wonder what happened to those poor people. Where are those defeated souls? Each time I remember them I say a prayer for them. I hope that they are doing fine. We learned a lesson from our own living experiences.

I was devastated by this experience. I felt so aggressively angry. My spirit was shattered. I asked myself, "Should I trust people again? Ever again?"

I was so frustrated. At that time, I could not bring myself to trust anyone else. However, I was still literally consumed with the desire for freedom, with the desire to escape out of the living hell.

A week later, I too returned home. My mother just took a deep sigh when she saw me at the house. She thought that I had gotten on the boat and escaped. She hoped that in a few more days she would somehow receive word that I had gained the gift of freedom and was safe in another land beyond the ocean.

Instead, here I was, returning home with greater depression than ever. I was very ill from malaria and the mosquito bites. With a heart filled up with sadness and depression, I was near the door of death. We didn't have any medicine to fight back the malaria. My grandmother had to come to help my mother treat my illness with her experience of natural remedies. Many nights, she prayed with me. One night, she thought that I was already asleep, and whispered in my ear, "My dear, you cannot give up hope and die like this. You have to fight to overcome the illness. You have to look to the bright future that is waiting for you in the land of freedom. Please, don't give up. I cannot live seeing you dying like this. Be strong my dear…"

I heard her words of encouragement, but I didn't say a word to her but cried inside my heart. From that very moment I said to myself that I couldn't create any more anxiety for my family. They had had enough of it already. I had to fight the illness to live. I couldn't allow all my family's sacrifices for me to be for nothing.

It took me several months to get the malaria out of my body. After I recovered from the illness and depression, I went back to work in the woods as I did before the last attempt to escape. I worked harder to take care of my family. While walking around finding dry trees to chop down to sell, I kept asking myself questions, "What is it that God wants to tell me? Why have things happened like that? How could I forgive others and myself? Should I give my vocation up and get married? Should I live with the Communists?"

Frankly, I was laughing at myself when I thought that I should marry someone, because my mother used to tease me when I was in the seminary, "Who wants to marry you? Ah, maybe a dog?"

I knew she was kidding, but I was so tired of trying to escape. It didn't work out for me. I was so tired of trying to carry on with the plans for my future vocation. In fact, I knew I could not be ordained as a priest in my homeland. All the seminaries in the country had been abolished. The Communist government controlled the Church. They told the Church who could be ordained and who couldn't. I didn't know how they decided this. We did not have freedom to exercise and nurture our faith anymore. The Communist government did not give us the opportunity to serve the people and to educate ourselves to receive the ordination of the priesthood. We were not even allowed to publicly practice our religion. I began to understand that because of the present circumstances, the meaning and values of my life depended on God's grace and my desire to achieve my goal of a vocation. To live and to serve others in the priesthood would only be accomplished with a successful escape. I became a quiet person and began to carefully plan for one last escape. I prayed that I had courage to accept God's will for me.

In early February of 1980, I had another offer by a dealer of dried wood in Saigon. I used to deliver wood from the jungle beach to his shop at wholesale prices. He got to know me for almost a year, and our relationship was normal as the business went. I always gave him a correct estimation of the amount of wood I sold to him. He never doubted my word. In fact, each time he measured the wood, there was more than I estimated. I never worried about it, and he always treated me with respect and kindness. In return, he allowed me to deliver wood to his shop any time, morning or night. In fact, he paid me very fairly.

One night, after delivering wood to his dock, I had to follow the tide to go home. Instead, he asked me to stay to talk about his plan. I was cautious because the offer was so sudden. Was he telling me the truth? Did I trust him? He wanted to take his entire family out of Vietnam. He needed someone who knew the way to lead the boat safely down the river to the open sea. He told me that he believed I was the one who could do this. I could accompany his family without paying. I agreed, and he began to build the boat. He placed me in charge of the project. He also allowed me to have several good friends to work with me, and we could escape together. While he took care of all the permits to build the boat, I hid the diesel fuel in the woods of the jungle beach. Each time I went to the jungle beach to chop wood I carried two five-gallon containers of diesel fuel in the boat. The local patrols at the checkpoints never questioned me about it. They thought they were containers of drinking water. I knew a good spot where we could hide the diesel fuel. It was a place we used to stock wood. We dug a big underground room, placed the diesel fuel in it and covered it with mud. We then stacked wood on top of the room. Each week, as usual, we took turns transporting wood to the city by our small boat. Two of us remained in the woods to chop dried wood and carry it to the dock where we had hidden the diesel fuel. All went as I planned.

In September of 1980, the boat was built. It was about twenty-two feet long and seven feet wide. The boat's owner contracted with the City of Saigon to transport ocean salt for the government's company. They gave him permission and a license to travel from the city market to other villages along the coast. With this setup, my friends and I could take the boat to the open sea without any fear the local patrols would give us any difficulties. They might suspect that we planned to escape, but they couldn't find any evidence to arrest us. They didn't know when we might try to escape. It was a game of cat and mouse between the local police and the inhabitants. Who would be the lucky ones? Using the business contract, I made the weekly trip with the boat from the city to the salt fields along the coast to pick up their production and deliver it to the distribution center in Saigon. We worked, acting as if we were real businessmen, for a couple of months. By this time, my friends and I had already hidden over three hundred gallons of diesel fuel. My friends continued to chop wood and guard the fuel. I continued to transport salt to the city. We all hoped that our dream would soon come true.

CHAPTER ELEVEN

Planning and Preparation, Departure and Disappointments

Even though my friends and I worked hard to gain the trust of the local officials, they were still watching us closely. Particularly, they did not believe that I had given up my plans of escape. They were right! They just waited for the right moment to catch us.

The owner of the boat made several contacts to hire a pilot with navy experience to drive the boat to Singapore or Malaysia. He informed me that he had been dealing with other customers to raise enough money to pay for the expenses of the trip. Also, he had approached other small boats about serving as taxis to bring the escapees to the location where I would stop to board them. Each taxi carried two or three people. Two taxis would bring water and food for the trip. In this way we hoped to safely transport the people and supplies. All we had to do was wait for the right opportunity. Meanwhile, we made preparations to assure a successful trip. We bought equipment such as binoculars, a small compass, a navy map, and a flashlight. We had to buy these secretly and hide them in a safe place in the boat. The local police could use these items as evidence against us, to put us in prison. Worst of all, they wanted us to pay a bribe.

Every now and then we received an assignment from the local officers to transport their things to a new location. These trips gave us an opportunity to learn more about the coast so that when we escaped we would have a safe spot to board people and safe places to hide if the local patrols pursued us. It required a lot of effort to remember these places, especially driving the boat in the dark of the night. If we made mistakes we could end up in prison or at the bottom of the sea. We had to find a route to get to the open sea from the jungle beach. Also, we had to memorize charts of the tide so we could lead the boat in and out of the inlets of the jungle. Once in a while, along the way to the open sea, I tried to test the ability of the boat by aiming toward the big waves of the ocean. The boat bobbed up and down. It wasn't at all like the way we drove the boat in the river. I knew it would not be an easy task to pilot the boat to land at the end of the horizon. The boat seemed too little compared to the ocean. I didn't know how the boat and all of us could survive the ocean crossing.

I began to face an inner fear in my mind and heart. My friends and I prayed to the Lord to help us to use the gift of courage wisely so that we didn't despair. In fact, we believed that the pilot would be able to drive the boat. That was his job, not ours. My job was to bring the boat loaded with people safely to the open sea. The rest of the trip would depend on the experienced pilot. We had to make all the preparations ourselves, and none of us had any knowledge of how to survive on the ocean. What would it be like out there in the sea? Could we make it? I had no idea, but I knew there were many difficulties waiting for us. On the other hand, freedom and a life to live also beckoned.

During prayers, my friends and I received comfort from the Lord, God of love and life. We agreed among ourselves that our priority was to get away from oppression and attain freedom, no matter what. Even if we died in the open sea, we would rather die out there than die at home because we felt that we were a burden for our families, for we knew how much they loved and cared for us. They couldn't bear to see us live in a country that had no freedom of religion. They knew we lived against our own will. They felt so powerless to help. On our part, we didn't want to be another hardship for our families. This thought revealed how desperate we were. I believed that if the Communist government gave permission to its people to leave the country freely, all would leave at once; even the streetlights would do the same if they had legs to walk.

I had to give it my best shot. I couldn't wait any longer. I would rather die than live facing an unknown future in fear and desperation. My poor mother already had so many problems to deal with. She had to raise and feed my sisters and their children and support my father who was in the reeducation camp. From my way of thinking, being the son in a Vietnamese family, with its cultural consequences, I was obligated to help my family and to fulfill my responsibility with honor. However, in this desperate situation, I would rather suffer myself than have anyone in my family suffer on my behalf. I couldn't deny that my family loved me very much and wanted the best for me. I had no words for them but the word of God: Blessed is the poor in spirit for the kingdom of heaven is theirs. I couldn't imaging how sad they would be if I didn't make it. My heart was torn to pieces. I didn't know what to do. Should I remain at home and accept the way life was? Should I go, even if I died in the ocean, to honor God's call for me?

Once in a while I had a chance to visit my family and bring what money I earned to help my mother and sisters. It was hard to leave them again, but deep in my heart I still heard God's call, "Follow me!"

In the silence of the night, before the crucifix of Christ and pictures of my ancestors, I was on my knees and prayed, "Lord Jesus, do you still want me to be your priest? Do you want me to give it up? I cannot handle this difficulty anymore. With your grace, I will try the best I can to embrace your will. I guess that I can get married, as many of my classmates have done, but if you want me to do otherwise, please give me a sign."

I didn't have to wait long for that sign: My maternal grandmother, who was ninety-six, expressed her desire to escape with me. I asked her if this was what she wanted. Without blinking, she said, "Yes."

We needed to learn how to escape from the city of Saigon to the port of Vung Tau. From Vung Tau we planned to reach the open sea and sail on to Thailand, Malaysia, and Singapore or to the Philippines. In the meantime, we collected more information on the geography of the rivers, canals, and location of checkpoints and islands.

We agreed that I would be the pilot in the river to the open sea. On each trip we all watched and searched for places we could use to hide along the river. We continued to gather information for a couple of months. We tried to remember every detail. We knew that this information could save our lives on the breakaway.

Working together as a group our confidence in each other grew. We attempted to drive the boat at night against the tide to see how fast the boat could go, and to see how the motor of the boat operated. Part of our plan was to limit the number of people who knew what we were doing. Also, we wanted to limit the number of people who would accompany us on the boat. However, during the preparations, several difficulties arose. Some people who knew we were trying to escape wanted to come along, too. If they were not included then they would be angry. If they were angry they might turn us in. In fact, we were reported to the police by the owner's relatives, but the police didn't have any evidence to arrest us. However, they paid closer attention to us. I felt there were eyes watching me all the time. I asked the owner of the boat for several weeks off to allow the situation to calm down. He agreed and we worked out a new way to pick me up to go to work at different places along the river. I didn't have to live on the boat any longer. We kept closely in touch by using my friends as the contact persons.

Paying a bribe to the local police, while waiting for the right moment to depart, I returned to my home to live with my family and help the local priest bring communion to the sick and direct the choir. I saw the sign that God had given me: my grandmother still wanted to go with me.

I knew the best time to escape was during the monsoon season. It was not safe at sea, but it was safer to depart from the port because the local patrols wouldn't expect any of us would be so dumb as to try to escape during the monsoon season. If we attempted our escape then, our chances of survival were about one in ten. However, we had to trust in God's protection, too.

At this time all of our funds and living expenses were used to buy supplies for the trip. Therefore, we had no choice but to accept additional passengers. We also needed money to buy off the police, if necessary. The boat could seat forty people in its interior. It was not comfortable, but we could stretch our legs. By the end of 1980 it was not hard to find people who wanted to leave the country, but we had agreed we would take no more than fifty people, including the nine of us. This was a small boat for ocean travel and the number of people was an important safety factor. Also, with fewer people, we could board them more quickly and minimize our chances of being captured.

While staying with my family, I was able to travel daily by bicycle to Saigon to help my friends with the final preparations. We hired people to stock food for the trip but the wet weather made it unsafe to eat. We couldn't keep food very long because we didn't have refrigerators. Fresh food only lasted one or two days. We didn't know what to do. We decided to use dried foods. Also, we relied on a lot of vegetables like cucumbers and sweet potatoes. These types of food could last longer. However, we had a big problem to face. We couldn't store much food on the boat. We didn't have permission to travel more than two days on each trip. If the police searched our boat and found food for more than two days for four people, they would arrest us. To solve this problem we hired people we trusted to transport the food in their small canoes. They would bring food and water to the place where we hid the diesel fuel. They knew this area well, but they didn't know we had hidden fuel underground. Along with the canoes to bring food and water, we hired more local people to bring the escapees to the same spot. Then, at last, I would drive the boat and meet them there to board together. We had fifty-four people to join us in this dangerous, desperate attempt to reach freedom.

We planned our escape for the first week of December 1980, if everything went well. No matter what, we could not delay beyond mid-December, as we sensed the local police were preparing to arrest us. For the safety of all, I left the boat in Saigon and returned to my village. My friends would come and get me when the time came.

On December 8, 1980, I attended the evening mass on the Feast of the Immaculate Conception. After distributing communion to the people, I came back to the sacristy to prepare to bring communion to the homebound. My friend was waiting to take me to Saigon. I didn't have time to say good-bye to anyone. I took off my cassock and rolled it up with my briary, and both of us got on his motorcycle. He said, "Bay Cao (the name of the owner of the boat) needs to see you tonight. The rest of our friends took people to the "hot spot" this morning. We have to flee as soon as possible. Something went wrong and we have to change our plan."

I didn't say a word. I know my friend didn't know the code of communication between the owner of the boat and myself. The phrase "see you tonight," meant, "it's time to depart." It was time for me to be in the boat, ready to take it to the open sea. In fact, it was not a good time to escape for the monsoon would get worst for the next couple of days. I was very worried, but I kept silent. What would happen next? Only God knew!

My friend and I arrived at the dock around ten that night. As we boarded the boat, Bay Cao told me he had ordered the taxis to take the escapees to our prearranged location that morning. However, the taxis could only pick up thirty-two passengers. Fourteen people had to return to their homes. "What are we going to do?" he asked.

I knew we couldn't let people hide too long in the jungle. It would jeopardize everything we had planned. I looked at him and

162

said, "Let us quickly review what we have and what we don't have. We will come up with a solution. Don't worry, my friend." As a matter of fact, I was as frustrated and confused as he was.

After we discussed with each other, we came to a conclusion as follows: Two of my friends would leave immediately to assure the people that we would arrive with the boat tomorrow. They could use a small boat we had, and following the tide, they would be there by morning. After they arrived, they would retrieve the diesel fuel.

In the morning, Bay Cao would go to the houses of the escapees to set the time, one o'clock that afternoon, to meet at the Saigon River Market's bridge. Normally, the police would take a nap after lunch. We would have about fifteen minutes to board. They had to be on time; otherwise, they would be left behind for good.

I would go to the salt company's office to obtain a work order with permission to travel. As soon as Bay Cao completed his task, he and I would take the boat to pick up the rest of them.

After my friends departed, Bay Cao returned to his house. I said my prayer as usual, but I couldn't concentrate at all. I tried to rest, but I couldn't. In the silence of the night I was thinking about the whole journey that I was about to take. I drew in my mind the outcome of the escape. What would happen to us in the open sea?

I figured that if we went from the Saigon River to Vung Tau Harbor, then to the open sea, we could reach Thailand within a week. If everything went well, we might make it in four to five days. That would be the best-case scenario. If things didn't go well we still had food for several more days, and we could go to Malaysia or Singapore. I dreamed about it. It rained all night.

In general, we were relying on two factors to help us escape. First, it was a miserable monsoon season, with a lot of rain and strong wind. Fierce, dangerous thunderstorms happened suddenly. Second, most people were preoccupied with preparations for the Christmas Season. Because of these two factors, we believed that the local patrols would not expect anyone to escape at this time of the year. It was risky at any time to try to get out of Vietnam, but we figured the patrols would think no one was crazy enough to do it during the monsoon season.

In the morning, we began to carry out our plan. Bay Cao took off to inform his customers and I went to the office to report to work. By ten o'clock Bay Cao returned to the boat. We checked the engine and were ready to depart.

The reason I decided to board everyone in the midst of the river market was that I thought the crowds of traders would distract the patrols. Our passengers would look like ordinary people in the market. The buyers and sellers would negotiate a price for their items, then, one at a time, carry their products on board. I also thought that, sometimes, the safest place is in the midst of danger. I didn't know what would happen. We would be boarding fourteen people at the Saigon River, across from the National Bank of Vietnam, right under the noses of the police. We might make it or we might not, but we had to take the risk.

I saw several policemen talking to each other as they pointed toward us. I couldn't hear what they were saying, but I knew that they were watching our movements, and waiting until everyone was on board. Then they would arrest us all. It was a bit of a game we played with them. They didn't know that the rest of the people were elsewhere already. They didn't know that we were only taking on fourteen people at this site. The police could see that fourteen people were a small number for a boat this large. They probably expected at least a hundred people to jam on board before we left.

As the passengers boarded, they talked to each other as if they were in real daily business like the other boats parked along the river. I told Bay Cao I was going up the street to get some cigarettes for the young men to help them stay awake at night, and candy for the trip. I went to a nearby street to make my purchases from one of many street vendors. At a prearranged signal, when I returned and untied the mooring rope to the boat, a friend would start the engine, and we would leave immediately.

I remember the face of the old lady who sold me the candy and cigarettes. She only had a few boxes of candy and a few cartons of homemade cigarettes. I bought them all. She couldn't believe her luck. Normally, she would sell only one or two cigarettes at a time. She looked at me and she whispered in my ear, "My dear, did you buy this much so you can escape?"

I looked at her smile and said, "Yes, grandma."

Addressing her as "grandma" was a traditional way to show respect to the elderly. I held her hands and whispered, "Grandma, pray for us."

She said, "God bless and God be with you."

I bought everything that she had. I knew the Vietnamese currency was not worth anything outside the country, so I gave her all the money I had left in my pockets. It would give her a chance to do good for her family. It was worth a couple of months' earnings for her. I felt good as I left her.

Chapter Twelve

Gunning for Territorial Waters

It was almost one o'clock, but the cloudy sky made it seem darker than usual as I returned to the boat. I had been gone about five minutes. Everyone knew my return was the signal to take off. My friend started the engine as I untied the rope from a big bamboo pole stuck in the riverbank, and we began to pull the boat to the middle of the river.

The police were caught lazing about, totally unprepared for our quick departure. They didn't know that we would take off so soon. Also, they couldn't believe we would do such a fool thing right in front of their eyes.

As the boat reached the middle of the river, we increased the boat's motor to its maximum and sped away. I could hear the whistles and shouts of the police in between the gunshots. The police got in their boats quickly and were after us. When I first looked back I thought that we were going to get away and that I could outrun them, but they didn't give up. We met two big commercial ships and passed by them. As they covered our wake, at a sharp bend in the river, we quickly ducked into a small canal to hide. Both sides of the canal were covered with water and coconut trees. It was a good place to hide for a while. It was raining heavily and the sky became darker.

We decided to stay in the small canal for a few hours, hoping the police would think we had gotten away and stop looking for us. It was low tide and we were stuck in the canal without enough water to move the boat. We were grounded, but we were safe for the moment. We kept pushing the boat toward the mouth of the canal. As soon as the tide rose, we would continue to the appointed place. However the moments of waiting were not an easy task to handle. How could time move so slowly?

As the tide came into the canal, we got the boat moving to the river. It was raining heavily and the wind had picked up.

We had no problem along the river after the last accident. Once in a while, the lightning allowed me to see the riverbank and its trees as a black wall along the river. The fourteen escapees were in the engine room. My friend was in front of the boat and I was behind the wheel. Both of us wore raincoats. The wind blew against our bodies as the boat kept moving forward. We looked like ghosts as we dashed through the darkness of the forest.

Finally, we came to the inlet of our meeting place. The small boats that had transported the escapees to this place two days before were parked around the inside of the inlet. Quietly, we parked the boat outside the inlet and turned off the engine. We didn't want the woodchoppers in that area to be suspicious about us.

I got into the river and swam to the canoe of my friends. They were inside a small tent at the middle of the canoe. They were glad that we got out of Saigon safely. I explained to them what we would do next. We needed to move the fourteen passengers from the big boat to other small boats. It was still too early to have them all on board. We didn't want to be caught together by the local patrols if there were any around this area tonight. Also, it was around this time of day that the woodchoppers would use their boats to pick up the wood they had chopped during the day. If they saw us it might create a problem. Most importantly, we had to go to the salt dealer's warehouse to load up the salt that we contracted for the office in Saigon. We needed to be there. Otherwise, they would telephone the main office and report our absence. In turn, they might send patrol boats to find us, as they always assumed we might attempt to escape.

We had to leave the gathering area as soon as we could. I asked my friends to put all the containers of diesel fuel in their canoes and be ready to load up to the big boat when we came back later that night. Also, they needed to have someone waiting for the two taxis that transported food and water. No matter what happened, someone had to wait for us at the inlet.

Four of us departed as usual to load the salt. It was eight o'clock at night when we arrived to the dock of the warehouse. We saw several patrol boats parked nearby. They had more boats than usual.

They were drinking in the restaurant and bar with loose women. We found the manager and presented the order for him to sign. He was full of beer. He raised his voice at us and demanded to know the reason we were late. He told us that he didn't have the full quantity of salt to transport back to Saigon. We could load what he had and go home. Two days later, we needed to come back for the rest of the work order. Hearing this good news I said to myself, "Thank God."

He asked us to buy beer and wine for the rest of his men. He said, "My friends, it is raining and cold. Why don't you sit down and have a few drinks with us." Of course, we wanted them to get drunk so we sat down with them and ordered beer and wine. I ate some rice and excused myself. My friend and I went out to load twenty fifty-pound bags of sea salt into the boat.

Close to eleven o'clock, we said good-bye and took off. On the way back, we prayed that no patrol boats would be in the area. It continued to rain. The strong winds that blew against the boat created a sense of fear in our hearts. We hoped that the winds would die down and the rain would stop. Otherwise, we were going to face an extremely dangerous journey to the territorial waters. None of us talked about the weather, but deep in our hearts we knew it was an advantage that would keep the patrols away tonight. We knew that we had to walk through the gate of death to enter into the door of life. Taking a deep breath, I silently prayed the sorrowful mysteries of the rosary while I drove the boat to the designated area.

We stopped the boat outside of the canal. We could not drive the boat into the canal for the boats of woodchoppers and fishermen were anchored there. Normally, with the wind's breeze they stayed near the sides of the canal to avoid mosquito bites at night. We would wake them up with the sound of the boat's diesel engine. My friend and I got off the boat and waded along the side of the canal. We needed to go to the inlet and find fifty people who had been waiting for us for over two days and two nights.

When we came into the inlet where people were gathered earlier this evening, we couldn't find anyone. Oh no! What had happened to them? Where did they go? I came to the spot where we had hidden the diesel fuel and found my friend waiting for us behind the loading dock. He quickly told us that patrol boats had come into the canal to patrol the area. They had to disperse and move themselves deeper into the other inlet. Some of the canoes were parked nearby, and people were hiding in the woods. "Thanks be to God," I said to my friends.

The three of us began to walk toward the nearby inlet to inform everyone that we needed to move out to the main boat. We needed to do it quietly and quickly.

On the way to the boat, I asked my friends about the fuel, food, and water. They told me that the fuel had been collected, but the canoes with food and water didn't come. We had been waiting for these two canoes for a couple of days so far but they didn't make it.

Reaching the main boat, I told Bay Cao bad news about the food and water. We had to escape without it. We had no time to debate. We couldn't delay the trip for we were in a dangerous situation. We needed to reach the territorial water before dawn; otherwise, we would be caught by the Communist patrols for sure.

We decided to get people on board as fast as we could. Each canoe approached the starboard side of the boat and delivered its people. We loaded the diesel fuel containers, and at the same time, two friends of mine unloaded the bags of sea salt into the river. Others helped the women and children get on board. They all tried to talk quietly and keep the children quiet, but it was impossible. Children cried and adults shouted at each other as they struggled from the canoes to the boat. The woodchoppers and fishermen parked nearby began to wake up from the noise. They called and told each other what was going on.

We had to load people faster. Otherwise, the patrol boats would come soon. I ordered my friends to draw up the anchor. The drivers of the canoes, after getting paid for their services, tried to depart from the boat as fast as they could. They shouted at us, "Good luck to you all, my friends." The last group of people got on board while the boat began to drift with the strong winds. An older gentleman, a parishioner that I knew, grasped my hands and shouted, "Be careful! Don't go near the riverbank! The police are there! Look at the lighthouse! Aim toward it and you will be at the gate to the open sea." Patting my shoulder, he jumped back to his canoe.

We began to spread a thick nylon cover from the head of the boat over its starboard side to the engine room, to prevent the wash from getting in the boat. If we timed it properly, we could catch the outgoing tide to the sea. It would propel the boat so that we could dash to the open sea easier. However, the engine wouldn't start. The boat was moving with the strong wind away from the jungle. I was behind the wheel, ready to drive the boat. My friends shouted at me from the engine room, "Hey, Quang, the engine doesn't work! What are we going to do?"

I shouted back at them, "Some of you come up here to take the wheel! Let me go down there!" I got down into the engine room, and there were two of my friends trying to turn the heavy flywheel of the engine. They couldn't turn it fast enough to start the engine. I told them to rest and give me the handle to turn the engine. I told my friend to push the knob of the starter in and release it when I turned the engine. After trying several times to start the engine, I was in a most anxious mood of fear and frustration. We didn't give up. We tried it again and again. Finally, the engine started. My face had turned red from holding my breath so long to use all my muscles to turn the machine. Throwing the handle to the floor, I rushed up to the upper level of the boat to catch my breath.

Seeing me coming up from the engine room, my friends moved

aside and gave me back the steering wheel. We turned the bow of the boat in the direction of the lighthouse to enter the open sea. This was our only chance. I remember that we packed the people to the front of the boat and the young men, the "sailors," were in the back of the boat near the engine room with me. We needed to control the boat.

Chapter Thirteen

Goodbye Lighthouse, Hello Flags

It was about one o'clock in the early morning of December 10, 1980. As soon as the engine started, I took the helm and steered the boat toward the open sea. We moved fast and rapidly left the river behind. We began to enter Vung Tau Bay. I had never been on a boat in the open sea. In the daylight I could see the sea and its horizon, but in the darkness of the stormy night it seemed bigger than life. Behind the steering wheel I could see only darkness in front of the boat. I aimed toward the lighthouse and pushed the engine to its maximum speed. We needed to get out of this bay before the dawn; otherwise, the Vietnamese Coast Guard would catch us. I didn't know how far we had to go to get out of sight of the coastline. So far, we didn't have any patrol boat chasing after us. Three of my friends and the boat's pilot were with me at the back of the boat to keep watch and double check the direction we were headed. As long as we still saw the light on the shoreline everyone had to stay under the canopy covering the front of the boat. The canopy deflected the water that splashed up as we hit the ocean waves. The window of the engine room was closed so that the light could not be seen. We certainly didn't want to get caught on the patrol's radar, or have any patrol boat come after us.

I asked the people under the canopy to stay calm and not panic. The wind and waves rocked the boat precariously from left to right. The people couldn't move for fear it would overturn. Their movement was even more dangerous than what the wind and the waves could do to us. The boat was rolling left and right and moving up and down.

I tried to assure people that in a couple of hours after we were far from the lighthouse, we would be safe. Children were crying. Women were beginning to get seasick, and men became aggravated. A lot of people were getting seasick and this simply did not help their fellow passengers at all. They vomited. They began to complain to each other as they tried to make room for themselves. It was four days since they had fled Saigon. They were tired and needed rest.

It continued to rain. The wind was so strong I could barely hear what people were saying. I had to yell into my friend's ear to be heard. I had never been in such a situation. The only relief from the total darkness was the beacon of the lighthouse. I could not distinguish the sea from the sky. The wind and the big waves made me feel so small and helpless I didn't know what to do next. It was a completely different experience to drive the boat on the open sea than on the river. The sea seemed to have no boundary at all. I couldn't judge the speed of the boat, but it seemed to be moving forward. However, the lighthouse was still in my sight. We were still in danger of being captured by the coast guard. Once in a while, my friend used a small flashlight to get a reading from the compass. He directed me as I tried to control the steering wheel. I tried to keep the boat heading toward the open sea. The compass was fixed on the top of the engine room on the right side of the steering wheel. We went on and on. My friends had been next to me since we departed from the jungle beach. We looked at each other with smiles on our faces. At least, after all our hardships and preparation, we had made this escape become a reality. What would happen next? I didn't know, but for now, I asked them to pray the rosary with me. We joined with each other in the prayer of meditation of God's love for the world and for us. I felt warm in my heart as we prayed together. I forgot that I was cold, wet, and hungry. Time went by slowly as we sailed toward the open sea.

At the edge of the horizon the glow of the rising sun appeared.

In the midst of fear and anxieties we were about to have a new day, perhaps our last day, to live. My other friends who were in the engine room took a break from their toil to join us in the Morning Prayer.

I never felt so wonderful as we prayed in the comfort of the Lord the Canticle of Zechariah:

> *Blessed be the Lord, the God of Israel;*
> *He has come to his people and set them free.*
> *He has raised up for us a mighty savior,*
> *Born of the house of his servant David.*
> *Through his holy prophets he promised of old*
> *That he would save us from our enemies,*
> *From the hands of all whom hate us.*
> *He promised to show mercy to our fathers*
> *and to remember his holy covenant.*
> *This was the oath he swore to our father Abraham:*
> *To set us free from the hands of our enemies,*
> *Free to worship him without fear,*
> *Holy and righteous in his sight all the days of our life.*
> *You, my child, shall be called the prophet of the Most High;*
> *For you will go before the Lord to prepare his way,*
> *to give his people knowledge of salvation by*
>   *the forgiveness of their sins.*
> *In the tender compassion of our God*
> *The dawn from on high shall break upon us,*
> *To shine on those who dwell in darkness and*
>   *the shadow of death,*
> *and to guide our feet into the way of peace.*
> *(Liturgy of the Hour – Morning Prayer)*

As the sun rose over the horizon we still saw the lighthouse from afar. We kept traveling east and about nine o'clock in the morning we could no longer see the lighthouse at the port of Vung Tau. Thanks be to God! We were safe for a while as we approached international water.

My responsibility was fulfilled. We were now in the South China Sea. The rest of the journey would depend on the experienced navy pilot. We asked for a break as we moved aside for the navy pilot to take the helm. My friend, Bay Cao came out of the engine room and informed us that the pilot was very seasick. He had become seasick as soon as we entered the open sea. Bay Cao, took us aside to inform us that the pilot had confessed to him he wasn't a real experienced pilot. He was in the navy, but he had never driven a boat before. Upon hearing this, my friends and I were in a panic.

"Who is going to drive the boat?" we asked the owner.

He looked at us with a guilty look on his face, "Please don't let the people know we don't have a pilot. You and your friends will have to do that job. We have no one else."

I looked at him and my friends, "I personally don't mind helping out, but I don't have any experience in the open sea like this. What if something happens? Who will take responsibility for our people?"

We talked back and forth about the problem for some time. Finally, I said to my friends, "We have to take over this job. I don't know much about driving this boat in the open sea, but if you all help me, we can do it together." All of my friends agreed to help. I took a deep sigh and shook my head in an expression of a great disappointment. My friends tried to encourage me by patting my shoulder, "Quang, we have to do this. We have no other options. Besides, you are the leader and we believe in you."

We took out the map of the Asian-Pacific Ocean to read the notes I had written before we left Vietnam. Using a ruler and a compass, I drew a line on the map to shows the direction to Thailand and Malaysia. We didn't know how to estimate how the wind would change the boat's direction, or how the big waves of the ocean would change the speed of the boat. We used our common knowledge to estimate the direction of the wind then we added a few degrees on the map to track the boat's direction, hoping we were right. We did the same to measure the speed of the boat. We estimated its speed and subtracted what we thought would be the force of the waves. We then estimated the number of hours it would take to travel the distance on the map. That was all we could do. The rest of the journey depended on God's blessing.

For me, driving the boat on the river was easy enough, but at the open sea was another challenge. It was a totally new skill to learn without any instructions. I was scared. I felt so unqualified to do this job.

I told my friends, "Hey, buddies, if we don't do it right the boat will overturn, or we may end up on Con-Son Island. We better pray that doesn't happen. Otherwise, we die for sure."

Con-Son Island was a maximum-security prison for political prisoners and those who committed serious crimes. If we ended up in there, we would never get out.

My friends had no comment on what I said. They focused on drawing the line on the map. We all knew the outcome of this extraordinary task: live or die. For now, we had to do what we could to survive.

The rain stopped as we continued east. We agreed on two-hour shifts to drive the boat and to rest, two by two.

By noon there was nothing around us but the open sea. This was the first time that the wind died down and the sun shone fully on the boat. The heat of the sun was so hot I felt we were being cooked alive. It was a scorching heat. I was very hungry and thirsty. I asked my friends to take over the steering wheel and I moved to the front of the boat to get a drink. On my way I lifted up one side of the canopy to pull back the tarp and give my fellow escapees some fresh air. I didn't have a chance to see all of them in the daylight yet. I wanted to say hello and see how they were doing. I also wanted to know who they were for we were now in the same boat. I intended to ask if there was anyone who had any seafaring experience. I hoped someone would know more about the sea than I did.

As I rolled up the canopy, I saw a group of people packed together as if they were in a container. I have never seen such an ugly scene in my life. People had vomited all over the boat. They were lying next to each other, shoulder to shoulder, even on top of one another. Nylon bags of personal belongings were everywhere. Over fifty people looked like zombies. I couldn't imagine how hard it had been for them to be under that canopy. It must have been awful for them to be stuck in the same room with fifty-some vomiting people. I thought that even if my stomach was strong enough to handle the motion of the waves, the odor could easily set you off. Obviously, the boat was too small to use to get across the ocean. It wasn't safe at all. However, in our desperate situation, it was the largest boat we dared to use.

The people were relieved when I announced that the lighthouse of Vung Tau was no longer in sight. They all tried to shout for joy. In their eyes I saw both hope and joy, anxiety and fear, for they knew it was just the beginning of the journey for life. So did I.

It was safe to roll up the canopy for fresh air. The wind had died down a little. The waves of the ocean were softening. People tried to stand up for the first time since we had set off early that morning. They couldn't help but to look at the sea with astonishment: "O my God! It is huge!" It was larger than life. I agreed.

We began to let women and children go to the rear of the boat to use the rest room. It was a small wooden box that hung off the rear of the boat. They cleaned themselves with seawater. I specifically ordered them not to use the drinking water for washing. We had to save the small amount of drinking water that we had left. We didn't know how long it would take to reach land.

The boat was running well. Up and down it went. We hoped we were in international waters by now.

People woke up as they tried to clean up and take advantage of the fresh air, the air of freedom. I asked them to help clean up the boat. Bay Cao and his family were in charge of the distribution of water and food. I knew we didn't have much food and water. I didn't know how we would divide our limited resources.

But for now, I needed to get some rest. As soon as I lay down next to the engine room, I fell asleep quickly. Too bad it wasn't vacation. I would have enjoyed the beauty of the ocean very much. I didn't have a chance to say goodbye to anyone in my family or my community.

The splashing of the waves awakened me. It was about four o'clock in the afternoon. I had slept for three hours and felt a little bit better. My friends told me, "Quang, go back to sleep. We can handle it."

I was sure that my friends had things under control, but I was awake. I rolled up the blanket and put it in the engine room. I came back to the helm to check our heading. Looking around, I realized the wind was increasing in force from the northeast. The boat was rolling left to right more frequently. The waves seemed bigger and higher than a few hours ago. After observing for a while, I asked my friends to adjust the direction of the boat a little toward the northeast. We needed to avoid the high waves that hit the boat from its side.

I hoped that my estimation of the wind and its force was correct and we would continue toward international water. Most of all, we had to get away from the Con-Son Islands. Letting my friends drive the boat, I sat down against the wall of the engine room to visit with Bay Cao about the direction that we were aiming. After reading the map and listening to my explanation, he went back to his family's corner. He trusted in me, but somehow, I didn't have much confidence in myself. I prayed that God's Spirit would guide me. If not for my sake, then for the other fifty-three innocent people on the boat. I closed my eyes to rest.

This was an opportunity for me to recall what had happened over the last two and a half days. I didn't know what to tell people because I didn't know what to expect. We could be lost in the ocean, circling around until we died. A nervous feeling dwelt in my heart. I felt like I didn't know what I was doing. I wished I had more knowledge of and experience with the sea. We were in a dangerous situation.

Looking around the ocean, there were no other boats to give us help or directions. Fortunately, we had our little map and a very small compass. I didn't know how strong the wind was or how much it would slow down the speed of the boat. I had no idea what the results of this journey would be. The only thing I knew was that we needed to keep the boat running and to keep heading for safety. I prayed the boat was heading in the right direction and we all had a safe journey. At this point I was about eighty percent sure the Vietnamese Coast Guard would not catch us. That gave me some hope. I had a deeper sense of trust in God's providence. I believed God would protect us always.

Even though we didn't have a real pilot, it seemed that we were safe. We felt better after we had cleaned up the boat. The people seemed to be in a little better condition. They tried to make room for each other to sit up and lie down. The first day was not that bad after all. People began to talk to one another and once in a while a child would cry. There were a lot of mixed feelings. They were happy that the coast guard didn't catch them. However, it was sad to leave their homeland and their loved ones. It was a bittersweet experience. For me, as I recall the memory of that day, I felt torn apart because I didn't have a chance to say good-bye to any of my family. Furthermore, as the "acting" pilot, I felt a responsibility for everyone on board. I kept these feelings inside my heart.

Luckily, the wind was not too strong and we continued on our journey. The ocean was absolutely blue. With the fresh air, blue water and clear sky, it was the brightest day I had ever seen in my life. If we weren't running for our lives, it would have been a perfect day. As we continued toward the South China Sea, our souls would not be at rest until we landed safely.

I had never seen a sunset at sea. The beautiful sun went down slowly, touching the water. It was absolutely gorgeous. We tied the steering wheel with the rope and gathered for evening prayer to say the rosary. After the evening prayer, darkness covered the surface of the ocean and I wondered what direction we were going. I said a quick personal prayer: "Lord Jesus, You are my light, my savior, my stronghold. Help me, not only for my sake but for the sake of the people in the boat with me."

It was eight p.m. on December 10, 1980, as I took over the wheel of the boat and told my friends, "Get some rest. At least grab a cucumber or something to eat. We have to make sure that we save the water for the children and the dried food for the people. We don't have much food and water with us, but we can handle it for a couple of days. So, hang in there."

I knew that we all needed food to survive and work. My friends and I needed to restore our energy, but there was such a limited supply on the boat. We wanted to make sure we could help the women and children as much as possible.

The first meal was served about twenty hours after we had set off. We cut one of the pumpkins. Of course, we had no way to cook it. Each of us had a small slice of pumpkin. I was hungry and I ate it all including the skin. The first pumpkin was gone. There were four pumpkins left, I figured we would be able to survive for four more days. Each of us had a small cup of water. I held it in my mouth before I swallowed. It tasted funny. We hadn't covered the container and seawater had splashed in. Still it was better than nothing. We continued to travel east to get as far away from Vietnam as we could. In the darkness, I heard the sound of the engine, the wind's breeze, and the splash of the waves against the boat. The boat, up and down with the waves, went forward.

I couldn't see the front of the boat. My friends were using a flashlight to see the needle of the compass. We didn't talk to each other much. We were quiet as we tried to save energy. Standing behind the wheel, I began to get in touch with my feelings. I believed that my friends and I had the same feeling of sadness in our hearts. We desired freedom and had pursued it at great sacrifice to our families. We couldn't wait to get out of Vietnam. However, I never anticipated the feeling that took place when we departed our homeland. It was a tough emotional moment when I first looked back and couldn't see the port's lighthouse. The land where I was born and grew up was no longer visible. I didn't know if I would ever see it again or not. This was a hard lesson to learn about saying good-bye. I felt I was being buried alive. I had cried for lost friends during the war and when I helped my pastor do funerals for children killed by bombs. It was sad and painful. I was trained with the mentality that "boys don't cry." I thought I had never cried for my loved ones because I hoped and knew I would see them again, but in this situation, saying good-bye to my homeland where the people I loved still lived, it was hard for me to hold back my tears. I didn't know if I would ever see them again. For the first time in my life I understood the meaning of the word, home. A home is a place where I live with my loved ones. We should be together, physically and spiritually. It is a place where my people are born and live. We should live together in peace, to love our home, to defend it, to die for it. For the first time in my life I thought about the meaning of the word. It was, and always will be, meaningful to me. No doubt, during all those years of war I grew sick and tired of the causalities in Vietnam and wanted to go somewhere else, to seek peace. But, as I departed from my homeland, I loved it more than ever. It will remain within me as long as I live. The most beautiful thing on earth that still makes me cry is the meaning and spirit of "homeland."

Vietnam, my homeland, held the people I loved. Many were still struggling with oppression, personal loss and persecution. Physically, I was gone. I had escaped from the injustice, but my heart was left behind. For the first time I cried for the people and the homeland I had left behind. It was something I didn't anticipate.

I had left behind everything, my loved ones and the familiar environment that was so close to my heart. All of the people who knew me and had suffered and grown together with me were there and I was not. It caused me so much grief I broke down and cried silently during that first night. No one knew why I cried. When my friends asked me what caused me to cry, I told them the wind and the seawater were hurting my eyes. They knew what was happening to me. I was lying. The grief came so automatically that I was not aware of it. I had taken courses in psychology and studied about grievance, but it was hard to accept the reality. I knew there would be anxiety and sorrow, but I never knew it would be so difficult. It seemed like the deep sorrow had its own bitter taste. We left everything behind, everything we were attached to, and opened ourselves to a new life we didn't even know. Sometimes, we don't know our future, but we must go on. It was a mystery of life. It is an amazing grace.

At the time, it was true for all of us on that boat. I was crying in silence. A deep sigh poured out. I never prayed so hard to God: "Lord God, take care of my homeland, my country and all its people. Here I am and my heart is left behind. I am waiting for you to give me a new heart because my heart is now broken. Be with me, Lord. You have to give me a new heart, a heart of hope and trust, a heart of faith and courage, a heart of love that always trusts in your providence." I shook my head and went back to steering the boat.

We estimated the boat's speed was about twenty-two miles an hour. We counted the number of hours we had been traveling east, then we tried to calculate how much the wind had delayed us. We counted and subtracted, all in our heads. We finally decided it must be time to turn south toward Thailand. I remember it was about one o'clock in the morning on the second day of the journey. We figured we were headed for the Gulf of Thailand.

The night was peaceful. Everyone was sound asleep, except the crew on duty. At dawn we began to see a cloudy horizon. The night had been very cold. The wind had blown and it was very humid. The humidity and the sea salt in the air turned our skin very sticky. Before the sun rose I saw what looked like mountains. It looked like a big cloud crossed the horizon, but I wasn't sure. I asked my friends, "Is that a pillar of cloud or is that a mountain?"

One of my friends took a look with the binoculars and cried out, "Oh my God, we better turn around, and run fast! It looks like we have ended up near the Phu Quoc Islands."

I grasped the binoculars and took a look for myself, "No. It cannot be the Phu Quoc Islands. It must be the Con-Son Islands. Look at the map! Is that Con-Son or Phu Quoc?"

These islands are in south of Vietnam's coastline near international water. These islands belonged to Vietnam and were where political prisoners were kept. We were so close to these islands. We could see them through our binoculars. Taking a closer look I could see a red flag with a yellow star in the middle of it. It was the flag of the Communist Party. The other flags next to it were half-red and half-blue with the yellow star in the middle. That was the flag for Vietnam's South Communist Military. The revolutionary prisoners from the south were there.

I knew all I needed to know. We had better run and run as fast as we could. As the mechanic increased the speed of the engine, I turned the boat a hundred and eighty degrees and headed back out to open sea. This time we hit the throttle so hard a pillar of black smoke came out of the muffler. We had to run fast, because if the Communists caught us we would be dead. They had a reputation to defend. That meant we wouldn't just be imprisoned there, we would be dead. Absolutely. Period. I had never been to the islands before, but from the newspapers and our geography classes we knew what we had seen. I thought to myself, "What have I done?"

Everyone woke up and after being informed of the bad news they were in fear. It was a mess!

We were back in the open sea by nine o'clock and we couldn't see the islands any more. Wow! Thank God, we didn't see any patrol or coast guard boats after us. I thought to myself, "God must have covered their eyes so they didn't see us." Maybe it was just that it was a cold winter morning and everyone was asleep.

I was so thankful. It could have been the end of our escape. When we felt we were out of danger my friends and I sat down and decided we better figure things out again. We realized that the boat was not capable of traveling at twenty-two miles an hour at all. It was more like twelve miles an hour or even less. What a shock to all of us! We recalculated where we thought we were. This time we realized we needed to go east toward the South China Sea at least for another day. We had to make sure we had entered international waters.

So the second day had begun and the people were getting a little bit used to their surroundings, even though there were big waves and a strong wind. The sun was very bright, direct and hot. More people were getting sick from the heat and the seasickness. They lay down in the bottom of the boat suffering from nausea and headaches. We began to get requests for water. First the children, then the older people began to cry out for water. I assigned two friends to assist Bay Cao with the water distribution. They were to be very careful and to give only a capful of water to each passenger. First the children were served, then, the adults. When I got my ration, it did refresh my tongue a little bit, but certainly wasn't enough to quench my thirst. I wet my clothes with seawater to cool my body and delay the need of water.

Using the canopy, we constructed a roof support from the engine room to the front of the boat. In this way we could get some shade from the heat of the sun and take advantage of a little fresh air. There were people with some skills who were able to use the bamboo that had camouflaged the boat before we escaped. The bamboo pieces were trimmed and slipped into slots along the sides of the boat, then bent over the middle to cover the boat. It worked very well. However, there was an open space at the front of the boat that allowed waves to occasionally splash into the boat. It wasn't very much water but, it caused some difficulties for people.

Some people did not want to sit where they would get wet. I had to tell them that this was all the space we had. We finally solved the space problem by having people sit across from one another then alternating stretching their legs out and folding their knees up. Every hour or so they would switch. The children spent most of the time sitting on the lap of their mother or sister. They were crowded together and got cramps in their muscles and stomachs.

They began to ask about the pilot of the boat. I had to tell them the truth. The truth was that we had a man in our boat that had approached us, declaring that he had been a captain of a ship in the navy. He said he knew the routes from Saigon to Singapore and to the

Philippines and all the islands of Indonesia. He claimed that he knew the sea and its routes very well. Because of his professional skill, we allowed him and his family to travel free with us. However, on the first day of the journey, we found out he was a fraud. He didn't know anything about piloting a boat. In fact, he was one of the first people to start throwing up. He looked like a zombie after thirty minutes behind the steering wheel. He was useless. I was angry with him, as were the others who knew what had happened. We put him in the engine room and I told him, "You stay down there and don't let me see your face again. The people may get angry with you and throw you off the boat. For your own sake and the sake of your family and the people on the boat, stay down there."

We didn't plan it this way. We had planned to be assistants to the pilot, but we had to take over. This was a huge disappointment.

It was extremely difficult for people to get to the back of the boat to use the toilet. Some of them had become so seasick they didn't even know they were soiling themselves. We tried to manage reminding them, "If anyone wants to use the toilet please let us know so we can help you to get there."

During the first three days we simply tried to cope, to help people get comfortable. We tried to clean up the boat and create a better environment.

Time went by. The first three days passed without crisis. The wind was normal, not too strong to severely affect our direction toward the Gulf of Thailand. We didn't know if we were going in the right direction or not, but we kept on. On top of lacking experience, we saw nothing but the ocean in every direction. There was nothing else. We continued south, using our little compass. Hopefully, we would soon reach the territorial waters of Thailand.

After the people would vomit, they would feel thirsty. The request for drinking water became more frequent and more urgent. By the third day we had already consumed the water in the first container. Mothers wanted their little children to be satisfied, but we were not able to give them enough water. They kept asking over and over for more. The people knew I was a seminarian, as were some of my friends. We tried to take care of the people as best as we could. Our helpers came to me and said, "We have problems. The people don't listen to us. Can you talk to them?"

I had to make the announcement that we had only one container of water left and we have to reserve it for the children. I suggested, "Adults, wet your body with seawater to get some relief. Hopefully, that will give some relief from the heat of the sun as well."

We distributed the third pumpkin. We had only two pumpkins left, several cucumbers, and some jam remaining in our cache. Because of the seasickness, people didn't want to eat. All they wanted was water. I hoped it would rain soon. Otherwise, we would have a huge dilemma to deal with.

Four of us, in pairs, took turns piloting the boat. I was so lucky that I didn't get very seasick. When I was piloting the boat I stood behind the wheel, and with the fresh air of the sea I didn't feel seasick at all. However, when I sat down to rest I would feel a little dizzy. We were also weakened by a lack of food and water.

We talked to each other to stay awake. At the end of the third day all we had seen was the open sea. From time to time we would check each other's physical condition. We talked less and less. I had never felt so hungry and thirsty. I wished for a bowl of rice to satisfy my hunger, or a large cup of fresh water to quench my thirst.

There was not much external expression of joy or hope from any of us. There was no sign of confidence in our eyes. Our spirits were very low. We just looked at each other with anxiousness, "What will happen tomorrow? When will we reach land?"

None of us had an answer. After the evening prayer, each of us continued to pray according to our own intentions. For me, I prayed, "Lord Jesus, you are my light. Help me to see your face, and show me the way to land."

CHAPTER FOURTEEN

A Light in the Sky

The third day was gone. The wind was mild and the waves gently rocked the boat up and down, up and down. It was like a series of musical notes. The weather was quite clear and the sun was beautiful, but there was no sunshine in our hearts. A sense of fear and worry gripped us. We didn't know what would happen to us. There was a deadly silence among us. We were lost in our own thoughts, withdrawn from facing reality. Yet, I still had hope that we would be fine after all.

People were exhausted from being sick and from lack of food and water. They sat down against the sides of the boat or lay down next to each other. They didn't care whom they leaned on, whether it was a man, a woman or a child. They just tried to get comfortable and get some fresh air. Most of the people tried to sleep, hoping that they could forget their hunger and thirst. Some shared with me that they wished for a long sleep, and upon waking would find themselves on dry land.

They didn't know how long the journey would take. All day long they were filled with anxiety as they looked toward the horizon and saw nothing but water in every direction. There was nothing else. During the day they forced themselves to sleep so they would not have to face such helplessness. If I didn't have to drive the boat, I would have done the same, but I was behind the wheel most of the time.

We were very lucky that one of our group, a former classmate, was a mechanical genius. He worked with the boat's mechanic to maintain the engine. Whenever he came out of the engine room and up from below, he looked so funny because he was covered with grime. His nose and his face were covered with black exhaust. We had a big laugh when we first saw him because all we could see were his eyes and teeth. He didn't say a word, just coughed out the exhaust. He just smiled at us. His smile was full of gentleness. I respected him a lot. He was an intelligent and good student. During the years I studied with him in the seminary, I never saw him get angry with anyone or complain about anything.

I realized he had been down in the engine room since we left Vietnam. He had been so busy helping the mechanic. It was hot and smoky in the engine room. I couldn't handle the smell of engine fuel. I knew I would get seasick easily if I had to be the one taking care of the engine. He was a wonderful guy. I didn't realize how important these two mechanics were for our journey. Without them, we would not have been able to pilot the boat at all. I thanked God for them.

The night arrived slowly as usual. We felt a little bit better as the sun disappeared under the sea. I was thirsty and hungry. I had had only a slice of pumpkin and a capful of water that day, but I believed I could endure for another day.

As the fourth day was about to begin, a strong wind arrived from the north. Early that morning we could see the waves were getting larger and higher. The boat's speed seemed to diminish as it struggled to move forward. We tried our best to eliminate the rocking of the boat. We didn't say anything to our people about our concerns.

Of course, our eyes were always fixed on the water container. There was only about two thirds of the second water container left. The people began to ask for more water. I knew we could not have more or we would die for sure.

I kept thinking about what we could do to make drinking water out of seawater. We had so little equipment to work with. I asked my friends to gather all the cookware we had in the boat. We had two cook pots and a couple of iron bars. I remembered from the survival skills I had learned in the Boy Scouts that there was a way we could make fresh water. We would have to use some of the diesel fuel to boil the water. If we could capture the steam we might have some water to drink, but we didn't know if we had enough fuel for the rest of the trip. I said to my friends, "Let's set it up and see if it works or not. Then, we will see what we can do about it."

My friends set up a spot to boil the seawater at the rear of the boat. They placed a cook-pot, filled with diesel fuel and pieces of cloth, on the floor. They laid two iron bars across the cook-pot. Then, they placed another cook-pot, half full of seawater, on top of the fire. They covered the top cook-pot and waited for the seawater to boil. Then, they took off the cover to let the water on the cover drop into a bowl. I counted the drops. There were sixteen drops of water. They tasted it and told me, "It's still salty, but it's all right to drink." I asked them to continue and save the water for when we were not able to handle our thirst any more. It would be better than nothing.

With a positive result from the effort, we began to regain our hope and confidence. I hoped the black smoke from the cook-pot would be a sign for other boats, if there were any. They might come and rescue us. My friends also had the idea to write three large letters on top of the cabin with grease: S.O.S. (Save Our Souls). We tried all these things to nurture our hope. I didn't think there were any airplanes to see us, but I kept silent for there was nothing wrong with hope. I was desperate as they were.

By noon the sun was oppressively hot. For the last couple of days I was wearing just my shorts. My shirt was always wet with seawater. The only way I could manage the thirst and the lack of water in my body was to keep wet all of the time. I knew I could get sick easily, but I desperately tried to delay the need to drink water. I couldn't ignore my thirst and hunger. Everyone on the boat was threatened by thirst. Our crew was badly sunburned. Time passed by so slowly, but we kept going forward.

At night I wrapped myself in a blanket against the wind and cold. Even though we had been born and raised in the coastal climate, the wind was too cold for us at night. We hadn't eaten enough food to produce the energy to resist the weather. The dew and the night fog cooled us off from the sun's burning heat, but it also added to our discomfort. Every once in a while one of us would check the compass to see if we were still heading southeast toward the China Sea.

As the sun finally set on the fourth day, we saw two glowing areas of light in front of our boat. Was that the light of a commercial ship? We excitedly approached the light. Perhaps, if it was a commercial ship and they couldn't rescue us, we could at least ask them for directions to the nearest country. Everyone woke up. They seemed to forget about their weakened condition. They shouted in hope, encouraging us to increase our speed. Fortunately, it was in the same direction we were already traveling. We watched and waited. We all wished for rescue. That would be great! For the first time, I saw the people in the boat expressed their hope. It was nice to see them regain their desire to live.

Because the sea was so vast, we could not tell how far away we were. How far was it to the lights? We all wanted to know. The glow of the lights reached high into the sky. We kept going and going, hoping this was the end of all our difficulties.

Early in the morning of the fifth day, about one o'clock, we started to make out the gigantic structures of an oil rig on the horizon. There must have been a huge well of oil because there was an enormous fire shooting up into the sky. We all became very excited, thinking how lucky we were. Surely, there must be someone there. Definitely, there must be people working there who would help us. We figured out that it was an oil company from Thailand or Malaysia. We hoped we were about to be rescued. Bay Cao asked the women and children to stand near the starboard side of the boat and yell for help. When we got within about five hundred yards we heard the gunshots.

Gunfire was not unfamiliar to any of us. We had grown up with it. We saw people in uniform running to the lights on the oil rig. A couple of spotlights were aimed at the boat. I saw several gunmen shooting their guns in the air. They weren't firing at us, but were firing as a warning to us. They said something on a loudspeaker. We could hear a message, on and off, but we could not understand what was being said. We kept moving closer. The wind was stronger, and the waves were higher near the oil rig. The message came again in English, "Stay away! Stay where you are! Don't come near."

We moved closer. This time they fired directly over our heads. We could see the shots being fired in the dark. We finally understood their warning. They were making sure that we didn't come closer. We stopped and wondered what we ought to do.

I didn't know how to speak English. None of us knew what the message was about. We looked at each other and I asked, "Does anyone here speak English?"

My friends looked at me and said, "You know we didn't study English. We studied French."

It was a huge frustration. We kept the engine in neutral gear and waited, bobbing about on the surface of the ocean. We drifted closer to the rig and the spotlights on the rig kept following us. We could hardly hear what they were saying. The wind was too strong and the splash of waves was too noisy. It was difficult to hear and to talk to them.

After about fifteen minutes a boat came out from the oil rig. I saw four guards with machine guns in the boat. I said to myself, "Oh no, what is going on?"

At first, I was afraid they would harm us, but they didn't look like Vietnamese guards. They came near the boat and two of them got on board and tried to talk to us in English. My friends talked to them in French and indicated that we couldn't understand English, but we could speak French. They signaled for us to wait and talked to the two who remained in their boat. The boat returned to the rig.

A little while later the guards returned with a translator who could speak French. We were told that we couldn't get any closer to the oil rig. It was dangerous. They couldn't help us at all because they didn't have authority from the manager.

After learning we were the boat people from Vietnam, they told us we had come close to the territorial waters of Malaysia. We realized that after we turned away from the Con-Son Island, the wind must have kept pushing us out to the Pacific Ocean instead of toward the Gulf of Thailand.

The guards pointed in the other direction and said, "If you go on in this direction for another two or three days you can reach Malaysia."

After verifying with us the direction to Malaysia, they returned to their post. They wouldn't allow us to come to the rig. They wouldn't rescue us. They would only give us directions. I tried to seek some assistance from them. I saw they were sorry they couldn't help us. We all felt so desperate. Couldn't they see how desperate we were? They just kept rejecting us, saying they didn't want anyone close to the oil well fire. There was a huge area of the sea that was lit up by the two fires. However, the light of the oil rig could not show us the way to dry land.

The darkness of the night became threatening for our group of helpless people. We didn't want to go out there again. The rig was like a little village on the ocean. We wished we could just get on the rig and off this tiny, little boat that we had been on for four days.

The women and children cried in desperation. The men were silent. They couldn't speak a word.

The security guards just kept shaking their heads, "No. There is nothing we can do for you and there is nothing we can give you. The only thing we can do is show you the direction. Aim your boat as we showed you and keep running and in another two or three days you will reach Malaysia."

I brought the map to the one guard who seemed like a gentleman. He looked at the map and told us where we were. He pointed on the map the direction for us to go and I adjusted the compass accordingly. He looked at the small compass shook his head in disbelief. He must have thought we were the most foolish people he had ever met.

We had no choice but to go on into the dark of the ocean. There was no way that we could change the hearts of these people. I thought perhaps they really did not have anything else to offer us. Perhaps they had some reason for not allowing us on their oil rig. Everything happened for a reason.

We aimed the boat back to the open sea. We had to continue on our journey. What a sad feeling! However, we departed the oil rig with the hope that we would come to dry land soon. It was about two o'clock in the morning on the fifth day of the journey.

CHAPTER FIFTEEN

"P" Is for Problems

The fifth day began. Everything was just fine. The container of water was about half full. Only one pumpkin left. Some of the people became desperate and during the night they grabbed something to eat and drank the water by themselves. I was upset but I understood. I asked my friends to save the water that was left for the children. We needed rain. We needed a miracle.

I tried to wet my lips with my tongue but I couldn't. My friends saw my thirst and they offered me a teaspoon of the steamed water we had made during the day. It was salty, but it wasn't bad at all. I held it in my mouth as long as I could to give my mouth some moisture. I told my friend standing next to me, "We are like a piece of dry sponge, eager to immerse into the water." He nodded, "I know. Persevere, my friend." I didn't know how much water I could drink at that moment. I thought I could drink a whole gallon at once. On the horizon, the sky began to clear. The rising sun was about to begin a new day for the world. I prayed in silence, "Lord Jesus, be with us always."

My friends took the wheel as I lay down on the floor to sleep.

Around noon, my friends woke me because they saw two boats. They looked like two big fishing boats. I stood up and tried the binoculars; I saw people on the boats. We hoped we were about to be rescued. I aimed our boat toward them to get a closer look at who they were.

Maybe they would take pity on us and help us. Perhaps, they would give us some food and water. At least, maybe they would help the women and children. I saw smoke rising from their exhaust. They were approaching us as we headed toward them. I thought this was a good sign. It meant they saw us. I hoped we would soon have some good news.

As we neared their boats, we saw there were about twenty men and young adults on board. Their skin was dark brown from the sun. They were waving at us. I didn't see any flag. We recognized some inscriptions on their boats' starboard sides and we assumed they were from Thailand.

As they pulled along side, one of my friends held the wheel while I scrambled up front to help throw our rope over to their decks so they could draw us closer. The boats were steel, about five or six times bigger than ours. They seemed like fishermen. Some of them boarded our boat. They helped some of the women on their boats. I wondered why they helped the women but not children. I sensed something wrong.

Suddenly, as the first woman reached their boat, four or five men grabbed her and tore her clothes. They pushed her down and began to rape her. We were terrified. The woman's husband was yelling and screaming, but we could do nothing. Quickly, they boarded our boat. One by one, they took the women. We begged them not to do this terrible act. We were all terrified. I begged them, "You can take anything, even the engine of the boat, but please don't hurt these women. Some of us have gold rings, money. Take them, but leave us alone. We are refugees. We are seeking freedom."

They jeered at us and pushed us around. We didn't understand what they were saying to each other. We tried to speak French to them. They ignored us. They just laughed at us. I wished I had the power and strength to knock them down and rescue our people, but we were so powerless.

One of them hit me on the chin with an ax. I fell, unconscious. I didn't know what happened after that. When I came to the pirates were gone. What a horrible scene they left behind. All the children were crying. All the women were bruised and naked, crying and bleeding. My friends were hurt also. The pirates had raped even the teenagers. I knew two of these teens and their families in Vietnam. They were sisters, sixteen and thirteen years old. I was really distraught. I didn't know what to say to them.

We tried to collect dry clothes and dress them. We did it in silence. I was afraid to say anything. They were hurt and didn't need to be hurt more by my words. Only God's word could heal their wounds. We helped them to the lower level of the boat. The men whose wives had been victims just hid their faces and cried. They felt ashamed and helpless. So did I. They didn't even know how to give comfort to one another. I could think of no words to say to them to ease the sadness. All I could say was, "I am sorry, I am sorry."

About twenty women had been brutally raped. With tears in my eyes, I asked my friends to clean up the mess. We had to go on with our journey for freedom.

The engine of the boat had been shut off during the siege. We didn't know if it was still working or not. We went into the engine room to try to start it again. Water had gotten into the boat through the engine's drain tube to the propellers. As long as the engine was running, the water was pumped out of the engine room. If the engine stopped, the water remained in the boat. Some of our people helped us bail water out of the boat while we tried to start the engine. After turning the heavy starting wheel, I didn't have much energy left. We took turns trying to start the engine. We kept bailing water to keep it from getting into the engine.

After awhile I said to my friend, "Maybe we should check everything before we try to start the engine for the last time. Otherwise, we won't have enough energy to turn the engine."

The mechanic cleaned the spark plugs. He did a total checkup of the engine so we would not waste our energy. In fact, we all were very low on energy from lack of food and water, and we were all depressed by the horror that had just taken place. Each one of us was in shock. It was devastating to us. I prayed, "God, if you really want us to survive, then let this engine start."

I did my best to turn the heavy wheel of the engine. The engine did eventually start. I was so grateful.

When I got behind the steering wheel, I couldn't remember which way we were supposed to go. We consulted with each other, looked at the map and the compass, and began our journey again. It was about five o'clock in the evening of the fifth day, the day of fear and injury, the day of sadness and doubt, the day of sorrow and anger.

We headed east. The sun was behind us. Everyone was mute. I felt like I didn't want to go on at all. I didn't care if I survived or not. I was devastated.

Each of us grieved our own way. Why did I have to face a situation like this? Why did people treat each other so cruelly? Above all, where was God? Why did God allow such a bad thing to happen to us? Deep down in my heart, I knew God didn't do these bad things. I knew God was near, but I couldn't escape the feeling that I had: I was angry with God. I looked straight ahead, but I didn't see anything.

The children were crying. They saw their mothers and their fathers grieving and they knew something was terribly wrong. The younger children had just experienced the most horrible thing of their lives. They didn't know how to give comfort to their parents, sisters, and brothers.

Most of the women, according to their cultural perspective, felt they had nothing left within them. Their honor had been taken away. Their dignity had been violated. Some of women, in their anguish, pushed away their children. They pushed away their husbands. They didn't want anyone to come near them. They felt they were not worthy to go on living. Life had ended for them. They were taught to be chaste until they were married, then to dedicate themselves to their husbands and families. The women, who were not yet married, had planned to offer themselves only to their husbands. They became the victims of these terrible acts, but they blamed themselves. Their self-image was destroyed and they felt there was nothing left to live for. They would have a hard time to be with their loved ones in the future.

I felt so bad for them. I wished I could cry to release my feelings, but I couldn't. The tragedy was a heavy load on my heart. It made me feel so numb and angry.

I didn't realize that the wound on my chin had opened again until my friend gave me a piece of cloth to stop the bleeding. It was bleeding all over my chest. It was painful. While cleaning the wound with seawater I thought to myself, "The wound on my chin will heal, but the wound in my heart will be there for a long time." I wished the light of the sun would stop shining upon us, and let us hide in the darkness, let us hide how broken and wounded we were.

I had never experienced such a deadly silence. No one spoke. I looked at my friends and they looked back in silence. I felt shame, emptiness, hopelessness, anger, and frustration. A thousand feelings had crossed my mind. I was overwhelmed. We risked our lives to attain freedom, to live in peace and dignity with other human beings. The price for life and freedom was too high, too expensive.

I kept blaming myself. If I didn't insist on seeking help from those pirates, then nobody would have been hurt. I kept thinking that if I had had the right knowledge and experience, we would not be in this awful situation. I shared this thought to my good friends. They felt the same way. They echoed my thoughts, "If we had had better knowledge of the ocean and how to cross it we would not have led these innocent people into such painful situations."

It was a heavy blame to live with. The blame we put on ourselves was hard to embrace from within, but it was shared: Only in God can we be healed and find rest for our souls. The prayer that night was offered to God in tears.

That night, when my friends took the wheel so that I could rest, I went down to check that the women were doing okay. Earlier, when I had put clothes on them, I knew that some of them were bruised and bleeding badly. It was such a sad scene. They were in tears and hiding their faces in their hands as they cried silently. I knew they had bitterness in their hearts. They bit their lower lips to keep the sound of crying from coming out. I wanted to say a few words of comfort, but I couldn't find a word to fit this situation.

They helped each other, applying ointment to each other's bruises. Some of them lay on the floor and slept. Their faces were covered with tears. I didn't know what to think or what to feel. All I knew was their dreams had come to an end.

I just kept patting each of them on the shoulder as a sign of comfort. They knew I was a seminarian and they accepted this offering of sympathy from me. I sat down in the middle of the floor as I just kept saying softly, "I am sorry that this happened to you, but our journey cannot stop right here. We have to go on."

I felt close to each one of them for I was one of them. Since this tragedy happened to us, I had almost given up the idea to go on. I thought this escape was the biggest mistake I had ever made in my life. I would rather have died at sea than to face all of these awful, guilty feelings. I was the one to insist that we needed to ask for help from the people on those two boats. If I had just driven away, these cruel people wouldn't have hurt us.

That night was the most difficult night of my life. In the war, when I saw the bodies of my dead friends, I felt so empty. The feelings of those times past were not easy to forget. I had been with their families when they stayed awake all night as part of the prayer vigils. But I had never felt such emptiness as I felt this very night. My people were being buried alive. I felt I was trapped in a tomb, experiencing death while still alive. The darkness of death covered me.

The night went on. I sat against the wall of the boat. Against the opposite wall were the two teenage sisters. In the light of the oil lamp, I saw the tears in their eyes. They didn't cry aloud. The tears stayed in their eyes. I couldn't say a word. I was afraid that if I said anything, it would hurt them more, and they would burst in tears. How helpless I was!

This was the first time I ever went downstairs to stay with my people. I wanted to share their suffering. They were more than happy to make room for me in their midst. It was warmer than at the back of the boat. I closed my eyes and fell asleep as I heard the Word of God in the back of my head, "Do not fear! I am with you always!"

My friend woke me up around three o'clock in the morning. I woke up right away, but my body was filled with pain. It took me a while to get up to the pilot's room. The morning wind was cold enough to wake me up. Cleaning my glasses with a filthy piece of cloth, I saw everything was the same. The surface of the sea filled up with big waves. The night sky was scattered with stars and a new moon. We still avoided talking to each other unless there was a necessary question to ask. Occasionally, there was a request for information about the engine to check on the amount of water that got into the boat. We only talked when there was a need. We didn't talk to keep each other awake. It was hard to describe how we felt. It was like the power of death had overcome each of us.

The wound on my chin had stopped bleeding. The survival skills I learned in the Boy Scouts helped me to treat the wound appropriately. The day before, I broke open a cigarette and applied the tobacco to the cut. I pressed the tobacco to my chin for a little while and wrapped the wound with my friend's shirt. The nicotine stopped the bleeding, numbed the pain and killed the bacteria. I didn't feel the pain in the open wound, but my jaw still hurt. I hoped I wouldn't lose any teeth. The seawater got into the wound and created a little pain when I washed my face. I was lucky. The blow wasn't strong enough to kill me or to break my jaw.

The sixth day of the journey began. People began to go to the back of the boat to clean up. It was the normal routine of the past five days. We passed each other, but we didn't talk at all. Everyone was quiet and finished their cleaning as quickly as they could. Bay Cao came into the pilot's room to talk to me. His family was badly hurt from yesterday's nightmare. There was sadness in his eyes. He asked if I would say something to the people. He said he couldn't stand the deadly sadness and the awful silence any longer. I was reluctant to say anything. He begged me to say a few words to give people hope. He also told me to ask people to clean up so that they wouldn't get sick. We agreed that after "breakfast" I would say something to the people.

Breakfast was a teaspoon of water and a thin slice of the last pumpkin we had left. The last resource of food and drink on the boat was about to be gone. We would have nothing left for the rest of the journey.

We rolled up the canopy so that we could have fresh air and light. I saw people trying to clean up the boat where they had lived for the last six days. They really tried to help one another.

After all of these preparations were done, I started to speak, "We all are in a critical condition for the rest of the journey. We all are aware of this desperate situation. We don't have any food or water left in the boat. The temporary steaming equipment we created is capable of producing only a cup of water a day. We need to reserve this small amount of water for the little children. If anyone still has candy or personal dry food supplies, he or she is invited to share it with one another according to his or her own will. We all experienced the horror of the pirates. Our hearts are broken and are filled up with sadness. We share that sadness with one another. It was no one's fault. It just happened to us. We cannot blame ourselves. We need to rise above our personal shame to comfort one another. After all, we are in the same boat. We don't know for sure that we are going to make it or not, but we will do the best we can. We have been traveling for almost six days. We have to be closer to the dry land. We all have faith and still have one another. We are going to make it. It is not going to be an easy task, but I believe that we are going to make it."

I felt much better after I finished the speech. I shared with them what I felt in my heart. I unloaded the heavy burden into the sea. For me, I believed that God would lead us to the land of freedom. I shared with my friends, "Remember the words of St. Paul? He said that we are going to run, but we will not grow weary, for the Lord will be near to those who call upon His name. Definitely, we will rise again."

My friends all agreed with me. I continued, "Please, don't give up, my friends. Maybe we don't care about ourselves, but we must do this for our people. We have to go on with this journey for the little ones. Let us get ourselves together."

I told myself I couldn't remain in mourning. I had to overcome these sad feelings. We were not dead. We had to help ourselves first, then allow God to do the rest. Looking at my people, I saw their sadness and anxiety. It made me become a stronger person for the sake of the people. They believed in me and I believed in them. I said to my friends, "We must go on."

We looked at each other and gave each other a smile of comfort. We were aware these smiles weren't real. We didn't know how to react to each other's sadness. We just tried to be polite because of the wounds each of us carried. We tried to restore our confidence and commitment to our journey, but it was not the same anymore. Yesterday was gone and there was nothing we could do to change it. We had to live with it.

During the sixth day we emptied the second container of water. My skin began to crack and dry up because I had not even had a teaspoon of water for the last two days. I felt so thirsty and hungry. I wished I could have a giant cup of fresh lemonade my grandmother used to make in the summer. If I could have it, I would drink it all and die in peace. I never knew how important water was. It had always seemed like a small thing in our daily lives. Now I knew what a big role it played in life. I wished the sky would open and rain down on us, just for a moment, so that we could have water to drink. My body was literally oozing salt.

I wrapped my head with my friend's shirt and soaked it with seawater. The open wound on my chin began to hurt but I didn't pay attention to the pain. All I wanted was a little bit of water to drink, perhaps just a little bit of food to eat. I was so hungry, so thirsty. I began to feel dizzy. I had to sit down to rest. Bay Cao stood next to me. He gave me a piece of chewing gum, then he disappeared. Holding that chewing gum in my hand, I looked at my friend who stood behind the steering wheel. I didn't even think twice and broke it in half. Each one of us would have a half of a piece of chewing gum. There were no words to exchange. We understood each other well enough to not say a word. It wasn't necessary.

CHAPTER SIXTEEN

Silence Equals Sailing

Around three o'clock in the afternoon on the sixth day, the boat's engine suddenly increased its noise, and then stopped. I asked the mechanic, "What happened?"

He said to me in his tired tone, "Quang, I don't know. There is something wrong!"

I went into the engine room to check it out. The fuel level was still good, the coolant water was still in good condition and there was plenty of oil in the engine. Still, there was something wrong. We had no choice but to let the boat float with the wind.

After a lot of exploration, we discovered that the propellers were gone and the drive train was twisted. We were in trouble. We had to fix it. It would take at least a couple of hours to straighten the drive train and replace its propellers. A week before we left we had taken the spare shaft to the machine shop but we didn't have time to go back to the shop to pick it up. We had no spare. Fortunately, we had a spare propeller. It wasn't a good one, but we had no choice. We had to replace it. I never dreamt we would have to change a propeller in the middle of the ocean. I didn't have any experience with this at all.

I tied the propeller with a small cord around my waist, and my friend brought a tool bag. We jumped into the ocean and attempted to replace the engine's propeller. We bobbed up and down, trying to keep enough air in our lungs to get the job done. We had a tough time using our tools because of the bobbing movements of the boat. Regardless of how well we could swim and hold our breath, we swallowed a lot of water.

After many attempts to replace the propeller, we had to give up. It couldn't be done under such difficult conditions. We returned to the boat to rest and find another way to do the job.

Finally, both of us went back into the water. We tied the drive train with a rope. The other end of the rope was tied to my waist. We had to unscrew the drive train from the inside of the engine room. As soon as it was unscrewed the drive train could be withdrawn from the underside of the boat. We prayed we wouldn't lose the iron drive train. We would never be able to retrieve it. Luckily, we managed to bring the drive train on board.

The mechanic replaced the propeller while we caught our breath. The amount of seawater we swallowed made us vomit. My friends used an ax to straighten the shaft. After the propeller was replaced, we went back into the water again. We were careful to tie a rope on the drive train to a knob on the side of the boat. We put the shaft through the hole to allow the other end to reach the engine. We took turns holding the shaft while we came up for a breath. Finally, everything was done. We got on board again and hoped the engine would start. In fact we had spent the last calories left in our weakened bodies. We were very tired, but we had another chance to go on.

None of us had much energy left. We weren't strong enough to turn the engine. We took turns trying, but the engine wouldn't start. We rested for a while, then tried again. We tried and tried to turn the engine, but it wouldn't start.

"One more try," we said to one another. I could see the anxiety on our faces.

Finally, my friend and I both attempted to turn the engine for the last time before we gave up.

"Thank you, Lord," we both exclaimed when we heard the sound of the engine kick in. Everyone felt so relieved. It meant we still had a chance. We got out of the engine room to get some fresh air. All my muscles and bones hurt. My friends felt the same.

The sun had already set, but its light was still shining on the horizon. We aimed the boat to the east and the journey continued. Once again, we were in darkness. My friends took over the steering as I lay down to rest. The evening prayer wasn't said–it was replaced with a question, "O Lord, how long will it take us to see the land of the living?"

The sixth day ended in thirst and hunger. The cool air of the night was the only source of comfort we received, and it didn't satisfy our needs. The people were getting tired and extremely weak.

Early in the morning of the seventh day, my friends woke me up when they discovered smoke coming from the engine room. The engine had overheated. My friend who had stayed in the engine room with the mechanic from the first day fell asleep from exhaustion. Both of them forgot to check the engine's oil level. The oil had drained off and the engine had overheated.

He said to me, "I am sorry. We will have to take it apart and clean it. Hopefully, we can fix it." In their weakened condition, my friend and the mechanic tried to take apart the engine and clean up the parts. I didn't know how to give comfort to them. The boat once again floated with the wind. It moved up and down with the waves of the ocean. It rolled right and left. I knew that anxiety was at a high level in our hearts.

The seventh day seemed to begin with the adversity of nature. The wind was strong and the sky became dark. We had to face a thunderstorm. High waves slapped the boat from all directions. A lot of water splashed into the boat. Women and children began to cry. I thought we were going to die.

Because the engine was out of order the sump pump didn't work. We asked people to clear the middle section of the boat to make room for us to bail out the water. We formed two lines along each side of the boat. Each line needed three people to bail out the water. Two were at the bottom of the boat with buckets. They lifted it up to the next person who in turn dumped the water into the sea. We forgot how tired we were, but we knew how dangerous it was for our boat. The boat could sink into the ocean in no time. Everyone was trying to help us the best they could. They took turns replacing us so we could catch our breath. Thank goodness! The strong, windy conditions only lasted for about an hour. It began to rain hard and we had to quickly figure out how to catch the rainwater. It seemed to take forever to find something clean to catch the rainwater. Finally, we used the canopy to catch the rainwater to fill up the container in the middle of the boat. However the rainwater was mixed with the seawater that came from the waves. At the rear of the boat we used a blanket, but it was old and it stunk. I asked the young ladies to hold the four corners of the blanket so we could catch the raindrops into a container. Then we tasted it! It was salty. There was just no clean fabric on that boat after six days at sea.

The water wasn't good, but we filled up one big container. It still tasted better than pure seawater. I took one of the empty water containers and stood next to the roof of the pilot room. The rainwater from the roof tasted a little better. After I filled it up and sealed it, I enjoyed a shower with the rainwater. I took this opportunity to drink as much as I could. The people did the same. I washed off the salt from my head to my toes. It was a real blessing to have a real shower after a week. All of us enjoyed that blessing. My clothes were washed clean. I felt much better for a moment.

The two big containers were full, then we filled up the empty fuel containers with the rainwater strained through the soggy, salty, dirty blanket. At the end of the thunderstorm we had about sixty gallons of water, but it was not easy to drink due to the seawater that came in from the waves. Some containers tasted of diesel.

The thunderstorm lasted about two hours. Many of us were able to drink a decent amount of rainwater. It felt so good. It made a big difference, but still it wasn't like having a real drink of fresh water at home. However, we were all grateful and remembered this stormy day at sea. After the thunderstorm, it seemed we all came to the realization we still wanted to be alive. We wanted to live, not only for our families and ourselves, but also for the communities we had left behind. We were ready to work hard, using all of our skills, to succeed and to survive. The rain had a very cleansing effect on us, but we were so hungry. We all wanted to figure out how to redeem ourselves from this hopeless situation.

We felt better even though we were all soaking wet. After we bailed out the rest of the rainwater we decided to just lie down to rest because there was nothing else we could do. We went to sleep with a promise to one another that on the next day we would fix the engine. We would fix it! So we caught up on our sleep. It was the first time in six days that I could actually sleep, since we could no longer control the boat. The surface of the ocean became very quiet. Without the sound of the engine the whole ocean was peaceful and silent. I just lay on the floor to rest, for to stand behind the steering wheel was meaningless.

Our encounter with the pirates a couple of days earlier left us with a bitter feeling. They took away our only binoculars. Many of us lost personal items such as rings, golden necklaces, and money. They had taken away my watch and my glasses with the gold frames. They also took the gold crucifix from the rosary I wore around my neck. It was a gift from my grandmother when I received the sacrament of confirmation at the age of seven. They took the crucifix but left the rosary on my neck. I still keep it with me. I felt uncomfortable without my glasses because I couldn't see well. They had taken ten five-gallon containers of diesel fuel. Thank goodness, they didn't destroy our boat.

Actually, I took this opportunity to review what had happened over the last couple of days. I looked at my friends and we spoke to one another without words. I could see that all of us were so sorry we had ever participated in the escape. We didn't mean to lead the people into these difficulties. We felt a sense of great depression even though the people did not say anything bad about us or accuse us of anything. However, in their silence and the way they looked at us, we recognized their sorrow and suffering. It reminded me of the story of the Exodus. The people of Israel had cried out their needs to Moses, "Why has the Lord God led us out of the land of Egypt to die in the desert? Why did he allow us to be chased by the armies and chariots of Pharaoh? Here in the desert there is no sign of life. Where is hope? Where is God?"

For me, I didn't know how the people of Israel dealt with one another, but in our own situation, our hearts were still beating. We still desired to live.

The day and the night of the seventh day passed, as we drifted with the ocean waves. I wished we could have some food to eat, or at least some fishing gear, but we had nothing. We could no longer sleep due to the lack of food. We agreed to try to fix the engine. We needed to do something. We couldn't face the hunger that persecuted us. We went down to the engine room. My friend and the mechanic were already there.

The engine was badly damaged. We cleaned and reassembled it. We refilled the fuel and the oil. We then attempted to start the engine many times, but there was nothing we could do to make it work. We gave up.

When the darkness came, I just stretched out and looked up at the stars in the sky. To the west was the closest star, the "evening star." To the east would be the "morning star." This star gave us our direction. I believed that if we aimed toward it we would reach dry land, perhaps Thailand, Malaysia, Singapore, or the Philippines. I shared this thought with my friends and they agreed, but the engine of the boat was out of order and we couldn't control the boat. How could we go there?

We had to use the wind. We had to make a sail. We could make a sail. We decided to take a length of four-by-four from the starboard side of the boat and use it to make a mast. We nailed the four-by-four to the bar that crossed the center of the boat. We nailed the edge of the blanket along the mast. We then took a hard bamboo stick to divide the blanket into two right triangles. We used a rope to tie the lower end of the bamboo to the mast. We tied the upper end to the blanket. We used another hard bamboo stick for the base of the sail. Finally, we tied a rope to the upper end of the bamboo and to the end of the base of the sail. We pulled the rope aft and adjusted both ends of the rope to receive the wind. Somehow, the wind caught the blanket and we had a sail. The boat began to pick up speed as the wind blew into the sail. The boat was breaking the waves. It moved forward and its speed was not bad at all. Our hope began to rise as we cheered for the new product of our labor.

We quickly got ourselves in position to control the boat. Two were behind the steering wheel, two were at the pole tied to the rope of the sail. They would pull and release the rope to catch the wind according to the direction of the "captain." We continued our journey for freedom. It felt good to see the people express renewed hope.

We used our laundry to seal the hole of the drive train to cut down on the amount of water seeping in. Two fellows were assigned to keep track of the water level and bail water. We aimed the boat toward the morning star at night, and to the sunrise in the daylight.

The eighth day began with a new sense of hope. The wind came up frequently and kept the boat running. During the day we kept a straight line between the sunrise and the sunset. The angle of the sun helped us keep the direction. We made sure the boat lined up opposite the sun. At least we felt we weren't going around in circles, but progressing in one direction.

The boat sailed on and we took turns resting. As a matter of fact, everyone was so tired the will to survive needed to be restored in each of us. I felt I needed to motivate people. They needed to hear positive things. I told the people about my grandmother's comment about me. I said, "You know, my grandma is old and she has had a long life. She is ninety-eight years old. She used to tell me that I would have a long life as she has. So, I am telling you that I am not going to die yet. And if I am not going to die now then you will survive with me."

My friends knew that I tried to encourage them. They smiled at me and didn't say anything. We didn't talk very much, though I was the most talkative person of the group. It seemed a time for silence to respect all the suffering that people had endured.

I remembered the scripture: "In the silence of the desert of your heart I will speak." I wished it would be a peaceful silence, but it wasn't. In our hearts we blamed ourselves. We still felt guilty. We felt so powerless and empty.

CHAPTER SEVENTEEN

Bring on the Boy Scouts

The eighth day continued with silence in our hearts. We had nothing to eat but water. We had collected water, but it tasted like sewer water because it was mixed with seawater and diesel fuel. Everyone just rested. I thought to myself, "My God, does this mean we are going to experience death right now?"

A thousand different questions went through my mind. A thousand different reflections happened in a moment. I didn't know how to sort it out. I felt as weak as a zombie, but I continued to pray we would be saved.

We really felt the heat of the day and we thought it would kill us all. The scorching heat, the depression of the situation, and the silence of mourning were too much for me to endure. We had no skills at sea, with the exception of what a few of us had learned in the Boy Scouts. I wished that other men in the boat knew how to drive the boat so that we could rest a little longer. In fact, we all felt so weak. I could no longer stand up behind the steering wheel for as long as I could when we began. Although I was weak and exhausted my spirit became stronger. I was tired of blaming myself for what had happened. I was tired of being beaten up by those guilty feelings.

The day passed by slowly. We were thirsty and had no choice but to drink the rainwater we had collected during the thunderstorm. It was a little bit salty and smelled of diesel fuel. I was again at the wheel of the boat so that my friends could rest. I was feeling a little bit better about our situation and a little bit relaxed. The wind continued to blow and the boat moved forward, up and down with the waves.

Around two o'clock in the afternoon, by the shadow of the sun, we saw another boat from afar. Once again, we thought we might be able to seek some help. We knew if they would help us, that we would not send the women or children to their boat. The last experience made us cautious.

We used white shirts as flags to send a message to them in semaphore code. We hoped they would see us and offer some assistance. With our flags we signaled S.O.S. We kept sending the signal S.O.S, S.O.S. toward them. There was no sign they had seen us at all. We placed a cooking pot filled with diesel fuel on the roof of the pilot's cabin. We hoped that would help them to see us, but they kept moving farther away. All we could see was their black smoke as they disappeared over the horizon. My friends stopped sending signals for help.

They came down from the roof of the pilot's cabin and looked at me with the words, "I'm sorry."

Patting their shoulder, I said, "Don't feel bad. At least we tried. Maybe it is not a bad thing for us. When we don't get what we want it may become a blessing. It may be a sign of God's blessing. What if it had been a boat of pirates? It may be that God has just delivered us from a disaster. Let's not give up hope, but go on!"

We checked the sun's light to see if we were headed east and kept sailing. It seemed everyone was feeling uncertain, disappointed because we had received no help. On the other hand, we wanted to know for sure what kind of boat it was.

The night drew closer and the eighth day passed by. Stars appeared in the sky. We were starving. We were about to get sick. We slept more and talked less.

We began the ninth day with the reality that we had nothing to put into our stomachs. My stomach hurt more often. I told my friends I was getting weaker and weaker. They said they felt the same. We had to depend on God's love. I knew how difficult it was to accept and to believe the statement of Jesus, "My flesh is real food and my blood is real drink."

Two young boys in the boat became very sick. They were brothers, aged about two and four. They were children of a nice young couple. For the entire trip they had not complained about anything. This couple just sat together and held onto their children. One of the boys cried for a while but he was so weak he really had no strength to cry. They refused to drink any of the water in the containers. The husband asked for advice, "What can we do to help you and to help one another? How can we find some food?"

I told him we had nothing on the boat to fish with. We had nothing at all. He was quiet for a while, and then he asked me, "In that case, what can we do to feed our children?"

I looked at him; "I really don't know what to tell you. Are you afraid to get hurt? If you are not, I think there is only one thing you can do to help your children survive. This is a horrible thing to say, but I can't think of anything else. Cut your finger deep enough and let your child suck your blood. This will help your child to survive."

He thanked me and returned to his wife. Both of them talked for a while. It seemed they would both do what I suggested. I closed my eyes and thought about what he and his wife would do. It was a painful picture to see, but I thought to myself. "This is such a powerful and meaningful image."

They actually fed their children with their own blood, their own life. I felt sad that they had to do such a thing for their children, but I would do the same thing.

In the darkness of the night, my eyes filled with tears. I thought of my family, my community. They were about to celebrate Christmas. I said a prayer for them, for us, and for the Church. I missed very much the celebration of daily Eucharist. I missed them all, but tonight I had seen the powerful action of parents' love for their children: to nourish them with their own blood.

For me, blood is a significant image of life. Physically, in the celebration of the Eucharist, we receive the real body and blood of Christ in the forms of bread and wine. It is certainly easier to receive the life of Christ in these forms than to receive it in the forms of the raw meat and real blood. Theologically, Jesus identifies himself with the bread from heaven. His body and blood are what we must eat and drink in order to receive divine nourishment. I always believe that to consume the very life of Jesus, the word of the Father is to unite oneself with Jesus in faith, hope, and love.

The two boys' hunger seemed to be satisfied by their parent's blood. They rested in their parents' bosoms. I knew the more they rested the more the parents felt weaker and weaker. At least, if only in the temporary place in their hearts, they were at peace when they saw their babies resting.

CHAPTER EIGHTEEN

Treasured Trash

It was about 10 o'clock in the morning of the tenth day. Two fishing boats appeared behind us, approaching very quickly. We were not aware of their presence until they honked at us. We didn't know who they were, but we thought, "Oh, no. They are chasing after us!"

Of course, we didn't know their intention, but there was no way that we could speed up our sailboat to check out their intention, or to run away from them. About fifteen minutes later they caught up with us. We hoped that they had seen us and recognized our need. Maybe they would be willing to assist us. Maybe this was our chance to be rescued. Maybe we would experience God's deliverance. We prayed that these boats weren't pirates. I had mixed feelings; I sensed something bad was about to happen. I was terrified of their boats as they drew closer. From their appearance they looked like another group of pirates. They pointed their fingers and laughed at us. We were all at the point of death. The women and children were crying. The rest of us were so angry because we had no proper way to defend our people. Why had it happened again? Where is God?

It was a devastating situation! The people had just lifted up their spirits, since yesterday. They had lifted up their hope for the future. They believed that "God will deliver us, the poor from all harm and evil. The Lord hears the cry of the poor." I tried not to deny my faith, but for now it was hard to accept.

They pulled along both sides of our small boat. They were strong, bare-skinned men. Again, the members of our little boat were about to be abused. It was horrible and terrifying. They tied us together and then took the women to their boats. We knew they became victims of all these animal-men. Several of them remained in our boat with guns and knives. They searched around the boat. What were they looking for? I didn't understand their language, but I assumed they used curse words to express their disappointment for they couldn't find anything of value to them. They were full of wine. They pushed the water containers around. Our only source of water, even though it wasn't good, began to run to the base of the boat. Being tied up we were helpless. Oh God! I hated them! How could You allow these things to happen to us? I had experienced all the terrible persecutions at the hands of the Communists in prison in Vietnam, but in the midst of the ocean, this morning, I felt I was buried alive. I felt completely hopeless and helpless. We had no more energy or hope within us. We had nothing. Why had this happened again?

It was worse than the first time we were abused by the pirates. The women had not physically recovered from the first nightmare. They couldn't defend themselves.

I couldn't open my eyes to observe things around me. I didn't want to face the reality of such cruelty. It was worse than death. Death would bring an end to the suffering. I felt so bad for these women. They were innocent and they received such cruelty.

We couldn't see what was happening on the pirates' boats because they were larger than our small boat. All we could hear was the laughing of these men, the screaming of the women. Those women were wives, daughters, and sisters. I wished I were deaf so I could not hear. I wished I were blind so I would not have to witness these awful things happening in front of my eyes. I wished I were mute so I wouldn't say any word against God's love for all.

I hid my face in my knees to pray because my hands were tied. I knew I would only be able to speak what was in my heart. I recalled the body of Jesus hanging on the crucifix. After Jesus was dead they didn't break his legs. One soldier used a lance and pierced his side. The blood and water came out. This image always gave me a sign of hope for the new spiritual life. The living water and the saving blood of Jesus became a strong image of the sacrament of baptism and the new life. It was a sign of salvation gained for us through the death and resurrection. It was to show God the Father's love for the entire world. I wanted to think of this image now. I needed to feel His loving presence now, more than ever.

These women had been put to death twice. First, when they left their homeland, they lost whatever was close to their hearts. Now, victims of cruel rape, they lost their hope.

The assault lasted about three hours before the women were released. They put the women on a little platform and lowered the platform to our boat. I will never forget that image. What a painful picture captured in my mind! I could hear none of the women crying. They were all dead inside.

After the women were returned the pirate's final act of cruelty was to dump their trash all over us. There were fish heads, bones, and banana skins. There were some open cans of food that must have been out of date. They laughed at us as they departed. I have to admit that when the people saw the trash they moved forward to find something for their belly. They washed it with seawater and ate everything they could. I couldn't believe my eyes. Leaving them, I went back to the rear of the boat to avoid seeing "my people" eating the enemies' trash.

I felt like I had entered in Sheol, the dwelling of hell. I couldn't believe people could do such horrible things to another human being. We tried to cloth the women with what we had and took their clothes away to clean. We helped them back to their places. Hopefully, they would be able to rest near their loved ones.

I wanted to refuse to eat the trash they had thrown over to our boat. It was not much, but it was something for us to eat. People ate in tears. Their trash became our food. I had no idea how to feel about this. I felt that I didn't have to eat that trash for now. I believed I could handle the hunger for a couple of days. Should I express my anger by refusing to eat? When I was young and wanted to express my rebellious nature to my parents, I might refuse to eat. In this circumstance I didn't know what to do.

I cried even more to see people share with each other what they found to eat from the trash. It was an incredible sight. They were showing love for one another. Love, kindness, consideration, and understanding, all still existed in our midst.

By three o'clock in the afternoon, we were totally exhausted. We were like zombies. There had been so much crying. So many bad memories still remained in our mind. Then we just fell asleep. Each one of us seemed to hide his or her face in the side of the boat. We didn't want to see the light. We didn't want to hear anything else. There was a profound presence of death in our midst. The beautiful sounds of the ocean became the sounds of death.

Everyone avoided talking or looking at each other. They were afraid that if they said something, people would burst into tears. Everyone faced death in their grieving. I sat at the rear of the boat with my knees pulled up to my chest and my head bent down on my knees. I tried to cry. In the past I had been able to cry in private, but I didn't have any more tears to cry. How painful it was to cry without tears. I questioned myself about how many people in this life have experienced these feelings. I thought of Mary, the Heavenly Blessed Mother who had tasted bitter, sorrowful experiences. The disciples of Jesus Christ had experienced the same feeling. The poor people of the world lived with these situations. I knew the feeling of the poor, the suffering, and the victim of injustice. I understood how they felt because I was there and was one of my people. Once again, I questioned, "Where were you God when I needed You? Why has my soul been cast down?"

I thought to myself, "Maybe our journey has not come to an end yet. Maybe our lives will not end with this tragedy." For me, in our daily lives, things happen, good or bad, to give us opportunities to exercise our freedom to choose to love or to hate. Whether we like it or not, bad things happen, but we shouldn't react to all these events based on fear or hatred. We still have our honor to uphold. The decision to give, to love, and to forgive is the only way to live our lives. But it is absolutely hard. How could I convince myself to practice what I ought to be, and what I ought to do?

I promised myself at that time, with God's grace, to love and serve people no matter what happens because bad things happen to good people at any time. When it happens, they become stronger in faith, hope, and love. In the Christians' daily lives, in their own unique ways, they were and are called to be martyrs: witnesses of the living Jesus. Each one of us, as Christ's followers, is called to become a witness of Christ's death and resurrection in our daily lives, whether in good times or in bad. The word "martyr" comes from a Latin root word that means "testimony": to witness.

I thought to myself, these women were called to live the martyrdom of their faith. They have been persecuted unjustly, because they were seeking freedom to worship God in better conditions and environment. They have been persecuted because they were hungry for life. Their journey to seek freedom was no different than mine. We sought only to live and enjoy the gifts of life in faith and hope. We sought an opportunity to live according to our own vocations. We sought freedom to do God's will and believe that God prepared each of us to be His own through His son's death and resurrection. It was a lesson of faith. I believe that I was immersed into the death and resurrection of Christ, to rise up with Christ to the newness of life as the children of God. But to live the life of God's children was so difficult. It could be done only with God's grace, because without God I couldn't do anything. In our daily sufferings and anxieties we are called to be in communion with God and others. It was a beautiful call for each one of us; in this desperate situation, I wondered what Jesus would do? It was so difficult to comprehend and practice what we believed. How could we, in the image of God, as the instruments of God's love and life, do bad things to one another? What caused the pirates to do such cruel things? I didn't have any clear answer. All I knew was I needed to forgive and to accept that God was there to suffer with us.

I had to find a way to forgive others and myself. I must let go of these painful memories so I wouldn't live in fear, anger, and anxiety. Maybe they did not know Jesus Christ. Maybe they had never received any goodness from people. Maybe they never learned how to give. I was not quite sure what caused them to do such bad things.

None of us had the courage to go on with our journey. We paid no attention to the boat. We simply gave up. We let the boat drift with the wind. The sunset came as a sign of our death. However, the wind continued to come to us, sounding like words of encouragement: "We must go on! The journey is not ended here." I was completely frustrated. My heart was broken. I knew from that moment on I would live with these painful memories.

CHAPTER NINETEEN

Night Vigil

That night, the young boys had passed away to the next life. The young boys had passed away to death. They died. All I could hear was the cry of the parents who had lost their young children. The night was filled with sad crying. These two boys had touched others. Those people cried for the boys and for themselves. That night was the most mournful of my life.

During the war, I could hide myself so I wouldn't hear the cries of the people. Here, I had nowhere to hide. I had no other place to mourn. In tears and sadness, I heard all their cries. We cried because of the deaths of two young boys, or because of the nightmare that had taken place. Above all, we cried because of lost hope. We cried to Almighty God for help. We addressed our sadness to Buddha. We invoked the assistance of our ancestors. We sought the consolation of our own God.

It seemed the sky and the weather expressed its anger. The winds blew harder. The stars seemed less bright. Still I knew there was hope. There was a future and the desire to survive. Deep in my heart was a desire to live.

I tried to control my emotions and the mourning to get our small group together. We had to work together to control the boat. The wind was strong and we had to take advantage of it. If we were not careful to turn the sail at the proper time, our boat would overturn and sink. I didn't want that to happen. We didn't deserve to die like this. I paid more attention to the boat than to the current human crisis.

We were already dead twice and now we must rise from all these hopeless situations. The future was waiting for us. I didn't know what would happen to us, but we had to overcome our own fear and sadness. I didn't know why I still had the light of hope. I believed that God wouldn't allow us to die in vain.

After their death, we tried to make room to lay the two little boys. We put some clean clothes on them. We spent a little time in prayer and gave comfort to the parents. Some of the people practiced ancestor worship, so they just cried out in their own belief. They recalled on the names of their ancestors who went before them and sought their assistance. They asked their relatives who had gone before them to make intercessions on behalf of the young boys and bring them to eternal life. Some of the people were Buddhist and they prayed to Buddha for these two boys to have a happy death and a wonderful reincarnation. They prayed the souls of the young boys would be free of the bondage of hell and they would return to a better life. The parents were Catholic and they knew me. We stayed awake with them for the night vigil's prayer. I led the prayers with the rosary without the crucifix. Most of us tried to use formal and traditional prayers to assist the mourning couple. There was nothing else we could do. I believe that in their time of grief the young couple recognized that although the people came from different religious backgrounds, they all share their loss. Death's bitterness was tasted by all of us.

From the beginning of the trip I had been treated like the boat's captain. The passengers knew the small group of seven of us. They treated each of us with trust and had confidence in us. We were seminarians and because of this honor we had the privilege to give comfort to the faithful and to all of them. They felt very bad to see me cry. I knew I had to be strong to pull all of us together. It seemed we approached closer to the door of death. We needed to walk through this door to come to new life. Some of the people could not sit against the sides of the boat any longer. Not only were they weak, but their bones hurt from sitting in the same seat. They had to lie down next to each other. Children now lay on top of their parents' weakened bodies. They hoped to rest and while they were at rest a miracle would happen. Some people asked me if they could urinate into a cup so that the children could drink from this. We had water from the night of the rainstorm, but it was so salty. Most of us hung on without drinking. We fell exhausted and we fell into sleep. The rest of my friends took turns controlling the boat and its sail. We kept heading toward the morning star.

As the sun rose the wind became stronger and we became more concerned about balancing the boat. We began to worry about losing the blanket, our sail, so we took it down. When the wind blew stronger and made the boat lean, the people moved slowly from side to side so we could maintain our balance. They were physically very tired and weak and this movement became more and more difficult. Still, they had to move back and forth to keep the boat balanced.

My friends and I had had some experience sailing the boat in strong winds and we were able to reassure the people. We wouldn't sink the boat or roll it over. We told everyone not to be so nervous because we knew how to sail. I assured everyone that these strong winds might make it possible to land somewhere soon. After a while, they got over being nervous because they were so weak and had little care about what was going on around them. They were also depressed because of the boys' bodies, which were still in their midst.

I gathered my friends together and told them, "I think we need to bury these two young boys." I was afraid that since everyone was so hungry someone might decide to cook and eat them. They agreed and asked me to talk to the parents about the burial. When I talked to them I told them it was time for us to bury these young boys. They cried, but gave permission to bury their sons. I said, "Let us gather together to pray for our deceased brothers."

I intoned the prayer and we released the bodies into the ocean. The bodies just flip-flopped on the top of the big waves as we sailed away. It was so sad. I was holding both parents in my arms. I couldn't find any words to say to them. I just kept holding them up until the bodies of their young sons sank out of sight. I knew at that moment, I needed to stand still so that I could hold them in my arms. I wanted them to have the last vision of their loved ones before they sank into the ocean. Later on when I thought of it and envisioned a weak young man was trying to help two sorrowful individuals, I didn't know how I did it. God's grace strengthened me.

After the burial we took our positions in silence. Many questions remained in our minds and hearts. What were the lessons for us to learn in all of these events? What shall be done? What would happen next? Would we reach dry land?

I think about the miracle of Peter walking on the water when he wanted to come to Jesus. His love and desire to meet Jesus were so strong he was able to walk on water. When Peter saw the big high waves and strong winds he was afraid and faltered. In his fear Peter shouted, "Master save me," and Jesus stretched out his arms and lifted him up. That was a good story to read, a nice dream to have, but at this moment I didn't think about those stories. I thought how sad it is for these two young boys. They didn't have a chance to grow and live their lives with parents and friends and play childhood games. In my heart I believed God gave the gift of love and life to all, to these children and especially to this young couple. They gave up everything to seek freedom. Now these children have died. The young mother gave me a good lesson about trusting in God's providence. She mourned and grieved because of all that had happened to her. She had twice been the victim of pirates and then she lost her two sons. Still, the mother kept saying two things. "The Lord gives and the Lord takes away." Then she whispered in her broken voice, "Lord, take care of my children."

That is all she said and that is all I remember. I thanked God for her faith, but I didn't say anything to her for I believed she had found peace in her heart. Frankly, I could not distinguish how I was supposed to feel. Should I feel angry? Should I feel sad? Should I feel frightened? Should I put all my faith and hope in God? I didn't have any problem putting my faith and hope in God, but at that moment

I was blank. All I knew was I was crying with these young parents.

I could see a new image, a new meaning of immersion at the celebration of the sacrament of baptism. The bodies of these young boys sank into the ocean as they died for their former life. I believed they would very soon experience new life in God's kingdom. In the water of baptism, we buried our sins in the death of Jesus Christ so we could rise up with Christ's resurrection into a newness of life as God's children. The death of the young children didn't make me happy at all. I knew God would take care of these two boys in the newness of life in heaven. Still, I was totally shocked. Many different questions crossed my mind. I wondered about the purpose of human life. The emotions were overwhelming. I remember that the young couple got heavy in my arms as they learned on me. At least I was there with them.

CHAPTER TWENTY

He Is Hidden

The twelfth day was quiet. Around two o'clock in the afternoon I had to relax. I asked my friends, "Have any of you seen my cassock and my breviary?"

I didn't recall seeing them since I got on the boat. It was the first time I had been without them for so long. I remember placing them together in a nylon bag and rolling the breviary inside my cassock.

After a while, one of the young girls said, "Here Brother Quang, I think this is yours."

Indeed, it was the nylon bag. I took it to the rear of the boat and dried them under the burning sun. They were soaking wet. My prayer book was almost destroyed, but somehow it was still readable. As I unfolded my cassock, my hand touched something hard under the cloth.

It was a small metal box used to hold hosts of the Eucharist to give communion to the homebound. I thought to myself as I opened the pix, "Oh my Lord, I believe I still have some Hosts in here!" My old pastor gave me the pix during my first year of theology so I could bring communion to the sick and the homebound. It was beautiful and well made. It had a symbol of the Eucharist with bread and wine on the cover, with the cross connecting them together. I hoped the water had not damaged the Hosts. I felt so guilty as I said quietly, "I am sorry Lord Jesus I had forgotten You were with us."

I remember that after I finished giving communion to the sick I would bring the extra Hosts back to the tabernacle in the church. On the way back to the church I put the Hosts in a little inside pocket of my cassock, near my heart. I didn't have a chance to place the

Hosts back in the tabernacle because the mass of the evening was not over yet. While I was waiting for the end of the mass, my friend picked me up with his motorcycle for our escape. I completely forgot that I had the Eucharist with me. I took my cassock and breviary with me. I rolled them up and put them in a nylon bag. When I reached the boat, I placed my nylon bag in a corner of the engine cabin, where, I totally forgot about it. My hand was shaking as I tried to open the pix. I couldn't believe I still had the Body of Christ with us. I hoped it wasn't destroyed. I prayed, "Oh my Lord Jesus, forgive me, for I didn't know you were with me."

I pushed the button on the pix and the cover popped open. My heart leapt in joy as I saw six small Hosts.

I called my friends and said, "I still have six small Hosts of the Body of Christ in my pix. Can you believe it? Let us do the Holy Hour together."

The eyes of my friends lit up and they shouted at me, "Are you kidding? Do you still have the Body of Christ?"

I explained how it had gotten on the boat and asked them, "What are we going to do with this?"

One of my friends answered, "Save it and maybe before sunset we can gather together and have a communion service."

We announced our plans to the people. It was astonishing news to all. I held the pix close to my heart for a moment, then put it back into the little protective pocket of my cassock. I kept all of these precious things close to me from that time on. When I took a little nap I held them on my chest.

I couldn't believe that the good Lord was still providing his presence and support in the presence of the Holy Eucharist. He had hidden in the midst of all the events that took place. It was the first time I could allow myself to have a little bit of joy.

A joyful feeling sprang from the depth of my heart. This was the first time in twelve days I had a light feeling of joy. A light of joy and hope began to shine forth again.

I don't recall how long I slept, but finally my friends woke me up.

The sun was just about to slip below the horizon and the surface of the sea was relatively calm. The wind was not really strong but strong enough for us to go on with our journey. I thought to myself, "This is the most beautiful picture that I have ever seen in my life."

I had seen many sunsets before, but I had never had any feelings about a sunset like that evening. It was because of the presence of Jesus in the Eucharist. I let go of the bad feelings about what happened to us in the last few days to focus on the future. I was beginning to understand the greeting at Mass, "The Lord be with you." The presence of these people and love of God was evidence enough to convince me of the presence of Jesus in the Eucharist.

We gathered together to celebrate the communion service. Even though we came from different religious backgrounds we gathered in prayer to receive the divine grace and nourishment. When the people had gathered together I announced, "I have six small hosts of the Body of Christ. We are going to pray that God will lead us into the land of freedom."

Everyone attended this prayer service. Even those lying on the floor asked others to help them sit up so they could respect the Lord. What a sign of reverence! Even in their poor physical condition, they were eager to attend the communion service. Even those who were not Catholic showed their respect to the Eucharist. They were hungry for the food of life. It was so touching. Those psalms of hope had never made so much sense or touched me so deeply as they did that night. It was December so we were celebrating the Advent season.

"Rejoice! Daughters of Jerusalem, rejoice! Behold your King has come in his vindication." I said to the people, "Rejoice in this moment of hope. The fear and doubt and uncertainty of suffering has ensnared us. Our future will be illuminated by the light of Christ to guide our feet into God's way. He will be nourishing us with the Body of Christ, the word of the Father.

I held the Eucharist in my hand and after the Prayer of the Faithful when we said the Lord's Prayer, then I raised high the Host and proclaimed, "Behold this is the Lamb of God who takes away the sins of the world. Happy are we who are called to his supper." My hand was shaking. I felt weaker and weaker, but the emotion was so strong it touched every nerve in my body. I had never held the Body of Christ so peacefully and so gratefully.

Some of the people were not Catholic. They said, "Brother Quang, can we receive the Host, too?"

I explained to them about the meaning of the real presence of Jesus and shared with them why they did not have to receive the Body of Christ physically, but were more than welcome to join with us in prayer. I declared, "This is the Body of Christ, His real presence. Do you believe that?"

Each one said, "I do."

It was the greatest "Amen" I ever heard. In my mind the sound of organs played the song of communion. We were about to receive the divine nourishment of the Body and Blood of Christ, food for the pilgrimage.

After we received communion, there was a most solemn silence of prayer. I thanked God for his love and the precious gift of His only Son. I said to myself, "Forgive me Lord but I cannot deny my people's needs." I asked my friend to help me break the six small Hosts into fifty-two pieces. There was just a little tiny piece of Host for each one of us. When I presented the Body of Christ, the faithful received it with great reverence. We looked up from the depths of darkness and saw the light of Christ shining forth. From that time, I knew we were going to make it. The presence of Christ was among us.

I wondered why it took me so long to remember that Christ is always among us? I had been distracted with so many things. I realized that without God we couldn't survive. Truly indeed, the mighty hands of God had protected us. The cry of our voices, in our need and desperation, had been heard by the Lord and the Lord had answered. He answered us in the presence of the Body and Blood of Christ.

Before the Blessed Sacrament was found, the presence of the Host was lost among the people's suffering. It reminded me that

Jesus emptied himself and shared our humanity to deliver us from our fear and sinfulness.

Later in life, as I recall the memories of that afternoon, I believe that moment really helped me to understand that Jesus emptied Himself and became one of us. Even though He lived among us without sin. He suffered with us. Truly indeed He is Lord of all forevermore.

Also, I believed that Jesus was and is always present in the tabernacle. How many of us really think that the Lord Jesus is really there? When I was in the seminary, I learned that St. John Vianey, the great patron saint of the priesthood, who loved to celebrate the sacrament of reconciliation, would cry out each time he passed the chapel, "Jesus is there, and He is really there!" He always adored the Blessed Sacrament in dialogue and prayer. I began to have a deeper appreciation for the lives of the saints and the tremendous devotion that the saints of the Church had toward the Eucharist. I began to understand the precious presence of the Lord in the Blessed Sacrament and in the lives of our brothers and sisters.

Truly, indeed, we should appreciate the blessing of the saints in our lives. Their faith is written in their hearts from the beginning of their lives. We can recognize how beautiful and holy a human being is called to be. We are called to be Christlike for we were created in God's image. For me, people are eager to know God's will for them so that they live accordingly. We hope that we can become a person of Christ in words and in deeds. "In persona Christi," is what we are called to be. By God's love and mercy we learn to give and to live freely as children of God and as a person of Christ in all we say and do.

I needed to learn that lesson. I understood that, but it never made more sense than at the moment we adored the Eucharist on the boat. There were Buddhists, nonbelievers, and Catholics. These people reminded me that God's children have many ways to express their faith. They honored their ancestors, they honored Buddha, but they loved and worshipped Christ Jesus. We were all in the same boat, all in the same world created by God's love.

I always feel very blessed to know my God in and through the person of Jesus Christ. It is much easier to have a real person to relate too. We already perceive ourselves as God's children, baptized in the fire and in the Spirit. Each of us has the right to live as God's children, to receive eternal life because the Son of God, Jesus Christ, died for us. It is up to us to accept God's love and live it in our daily lives.

After the prayer service and communion, we closed with a final prayer. The people were filled with hope and trust in God's love and mercy for them. For me, it was a sincere trust that people have in an invisible God they cannot see. All we could see was the real presence of Jesus in the lives of our sisters and brothers. I intoned the blessing, "May the Lord bless us, protect us from all harm and evil, and bring us to the everlasting life." I made a sign of the cross with the words, "In the name of the Father, and the Son, and the Holy Spirit." I felt good even though I knew the journey might have more difficulties to come. I wasn't afraid anymore.

It was the first time some of these people had been blessed in this way. They watched what I did, then made the sign of the cross, too. This was the most beautiful thing that people had done for me. We are all God's children even though we come from different religions and cultures. So many people have not heard about Jesus Christ as the Son of God. They never have heard about the Good News of Jesus Christ. On the boat, this very evening, a few had an opportunity to recognize the presence of God and who God is for them.

"God the Father loved the world so much that He gave His only son to be the savior of the world." This was the Son of God, present with us in the small pieces of sacred bread we broke and shared with one another, just as Jesus had done at the Last Supper. "Do this in memory of me." For me, this is an imperative order that must be done in our lives.

The rest of the night went pretty well. The weather was mild and the wind was calm. This was the first time that I paid attention to the rhythm of the big ocean waves as they touched the boat. It was like a song. Tonight, at the gathering we had been enlightened with the light of God's love and of one another. We were one with nature's beauty on the surface of the ocean. Together, we had a most beautiful and prayerful communion service.

The water, the boat, the wind, and the big waves performed a musical rhythm. The waves created a series of notes, like a harmonious piece of music. I kept it in my mind. I wanted soft music, with a series of notes, up and down in its movement like the waves of the ocean. It was a rhythm of our lives. For me, a song is a composition to express one's heart. It is a series of events of our lives, whether in good or bad, to express our emotions. It was written to give thanks and praise to God. The sanctuary in the heart of people is beautiful enough for God to enter. In one's heart is a connection between heaven and earth, a place for each individual to meet his or her God.

The day passed peacefully. We didn't know where or when we would be rescued, but we were hopeful. We knew it would happen. It was what we hoped and prayed for. It seemed we had had a whole day of retreat after having found and consumed the Holy Eucharist. We were able to recall God's love and strength. We knew God would help us, and deliver us from all harm and evil.

St. Paul wrote, "It is in our weakness that we find God's strength." I believed that only in God would my soul be at rest. When I was younger I never thought about it, even in time of war when I experienced death and suffering. I couldn't deny that God's strength was with us to help us to survive. Now and then, we get frustrated as we live in the chaos of our life. Sometimes, we don't know how to sort our feelings out. The lack of order distresses us, and in those times God provides us with his Holy Spirit. It serves as a reminder to us, "Do not be afraid for I am with you always until the end of the world."

How could God be with us, with every single human being on this earth until the end of time? That is the truth of the celebration of the Holy Eucharist and the sacraments. In the ministry of pastoral care we experienced the presence of God in many ministries, whether in works of charity or a life of prayer, we remind each other that God's presence is among us. He is in our midst even in the moment of suffering and death. The moment of death transforms us into eternal life. The line between life and death as I have experienced is very thin. We have to keep in our heart the desire to recognize God's presence in our daily lives so that we are faithful to God's promise until the end.

Chapter Twenty-One

A New Voice

The afternoon of the thirteenth day passed by just fine until about six o'clock in the evening. Suddenly, we heard a women cry out, "Please help me, help me!" I heard the voice and said, "Oh my goodness, did someone die?"

I forced myself to move from the back of the boat. I tried to push people aside so I could walk through. The people could hardly move any more. Occasionally, I stepped on the leg or hand of someone. All I could say was, "I am sorry, I am so sorry."

When I came down to the base of the boat. I asked people in a loud voice, "What has happened? Who are you? Where are you? Keep talking so I can find you.

People were lying on the floor of the boat, as zombies, due to the lack of food. Finally, I reached a young lady who was pregnant. I asked her, "What has happened?"

She said, "I think my baby is coming, my water has broken."

I thought to myself, "Oh no, no way!" Not now! But, I asked her anyway, "Are you serious? Do you really have to give birth now? Who are you with? Are there any relatives or friends with you?"

She replied, "My husband is with me."

"Where is he?"

She said, "He is right here, but he has been unconscious since yesterday."

"Oh no!" I replied. "What can I do to help you?"

I managed to find a space to sit down next to her. She held my hand and said, "I need fresh air. I have to get out of here."

I asked people to move aside. I had to push them aside to make room for this young woman. Then, I took her hands and helped her sit up. She needed to get away from the others lying on the floor of the boat. Little by little, we moved very slowly to the back of the boat. Two of my friends helped pull her up from the base of the boat. She was quite young, in her twenties. We managed to make a little room at the rear of the boat for her to lie down.

Definitely, this was the first time I had experienced a woman in labor. I didn't know what to do to help her. I learned many subjects in the seminary but nobody taught us how to help people in labor. It was scary! She seemed to be in great pain. I murmured to myself, "Oh man! It is the wrong time, the wrong person, and the wrong place!" I asked my friends to help, but they didn't have any experience with this either.

I said to her, "Hang in there, my sister. Hang in there. You are almost at the rear of the boat. You are going to have some fresh air. By the way, do you have any experience with this?"

She looked at me in her great pain, "No. This is my first baby." I was terrified. Her painful expression made me very nervous. I said to myself, "Calm down, Quang. Think! Think!"

Of course, I had no time to think about basic biology. I had no idea how to help this expectant mother. What was I going to do? After I laid the lady down on the floor, she rested for a while. I was very tired and weak. I went down to the base of the boat and I asked everyone, "Is there anyone with experience in delivering a baby?" I was eager to find someone to help me to deliver the baby.

There was no answer. I asked my friends, "Do you guys remember anything about CPR or anything at all from the books about human biology and maternity? How are we going to help this lady?"

I was afraid that if we didn't have anyone to help this woman she probably would die. My friends looked at each other and answered, "Hey, Quang, we were in the same classes as you. You know very well that we didn't study about maternity."

Again, I asked the people in the boat, "Can any of you help this lady?"

They just looked at me and kept shaking their heads and shrugging their shoulders. They replied, "Sorry, we can't help you. The only thing that we can do is to pray for her."

I thought to myself, "Sure! This is great! All they can do is to pray! This is not fun—not fun at all."

I thought, "Well if there is no one to help her, I'll do my best. Before I do, let me ask the others again."

So, I went back to the base of the boat. One by one I asked all the people, "Are you a nurse? Are you a midwife? Are you a doctor?" Each one of them responded, "Not me."

At last, I came to an older woman in a corner of the boat. She woke up and learned that I needed her help to deliver a baby. She told me that, a long time ago, she had been a midwife in a small village. She said, "I have delivered babies before, but I don't know what I can do to help you in my condition. I am so weak I cannot even lift my arms."

I took a deep breath to relieve my anxiety. I said to her, "Don't worry! I will take you to the rear of the boat so you can lie next to her. You will have to tell me what to do. I can use your experience to help this young lady. Would you mind doing that?"

She blinked her eyes, "I would be delighted to do so, but I don't know how much I can do."

I assured her, "Don't worry! We will work it out. We will work it out."

That was what I kept telling myself as I helped her to move to the rear of the boat. WE WILL WORK IT OUT.

I was thinking, "Quang, you must be crazy. You don't know what you are doing. You should let this happen naturally."

I didn't know what to feel. It was an ordinary event under extraordinary circumstances. I didn't know if I was supposed to cry or laugh. All I wanted was to help her the best I could. In the midst of my personal frustrations, this poor expectant woman grasped my arms and cried out, "It hurts! It really hurts!"

In her pain, she called the names of her God, her parents, her husband, her brothers and sisters. Her fingernails dug into my skin. Yes, I was hurting, too.

"Are you in your full term?"

She opened her mouth wide to breathe, "No. I'm in my eighth month."

I thought to myself, "Oh no. She doesn't have any experience either."

The Boy Scouts had not prepared me to deliver a baby, but at least they had trained me in CPR. I realized that if she fell into unconsciousness, in her weakened condition, it would be very dangerous for her and the baby. She would probably die, and if she died the baby would probably die, too. The more I thought of the possible outcome, the more worried I became.

After the two encounters with pirates, we had nothing left on the boat. We didn't have any knives. We didn't have any scissors. We didn't have tools that would be helpful if I had to perform an operation to save a baby. What if she was so weak she was unable to push? What if she passed out? Then what should I do?

I asked one of my friends to help. I was on her right side and one of my friends was on the left. We pushed her up and down so that she could breathe and push. I didn't know how long it was supposed to take from the time a mother's water broke until a baby would be born safely.

My friend wasn't able to help her to sit up and down. He was very tired. I asked him to find a blanket and other clothes to make a pillow. I didn't know that a woman in labor could endure such physical pain. I began to appreciate my mother and other mothers. They surely endured great pain for us to be born. I knew for sure, if I tried to help her, I would spend all the energy left in my body. If I didn't help her, I might last long enough to be rescued by someone. The thought crossed my mind, but it made me angry, "Quang, you have to be ashamed of yourself. You cannot be so selfish. You cannot think like that."

I asked God to forgive me for such a selfish thought. I felt much better because I made up my mind to help this expectant mother no matter what happened to me.

Definitely, there was a sense of fear and a feeling of reluctance to get involved in helping this lady. I was reluctant to help her because I had no experience. I wanted to do things I had experience in so that I could do them with confidence. I wanted to be able to trust myself, to know exactly what I was doing. I was fearful because I didn't know how long this process would take. I didn't know for sure if the newborn baby could survive. It was really a great risk. I didn't really want to be responsible. These were the things that were going through my mind. I said to myself, "What am I to do in an emergency like this?"

The midwife was able to keep herself awake, but she had no energy to lift her arms to help me. I asked, "What are we to do first?"

The woman said, "We need to have clean, hot water and clean towels."

I took one of the cooking pots and threw some old fabric into it and soaked it with diesel fuel. I laid two iron bars across the pot of fire. I set a second pot filled with water on top of the iron bars to heat up the seawater. It was very salty and although it got hot I couldn't make it boil.

The midwife was with the expectant mother. She cried more frequently and intensively. She twisted and thrashed. Her pain seemed worse than before. I knew that whatever happened, I must keep her awake. We struggled for quite a while. The moon was up, but was dark because of the clouds. It was about ten o'clock at night. It was like camping with the fire from the diesel pot.

She was getting tired. Her crying was softer than before. I had to be alert to make sure that she didn't pass out. We didn't have any clean towels on board so I took some shirts and put them in the hot cook pot. I drained the shirts and hung them on the little cabin to dry. It seemed like everything was ready.

Around two o'clock that next morning, the expectant mother's pain became more frequent. She pushed harder and harder. The time of delivery had come.

The midwife told me what to do. I was completely ignorant. "Do I have to do that? Do I have to do this?" she yelled at me often.

I encouraged the new mother, "One more try. Breathe in deep. Just have one more push."

In fact, I was more scared than she was. She struggled to push for a while. Finally, the baby's head appeared, so soft and so small. I thought to myself, "Oh my goodness! I never saw such a wonderful thing in my life." A new human being was about to be born into the world. A baby, with God's blessing, is the fruit of love and life of the parents. It was truly a miracle of love and life.

The birth of a baby on the boat was completely awesome; terrifying, but awesome. The baby was a gift of new hope in the midst of our hopeless situation. It was terrifying because when that little baby was about to be born the midwife told me, "You have to pull the baby out. You have to pull the baby out. Quickly, but gently."

So I did. When my hands touched the baby's head it felt like an electric shock went through my body. It was an amazing feeling I was holding the gift of love and life in my hands.

Finally, I said to the mother, "You've got a girl. It's a baby girl." I was crying tears of joy.

I laid the baby girl on the mother's chest. I had to cut the umbilical cord. This was a problem. I couldn't tear it with my fingernails. I didn't dare bite it off either. I asked the midwife, "How do I do this?"

The midwife smiled and said, "You will need to use something sharp and clean to cut it."

I responded, "We have nothing. There are neither knives nor scissors." I showed her our hatchet, "Can I use this?"

Her eyes opened wide, "Oh my God! I guess we have to use it."

I put the hatchet in the hot water to clean it. I placed the umbilical cord on the floor of the boat and I cut it. Next, the midwife told me to tie the umbilical cord for both the mother and baby.

I got a little thread from my shirt. I carefully placed it into the heated water, then used it to tie the umbilical cord for both the baby and the mother. I let the mother rest for awhile. She was very tired, but she seemed all right. I place the baby girl in my shirt and brought her to the side of the boat to clean her up with seawater.

The midwife told me, "You have to turn the baby upside down. Clean the inside of her mouth so she cries. That will help her breathe."

I replied, "You must be kidding, right? My finger is bigger than her mouth. I don't want to hurt her."

"Just do what I said!"

I murmured to myself, "Yes, Madame!" What a lady! But, I did what she told me.

I had to change the water in the container several times to clean the baby up. Finally, the baby cried. Her crying gave me back all the energy I spent in the delivery. I was so glad that she was born unto us. I wrapped the baby in the shirt and laid her right in her mother's arms. The little girl opened her eyes. Her tiny mouth kept open, as she wanted to be nursed. She cried. She gave us hope.

I checked on the mother. She seemed to be asleep, or maybe she was unconscious. I needed to wake her up so that I could help her to clean up. Also, I wanted to make sure she was all right. She woke up and the first thing she wanted was to see her baby. It was a moment full of joy and love. The mother asked me if I would baptize her baby, for she was afraid that her baby and all of us wouldn't make it. In this case of emergency I was honored to do that. My friends attended. They were very weak by now. Some of them lay on the floor. Others sat against the wall of the pilot's room. I filled up a container with seawater. We celebrated the sacrament of baptism with joy. I asked the mother to give her baby's baptism name. She did not hesitate to name her after St. Catherine (of Siena) for it was the mother's baptism name, also. After making the renunciation of sin, we made the profession of faith. Then, I baptized the baby girl by pouring water on her forehead while saying the formula of baptism, "Catherine, I baptize you, in the name of the Father and of the Son and of the Holy Spirit."

We then said the Lord's Prayer together to thank God for giving this baby girl a new life in Christ.

After the baptism I asked one of my friends to hold the baby while I helped the mother to clean up. Then, I wrapped her and her newborn with a filthy blanket. Both of them lay down against the wall of the pilot's room to rest. I kept looking at the baby girl's face. She seemed such a fragile little human being. She was so tiny and so soft. I realized how fragile and precious each one of us is. She moved her hands, her arms, and her little legs in her mother's arms. I didn't know how to hold her. I thought if I made a wrong move, she might get hurt. Still, there we were. I had a precious human being in my arms.

After I placed the little girl in her mother's arms, I tied a rope around my waist and jumped into the sea for a bath. I had blood all over me. I laughed at the fact I was taking a full bath at two o'clock in the morning in the ocean. I drifted along with the boat and cleaned myself from head to toe. Suddenly, I felt a fish come up and bite at my leg. This certainly scared me and I thought, "Oh no! I hope it's not a shark."

The moonlight lit up the surface of the ocean, but it was still dark in the shadow of the boat. I didn't know if there were any sharks around the boat because I hadn't seen any in the last twelve days. When you are touched by an unknown creature in the ocean, you get scared. Was I ever in a hurry to pull myself back to the boat! I was terrified and told my friends that a fish tried to eat me. My friends had a good laugh. They told me it was not a good idea to get into the water in the moonlight because that was when the fish would be around looking for food. I didn't believe what they told me, but I had a good laugh, too. In fact, at the delivery of the newborn baby, I still had bloody shirts. I could use it to catch fish. I asked my friends, "How can we catch some of those fish?"

We didn't have anything, except one clothes hanger. It hung inside the engine room. I thought I could use this as a hook to fish. I used the hatchet to press one end and make it sharp enough to hook the fish. I tied another end with a cord. I wrapped the sharp end with part of a bloody shirt as bait and put it into the water. I hoped that if a fish swallowed it I might have a chance to catch him. Otherwise, the hook wasn't strong enough to hold the fish. Suddenly, a fish hit the hook and we struggled back and forth and finally I pulled it into our boat. I couldn't believe I could catch a fish with such tools. When the fish swallowed the hook it went right into his stomach and the fish was not able to get off the hook. I caught a second fish. They were about ten pounds each.

I used the little hatchet to kill the fish and chop it into pieces. We put them in the cooking pot without any water. I tried to steam the fish to avoid the salt from the seawater. We cooked it for a while. When my friend took off the cover we found the food smelled very fishy. Still, I distributed it to the people to eat. Some of us could eat the fish, but some were unconscious. I caught the fish too late.

I was especially concerned for the new mother. I woke her up and tried to feed her. She didn't want to eat, but I told her she had to eat so she could take care of her newborn.

"You have no choice. You have to eat and live to take care of your baby!"

Her eyes opened wide as I mentioned her baby. She began to eat. I fed her slowly, a small piece at a time. While she was chewing, I ate some fish, too. I was very hungry. I thought I could eat a whole cow at that moment.

After the fish was cooked and distributed, I realized it was still possible to continue to make drinking water by collecting water vapor from the rainwater. I thought this would be a lot better because it would not be so salty. My friend made some fresh water for the newborn.

After the woman was fed, she tried to sit up. She asked, "Can I see my baby?"

I told her that she was already in her arms. I helped her sit up against the side of the pilot room.

The moon reappeared in the sky. The moonlight was gentle and clear. One side of the boat was totally dark, but the mother sat on the side that was full of moonlight. She was exhausted and looked like a zombie, but when she saw her little girl, she had the most beautiful smile for her child. It seemed like she had forgotten all of the hardship, but her little baby girl. She bent down as she lifted her little baby to her face to give it a kiss. I thought that was a beautiful picture to describe the meaning of love and life. It was like the beautiful image of Blessed Virgin Mary and the Baby Jesus in the Christmas manger. This Christmas season we celebrated with the Advent's preparation to see God's face. I thought of Christmas day. There were only a few more days to go. I wished my family, my community, my friends and all a blessed one.

Every year at Christmas we celebrate the feast of Jesus, the only Son of God, being born into the world. The Prince of Peace brought joy to the whole world. I thought of this newborn, this little baby girl, being born in the midst of our hopelessness and frustration, in the midst of the power of death. For the sake of this tiny baby girl and others in the boat I had to go on, to see the land of freedom. I had to survive. I sat there and looked at the baby. "You are so beautiful," was all I could say.

The mother seemed to be getting better. She asked me to name her daughter and I named her with the combination of her parents' last names, Tran-Hoang. Her first name was Nguyet-Mac. In Vietnamese, her name means "A girl who dresses with beautiful moonlight." She looked gorgeous.

I prayed, "Thank You Lord, that in the midst of death, in the midst of frustration, and hardship, You are always with us. In Your kindness You give me a sign of hope. The baby is born to be a sign of new vision and a light in the darkness of our lives. Lord, I can see your presence is among us in the presence of this newborn. Thank You Lord for Your love and life."

I sat there to observe the baby as she opened and closed her eyes. Her mouth kept making a little noise as if she was going to be nursed. I gave the mother a couple of teaspoons of fresh water we had just made. She stuck her finger into the small cup of water and dropped the water into the mouth of her child. The little tiny mouth opened and drank the water. I kept encouraging the woman to eat the fish because I had read in a book that after a mother gives birth, if she had enough nutrition, she would produce milk to nurse her baby. I wondered in this case if the new mother could do it or not. They seemed to enjoy the moment with each other.

I tried to get a little rest and my friends did the same. Normally, we did two-hour shifts, but we were not able to stay awake that long and our shifts were reduced to an hour. We continued to take turns. None of us had enough energy to drive the boat for long anymore. We knew how weak we were, but we didn't say it aloud. The wind blew softly and the boat drifted along. The sail was still in good condition.

I had a little doubt before helping the woman deliver her baby that we would be able to survive. Now, I didn't think that God would allow the baby to die with us. This was not the theology of God's love I had learned. How could God allow this baby to die? If God in his holiness and goodness gave this baby a chance to survive, then we all would survive. I believe that God would deliver us from all harm. I fell asleep giving thanks to God for allowing me to witness a miracle.

CHAPTER TWENTY-TWO

Thirteen Is Not an Unlucky Number

Early the next morning, the wind picked up. The waves slapped loudly on the side of the boat and I woke up. I was very hungry and thirsty. I had eaten a lot of fish meat that night. How come I was still hungry? I prayed, "Oh God, if I have only one wish before I die, I would like a big cup of fresh lemonade, like my grandmother used to make for me. Then I will die in peace."

I knew I was losing control of my vision and the ability to think. I tried to stand up, but my legs were shaking. I held on to the wall to stand. My hands touched the dew on the roof of the pilot cabin. I tasted it. It was salty.

"O God, don't let me die like this. Let me have a cup of water before I die."

The reality was we were still in the middle of nowhere. We needed to land somewhere soon. Otherwise we would die.

I was getting a little worried. The people seemed quieter than yesterday. I checked on the new mother. I woke her up to make sure she was not unconscious. I asked her if she would like to see her husband. Some of us had gone to the bow of the boat to bring him to her. She was eager to see him.

We took off the canopy that covered the boat. We needed fresh air and sunshine. I tried to walk carefully among the people. Many of them needed to clean up. Everyone needed nourishment, but for now we had to keep them awake. If they fell into unconsciousness I thought that they would never wake up again. We gave them clean seawater to wash their faces. We cleaned up the floor of the boat. We bailed the dirty water out and used fresh seawater to wash the floor.

I had to sit at the back of the boat and hold my knees. I had a tremendous will to survive. I kept fighting to not give up because I couldn't accept failure.

I had become the leader of these people during the past twelve days and I could not allow myself to show any sign that I was about to give up. They could see how tired and weak I felt, but I wouldn't give up until we found land. They seemed weaker than I was. I began to realize that I was probably in better physical condition because I was always at the rear of the boat. I always had fresh air and had not been forced to breathe putrid air and diesel fumes.

As the sun rose and the heat increased I, too, became weaker and weaker. Whenever I tried to walk my legs trembled. I became distressed that I, too, was being seriously affected by the hardships and lack of food and water.

I made sure we were still steaming the water vapor for the new baby. It was hard for us to complete this process. It took us all day to make enough water to fill two small cups. We distributed it very carefully to the children first. Luckily, we still had a few containers of diesel fuel to heat the seawater. We planned to burn more at night in case some good people on boats would see us. It was a little ray of hope we had left.

It reminded me of the pillar of fire in the story of Exodus. The people of Israel walked in the direction of a pillar of fire at night. During the day it was a pillar of the cloud. With the presence of God in these forms, Moses led the people of Israel to the Promised Land. Moses looked up to see the pillar of clouds, and knew that God was there. But, that was in the story of Exodus. Here, in the middle of the ocean we had nothing, but each other and the fire. The fire warmed us and served as an emergency signal.

The thirteenth day was not exciting. As the day progressed the mother began to express her concern that the baby needed more water or milk. I suggested that she should try to breast-feed her baby.

She did. The baby eventually stopped crying, but I honestly don't know if the mother had milk or not. I didn't know how to ask her.

With each passing hour, I felt weaker and weaker and weaker. I asked my friends to take over steering and to wake me up when they got tired. They couldn't do any better. We were all about to collapse. I didn't think I could control the sail and the boat any longer without some rest. I needed a little rest.

I crawled to a little place in the corner of the boat and made a pillow with my cassock and prayer book. It was about noon and I felt so weak. I said to myself, "C'est fini." I didn't mean to say what Jesus said, "It is finished," just before He died on the crucifix.

I fell into a deep sleep. My eyes closed and my ears shut down. Just before I fell asleep I heard the baby's crying. I could see my friends trying to get comfortable. We had released the rope that controlled the sail because none of us had the power or energy left to direct the boat. None of us could stay awake. Little by little we fell into unconsciousness.

I still heard the baby's cry. It was strange because her cry made me smile when I said, "C'est fini."

The wind still blew. The ocean waves still splashed. The boat still rocked. Good-bye my loved ones! I fell into a deep sleep. I didn't wake up for the next couple of days. To the best of my knowledge the boat with license plate SS1037IA, with 53 people on board, was about to be lost in the Pacific Ocean. It was December 23, 1980.

I didn't know how long I lay there. When I woke up I heard the baby crying. I also heard someone speaking in a strange language. I thought to myself, "I am dead. Now I am in the other world."

I tried to open my eyes, but I believed that I was already dead and in the other world. I tried to move my arms and my legs and I realized there was somebody lying next to me. "Where am I?"

I started to check my senses. It seemed everything was working. I bit my tongue: It hurt. I pinched the skin on my thigh: It hurt. I still wondered, "Am I alive or am I dead?"

Finally, I opened my eyes and saw a friend of mine lying next to me. I recognized other people lying there with us on the sand of a beach. I figured we were on a small island and that we had landed by some miracle of faith. If I was alive then God must have had something to do with it.

I tried to stand up, but I fell on my knees. How come I felt like I was on the boat? The ground seemed to sway back and forth. It turned from left to right as if we were on the boat. I grabbed a handful of sand and brought it closer to my eyes.

I decided it was true that we were alive. There was life everywhere. The baby was still crying. My skin hurt. My mouth tasted the sand. There must be life in my physical body.

I screamed out loud, "I am alive, I AM ALIVE!" It was unbelievable. I didn't know where we were. I didn't care. I was so overjoyed to be alive. I called the names of my friends. No one answered my calls. I wondered if they were all right or not. Later, I heard someone call my name. Immediately, I recognized his voice. One by one, the members of our group regained their consciousness.

I began to wonder who rescued us and how we had gotten to this beach. There must be some explanation. When I tried to get up I could not stand. It had been a long time since we had given our legs any kind of exercise. We had to take time to get used to stable ground. We had grown accustomed to the swaying and bobbing of the boat. It took me several tries to get up and walk. I couldn't control myself. I kept falling down.

Eventually, some local people came to our group. They tried to speak to us. We couldn't understand what they said to us. We tried to speak among ourselves to find out who these people were. I guess they were the fishermen from a local village because I saw fishing boats and fishing gear along the beach. I tried to speak to the person who was in uniform. He was carrying a gun and a badge. His head was shaved clean. I thought it was an English style.

My friend tried to find out, "Where are we?" There was no response.

I spoke French to them and had better luck. The policeman

answered, "Malaysia, fishermen found you."

After this short conversation, we were escorted to the police station. We were held in the courtyard of the police station. They didn't talk to us much, "You all wait here!"

We had difficulty communicating with them in French, also. They seemed kind and gentle, but they didn't come near us. They were busy talking on the telephone.

The local islanders brought us all kinds of coconuts and food. They stood outside the fence of the police station and they threw food to us. We ate a little. It was hard to chew the old coconut patties. We drank its juice only.

The adults and children of the local community gathered around the fence to observe us. We probably looked pretty bad. Some of the children reached out to hand us food. They handed us little bits of coconut, rice cakes and fruit. We didn't understand what they said, but we saw their smiles and their gentleness and we felt that we were now safe.

The courtyard had a tall chain-link fence around it. It felt like a prison and I couldn't help thinking, "I have escaped from one prison only to be in another."

I hoped it was not true. None of us were able to speak English and I realize that English was the language that was being spoken to the officers. We had no choice but to wait.

We waited and waited. No one made any movement toward us. We ate the food the police provided for us and tried to rest. We checked each other. Some of our women and men were ill. The police brought these people to their local clinic for emergency treatment. Otherwise, we were all right.

From where I sat in the courtyard I could see a clock in the main police office. Around three in the afternoon, a little larger boat arrived and it was filled with police and a few ordinary people. A young woman introduced herself to me and spoke Vietnamese. She was Vietnamese. She was a boat person like us who was acting as a translator. She talked to the local policemen and told us what had happened: Early in the morning the local fishermen went out fishing. They found our little boat in their territorial waters. They had a big fishing boat. We were drifting with the wind. They approached us and got on our boat and there was no one awake. All they could hear was the little baby crying. We all were in terrible physical condition. They towed our little boat back to land when they recognized we were a group of Vietnamese refugees. They knew who we were because there had been many groups of escapees before us who had floated into their waters. They were so kind to rescue us. We were so lucky to be found.

The woman told us that the government of Malaysia had passed a law forbidding refugees from Vietnam. The present policy stated that if refugees arrived from Vietnam they would be nurtured, given food, water, and supplies and then be escorted back to international waters. They would be abandoned and have to find somewhere else to go. The Malaysian government did not want to be responsible for any more refugees in their country.

"Normally, you would have had to find another place to seek refuge," she said to us.

However, the villagers and local fishermen who were kind enough to drag us ashore were also clever enough to break the bottom of our boat by landing it on big rocks. They brought us to the beach and then contacted the police. It was set up that way to tell the local authorities we were lost and our boat had sunk. The local government had no alternative but to accept us as refugees. They contacted their main office in Kuala Lumpur, who in turn sent a boat to bring us to the refugee camp Pulau Tangah.

I could not express how very grateful I was to those villagers and fishermen. They offered us the most perfect hospitality and the goodness of the Lord. They were so thoughtful. We were brought to the police station because we were illegal immigrants. We had entered the country of Malaysia without proper papers and were considered illegal persons on Malaysian soil. We were granted asylum as Vietnamese refugees.

I had no idea what the rest of my life would be like. Still, I knew the people on my boat would begin a new life in a new situation filled with promise and excitement. It also involved a lot of fear and anxiety. The young translator explained that we were to be taken to a refugee camp about two hours away. This refugee camp was on another island. She mentioned this island held many refugees. She said that we were lucky to go to that main camp, Pulau Tangah. About 8,000 refugees already lived in the camp. We were free to walk around the island. She said it was a very nice island. She welcomed us and wished us well with our new life.

CHAPTER TWENTY-THREE

Joining Others for the New Journey

The United Nations boat brought us to the refugee camp named Pulau Tangah. On the way there, we looked at each other with joy. Finally, together we had made it. We lost two young boys, but had a newborn girl. A group of fifty-four people at the beginning of the journey were now fifty-three.

The police and the local fishermen brought us our personal belongings. I retrieved my cassock and breviary. That was all I had. They escorted us to the boat. On the way to the refugee camp we said good-bye to our own boat that embraced us for the entire trip. She was sinking and landed on the rocky beach. I looked the other way to hide my tears. She was faithful to her call. She did her job to bring us across the ocean. I closed my eyes to rest for a while, but my friends knew that I was in tears. I asked them to wake me up when we arrived to the camp.

About two hours later, I woke up because my people were screaming with joy as we approached the camp. From afar I could see a vast number of people on the beach. They were waiving at us with signs of welcome, "Welcome to Pulau Tangah! We're glad that you made it!"

The boat docked at the port for us to get off. Volunteers from the camp helped us walk to the center of camp. The whole refugee camp was decorated for Christmas. I asked one of the volunteers the date. He said, "It's 4:27 p.m., December 24th."

We were all brought to the detention area to live for a week. We needed to have all the necessary vaccines before they assigned us to live with others in the camp. Two Malaysian policemen and several Vietnamese men and women came into the barracks to search our personal belongings. They came to my bench and emptied my nylon bag. As they were unfolding my cassock one of the gentlemen asked me, "Are you the priest?" I shook my head, "No, I am not. I am a seminarian."

He continued, "We don't have any priest, seminarians, or sisters at all. The only seminarian we had transferred to another camp yesterday. We're looking for more religious people to help us."

I introduced my friends to them. They were happy to see all of us. One group after another came to the barracks to do their work on us. Around nine o'clock that night I had another guest. There he stood, Father Pierre Gauthier, my former professor from our seminary in Vietnam. He embraced me with a big joyful hug, "Oh la la! Pierre (my baptism name)!" Everyone woke up and wondered what was going with Brother Quang. He told me that he came in this evening from Kuala Lumpur and had just learned that a new group of refugees arrived in the camp, and there were some seminarians among them. He informed me that Father Petit Jean, another former professor, was with him as well. He wanted me to pack everything and go with him to the camp's parish hall and rectory. I would sleep there tonight. He would come back tomorrow to celebrate the Christmas Mass for the refugees. He didn't have permission to stay overnight in the refugee camp.

I was left alone in the parish center for the first night in the camp. I was overwhelmed. I couldn't believe that I had seen those priests again. They taught us in the seminary for many years. The communists expelled them from Vietnam after the fall of Saigon. They came to Malaysia for their missionary work.

Around 10 p.m. the choir and people gathered together for Christmas carols and the communion service. I didn't know that I had to do it for them. I was glad to see them all in the church and prayed with my brothers and sisters. They welcomed me with joy. It was my very first Christmas away from home. I couldn't believe that God gave me another chance to live, to love, and to serve Him again. It was evidence of God's love for me and for all.

Next morning, Christmas Day, Fathers Pierre Gauthier and Petit Jean arrived at the camp around nine o'clock. They celebrated Mass for us. I served them in Mass as a translator for the homily. I knew in my heart I had to give thanks and praise to God for the rest of my life, for God had saved me and delivered me from death. My friends joined me to serve people in the camp. We re-established ourselves with people of God in the camp. We all knew that someday we would depart from each other for new lives in other countries that accepted us, but for now, we made a home for one another. Thanks be to God!

After meeting with Father Petit Jean I accepted his invitation to serve the people as a leader for the Catholics in the refugee camp of Pulau Tangah, Malaysia, even though I was a young seminarian. There were about five thousand Catholics among twelve thousand refugees. We would be busy in pastoral work again. It seemed like the old days.

After the hard trip, my spirit, my physical and mental conditions were not back to normal. I needed to take time to rest and to grieve. I didn't have much time at all during the days, but at night, I walked along the beach to pray and to grieve. I missed home very much. Somehow, I was gaining back myself and still able to take the word of obedience to serve the people of God. It was my joy. It made me happy to serve the people in my own capacity. Even though we lost our names—the immigration office gave each of us an ID number for a name—the people in the camp and the people of my boat, whenever they needed me, still called me Brother Quang. The people who arrived at the camp before us had already formed different groups that included a youth group, Eucharist young adults, and many different kinds of services for all the people. I just took time to integrate myself into the life of the community.

At the beginning of the day we joined with the people for the morning communion service. They gathered together to pray the traditional prayers and worship from Vietnam. Many people came from different areas in Vietnam. However, we gathered together and began with the morning prayers, followed by the rosary. I concluded Morning Prayer with the communion service. We started with the ritual and distributed the communion, then went home to continue the routine of the day.

Father Petit Jean had expressed his wish that he wanted me to immigrate to France to continue my study in the seminary. He worked with the delegation from the French embassy to immigrate me to France. I agreed to go to France. For me, it was a better opportunity to continue my study for the priesthood. I began to review my French courses. I didn't take any class to study English at all. I had no clue I would end up in the United States. I made every effort to relearn French since this was where I thought I was going to be resettled. I even ended up teaching French to those families that had been designated to go to France.

I spent some time each day with the youth and made up a schedule for what we would be doing each day. We visited some of the poor people who had just lost their loved ones during the trip. We assisted children who needed special care. Some people had lost all their family members because of tragedies that took place during their escape. In some boats, only one or two people survived. We often shared with each other our own story of escape from Vietnam. We shared many stories of our journey. These people had been in the same situations that I had been through.

The three months that I spent in the refugee camp, Pulau Tangah, I would never forget, because this was a most beautiful people and a peaceful time for me. We were in the middle of the ocean surrounded by people who share a common background. We had all struggled for life and established a bond of faith together even though we arrived at the camp as total strangers. We accepted each other as brothers and sisters. I could identify with their sufferings because I had been there. I was one of them. I knew what made me become so close and be one with them. I could say to those suffering people, "I knew and I understand."

I was so blessed because I was given an opportunity to bring God's love, comfort, and healing to them. The spirit of my ancestors was with me and I became the fruit of their courage, faith, and tradition. I vested myself with Christ's love, with the kindness and generosity that people had shown me. Without people's generosity, kindness, and support from the beginning, I would never have come to this moment and my dream would never have come true. The people have showed me that God loves me very much. How? They showed me God's love in their own love, helping me to start a new life, the life of the ministry. I grieved, but I also looked forward to beginning my life again. I was able to enter into an unknown future with great confidence in God's love for me.

We lived in the refugee camp for three months before the United Nations closed the camp and move us. Most of the refugees were transferred to Pulau Bidong camp. I was on the list of people to transfer to the Sungei Besi transit camp in Kuala Lumpur. Again, I served the people of God in the transit camp. During this time, I received word that I was to have an interview with the delegation from the United States of America. Even though people were accepted to immigrate to France, Australia, Germany, Canada, or different countries, the final decision was made after meeting with the delegation from the United States. The United States functioned as the chair committee and coordinated with all the different countries to help settle the refugees. So I was scheduled to go to the United States embassy in Kuala Lumpur for the final interview. I went into the interview with my papers and documents that showed I had been accepted to go to France. The lady and the gentleman from the U.S. delegation interviewed me, after reading my file, said, "We want you to go to the United States."

I was stunned. Of course, I was speaking to them in French at that moment, "Mais, je ne parle pas Anglais." (But, I don't speak English.)

The gentleman said, "Don't worry! You're going to pick it up later."

I didn't have any clue what made them want me to go to the United States. I wished that I could go to France because I at least knew the language.

They began to make the arrangements of seeking a sponsor from different charitable agencies. My aunt, through the United States Catholic Conference, sponsored me. In order to transfer to the United States, I needed to enroll in an orientation program. I needed to transfer to the Philippines to prepare myself for the United States. They gave me the date that myself and others would transfer from Sungei Besi A, Malaysia, to Bataan, Philippines.

I didn't have much time left in the camp so I spent the time passing on the leadership to other seminarians. I had mixed feelings about immigrating to the United States. First of all, I was totally excited, saying to myself, "What does the U.S. look like? What am I going to do in the U.S.?" I knew that everyone in the camp wished to go to the U.S. because they said that America was really a good land to begin their new life. This country was the richest nation in the whole world and the land of opportunity. They said, "You would have freedom for you to start your life over again."

I heard all those promises. However, I knew that someday I would need to say good-bye to my people. Even though I knew that I would come to know new people in the different refugee camps in the Philippines, I would miss those people in the camps of Malaysia. In fact, some of the refugees who lived in Malaysia had been transferred to the Philippines a few months ahead of me. I was going to see them again. It was quiet exciting, but I knew the feelings of saying good-bye to loved ones once again. It wasn't easy to accept as a fact of life.

The day of departure came. I walked to the gate where the bus was waiting for us. Many of my friends gave me a kiss, a big hug, said good-bye, or took pictures. Some of them were crying. Above all, it was overwhelming for me. I didn't know how much the people loved me until I had to say good-bye to them. They called my number and I walked out the gates of the camp. I turned and looked back. I felt so sad because my people were crying. I wished that I didn't have to go. In my heart I said a quick prayer for them. The bus departed for the Kuala Lumpur Airport. On the way I said quiet prayers. The first prayer was for the people of Vietnam still living in oppression. It reminded me that I was very blessed and lucky to start my life over again. Many people in my homeland were still stuck there and didn't have a chance to start their lives over. They didn't have a chance to live with human dignity. The second prayer was for those people who remained in the refugee camps, that one day they would be able to start their lives over again. The third prayer thanked God, for He had given me another lesson to love my people. In and through Christ I made connections with their lives. I thanked God for sending them into my life.

My life was beginning with another journey. On July 7, 1981, I got on the airplane for the Philippines. The journey of faith toward love and life began with new challenges. As long as I placed my faith and hope in God's providence, I would be fine. On the airplane we shared with each other some pictures and stories. Some people asked me, "Brother Quang, when we come to Philippines, will I be able to stay with you in the same dorm?"

All I could say to them was, "Why not?"

We arrived in Manila early in the morning and from there we got on the bus for the new refugee camp, Bataan. It was a similar environment to Vietnam. There were different kinds of fruit trees, rice fields, water buffaloes along the route. I felt closer to Vietnam. People honked their horns to say hello to each other. It reminded me of when I was in Saigon. It was the same way of living. It was noisy, just as it had been at home. I laughed to myself. It was the first time since I left home that I felt at home. It was very exciting in the city. The traffic was full of cars and motorcycles. We came to the countryside and I felt more peaceful when I saw the rice fields, water buffaloes, and the people working in fields.

We arrived at the refugee camp, Bataan, in the afternoon. We arrived at area #1. (The camp was divided into 10 different sections.) There were no fences around the camp. The people who worked in the administration office came out and greeted us. They assigned us different shelters to live in. I was assigned to live in area #6, the center of the camp. I met a group of seminarians from Thailand, Indonesia, and Malaysia. We were all together in this camp to receive orientation for the new life in the United States. It was good to meet each other. We had a daily schedule to go to the classes about life in America.

In the camp I had met about fifteen other seminarians who had arrived from different seminaries in Vietnam. Somehow, we felt right at home with each other. The church was located in area #8, which was close to the foothills. We were able to go hiking to the different streams in the camp. However, the schedule was very tight for people because of ESL (English as Second Language) classes and the orientations about the country that we would live in. The ESL was in the morning and the orientation class was in the afternoon. We studied about seven hours a day.

I was assigned by the resident priest to direct the choir. Each Friday night we gathered together at the church so that we could rehearse. The celebration of the Eucharist was amazing! The church was full of people. They had to stand outside of the church. I could see the hunger for faith, and the hunger for the nourishment of the Eucharist. We had two masses on Sunday and many local villagers came to join us. The local residents were able to walk to the church and participate at Mass with us. Also, they invited us to do the living rosary, the processions of the Sacred Heart of Jesus, the Blessed Virgin Mary, and the Blessed Sacrament. We joined them to celebrate the feasts of the Church with excitement and joy. Each day we waited for the new opportunity to learn about the faith and the new life. We made a lot of friends and life was good to us.

I got the notice of the flight to the United States on November 30, 1981. My destination was Denver, Colorado, United States of America.

I knew I had to learn how to say good-bye to my friends again. My journey of faith toward love and life began again, with new challenges. I looked forward to finding out what God wanted me to be. If God wanted me to love and serve him in the life of the priesthood, I would like to say, "Yes, Lord. Here I am. I come to do your will."

Rescued Seminarians — Arrival in Malaysia

Leaving Malaysia for the Philipines,
and on to the United States

As a young seminarian — After Easter Mass, I posed with Archbishop Dominic Vendragon of Kuala Lumpur, Malaysia — 1981